# The Wesleyan Quadrilateral

*Scripture, Tradition, Reason & Experience as a
Model of Evangelical Theology*

Don Thorsen

Emeth Press

*The Wesleyan Quadrilateral: Scripture, Tradition, Reason, & Experience as a*
*Model of Evangelical Theology*

**Library of Congress Cataloging in Publication Data**

Thorsen, Don
    The Wesleyan quadrilateral: Scripture, tradition, reason and experience as a model of evangelical theology / Don Thorsen
        p.    cm.
    Includes bibliographical references and index.
    ISBN 0-9755435-3-9 (previously 0-310-75341-4)
    Wesley, John, 1703–1791. I. Title
    BX8495.W5T54      2005                                      90–40101
    230'.7'092–dc20                                              CIP

The picture of John Wesley at age 75 on the cover is by Richard Douglas. Used by permission.

*To my parents*
Rodney and Esther Thorsen
*whose loving steadfastness, trust, and
generosity served to establish
my life, my faith, and my vocation*

# Contents

# Preface

This book has several purposes, the first of which aims toward a deepened understanding and appreciation of the theology of John Wesley. His work has been increasingly considered more complex and subtle than was previously thought, due in part to the gradual publication of the scholarly edition of Wesley's *Works*. This book offers one more approach to unlocking insights into Wesley's thought. Perhaps it will contribute one more key so that his full theological contribution will become understood and appreciated by more than just "Wesley scholars" who have studied his writings firsthand.

The second purpose has to do with trying to understand a term that has become increasingly intertwined with Wesleyan thought: the *quadrilateral*. This term can be either enlightening or confusing; but because it has become popular, it needs to be viewed in a way that is historically faithful to Wesley, yet contemporized in a way that is theologically clear. Whether regarded as a model or as a heuristic tool for investigating Wesley's understanding of theological method and religious authority, the quadrilateral will serve to improve on our knowledge of the great man's thought.

Finally, this book has to do with evangelicalism, or the presentation of Christianity in conformity with Scripture and classical orthodoxy. Consequently, it also has to do with the vitality of a personal relationship with God in Jesus Christ through the indwelling of the Holy Spirit. We seek to present evangelicalism in terms that most self–described evangelicals would affirm; we do not attempt to remake evangelicalism in the image of Wesley. But this book does try to situate Wesley firmly within the evangelical tradition and demonstrate some ways in which Wesley contributes to that tradition. Just as Wesley helped to initiate the Evangelical Revival in eighteenth–century England, so his thought may serve to initiate revival today. And just as he stimulated a germinal revival of theology in his day, so his views of theological method and religious authority have value for those who wish to affirm evangelicalism in a way that encourages genuine catholicity.

It is hoped that this study will fulfill these various objectives, yet in no case will it claim to answer all the questions that arise in doing theology. Wesley's genius lay partly in his conviction that we should continually seek to make our beliefs more comprehensible and compelling to the world. This book merely seeks to become a part of the greater process of clarifying the saving truths of

Scripture and classical orthodoxy.

I wish to acknowledge several people for their part in helping me to complete this book. Throughout the entire project, Dr. Thomas Oden guided my research, critiqued my manuscript, and encouraged me to have it published. He also served as a mentor and role model for undertaking scholarly research with fidelity to Scripture and classical orthodoxy. Dr. Kenneth Rowe and Dr. Daniel Clendenin provided valuable editorial and bibliographical advice; both gave timely encouragement during the long writing process. I also wish to acknowledge Azusa Pacific University for the financial assistance it provided through the Creative Educational Project Fund and the Academic Internship Program. At the university, Dr. Roxane Lulofs offered helpful editorial advice, as did my research assistants Roy Taylor, Jason Zahariades, and Laura Muchanski.

My parents and siblings have been a constant source of stability and encouragement throughout my years of study and writing. My parents, Rodney and Esther Thorsen, could not have been more loving and supportive, which is why I have dedicated this book to them. I thank my siblings — Judy, Carl, and Norman — whose affirmation sustained me more than they realize. Finally, I wish to thank my daughters Liesl and Heidi for having brought a great deal of joy into my life.

# Abbreviations for
# Basic Wesley Texts

**Christian Library**    *A Christian Library: Consisting of Extracts from and Abridgments of the Choicest Pieces of Practical Divinity Which Have Been Published in the English Tongue.* Edited by John Wesley. 50 vols. in 30. 1750; reprint, London: T. Blanshard, 1819.

**Journal (Curnock ed.)**    *The Journal of the Rev. John Wesley.* Edited by Nehemiah Curnock. 9 vols. London: Epworth Press, 1909–16. The standard annotated edition of the journal, most recently reprinted by Francis Asbury Press, being replaced by the Bicentennial edition.

**Letters (Telford ed.)**    *The Letters of the Rev. John Wesley.* Edited by John Telford. 8 vols. London: Epworth Press, 1931. The standard annotated edition of the letters, most recently reprinted by Francis Asbury Press, being replaced by the much expanded and more accurate Oxford and Bicentennial edition.

**Natural Philosophy**    *A Survey of the Wisdom of God in the Creation; or, A Compendium of Natural Philosophy.* 2 vols. 1763; reprint, Philadelphia: Pounder, 1816.

**Notes upon the New Testament**    *Explanatory Notes upon the New Testament.* Salem, Ga.: Allenson-Breckinridge, 1950.

**Notes upon the Old Testament**    *Explanatory Notes upon the Old Testament.* 3 vols. 1765; reprint, Salem, Ohio: Schmul, 1975.

**Standard Sermons (Sugden ed.)**    *Wesley's Standard Sermons.* Edited by E. H. Sugden. 2 vols. London: Epworth Press, 1921.

**Works (Jackson ed.)**    *Works of the Rev. John Wesley.* Edited by Thomas Jackson. 3rd ed. 14 vols. Grand Rapids: Baker Book House, 1978. Reprint of the Jackson edition, London 1829–1831. The most complete edition in print, being replaced by the Oxford and Bicentennial edition.

**Works (Oxford and Bicentennial ed.)**    *The Works of John Wesley.* Oxford and Bicentennial ed. 10 vols. to date. Oxford: Clarendon Press, 1975–1983; Nashville: Abingdon Press, 1984–.

### Current Volumes

Vols. 1–4: *Sermons I–IV.* Edited by Albert C. Outler (Bicentennial ed.)

Vol. 7: *A Collection of Hymns for the Use of the People Called Methodists.* Edited by Franz Hildebrandt and Oliver Beckerlegge (Oxford ed.)

Vol. 11: *The Appeals to Men of Reason and Religion.* Edited by Gerald R. Cragg (Oxford ed.)

Vols. 18–19: *Journal and Diaries I–II.* Edited by W. Reginald Ward and Richard P. Heitzenrater (Bicentennial ed.)

Vols. 25–26: *Letters I–II.* Edited by Frank Baker (Oxford ed.)

**Forthcoming Volumes**

# Introduction:
# Wesley and the Wesleyan Quadrilateral

As John Wesley emerged as a principal leader of the Evangelical Revival in England in the seventeenth century, his hopes for revival extended beyond evangelism and discipleship. He wanted to blend what he called "heart–religion" with a firm theological grounding in scriptural Christianity.

Although he did not limit his ministry to the study and writing of theology, Wesley demonstrated a holistic understanding of the Christian faith that superseded his particular skills as a biblical exegete or systematic theologian. The theological gestalt he developed drew from the theological method that he inherited from the Reformed and Anglican traditions, along with a catholic spirit that sought to incorporate a wealth of insights regarding true Christian tradition. This did not merely result in an eclectic miscellany of assorted beliefs; Wesley sought to formulate theological ideas consonant with Scripture. But in order to describe the wholeness and dynamic characteristic of true, scriptural religion (a phrase he liked to use), Wesley appealed to tradition, reason, and experience as complementary sources of religious authority. These sources, together with the primary religious authority of Scripture, contributed to an approach to theology that continues to provide insight for Christians today.

## John Wesley as Theologian

The stature of Wesley as a theologian has risen in recent decades. What is it that inspires contemporary readers to delve into Wesley's theology? Many seem impressed by the practical relevance of his theological enterprises. Albert Outler, editor of the scholarly edition of Wesley's sermons, describes him as a "folk–theologian." This description suggests a view of Wesley as "a technically competent theologian with a remarkable power of creative simplification."[1] Some, like Colin Williams, interpret Wesley's theology in relation to the contemporary ecumenical movement.[2] Others point out the theological quality of Wesley's writings; for example, Randy Maddox argues for the reconsideration of Wesley as a systematic theologian.[3] Still others cite Wesley's contributions to doctrines such as Christology, salvation, and sanctification.[4]

Mildred Bangs Wynkoop offers a different and intriguing interpretation of Wesley in *A Theology of Love*. Her creative approach identifies love as the hermeneutical theme that runs throughout Wesley's works.[5] In so doing, she presents Wesley's theology in a way that "commends itself to modern man's new understanding of nature and furnishes a ground for the Christian meaning of life which all men seek, whether or not they know what it is they seek."[6] One of Wynkoop's many contributions to Wesleyan scholarship is the prominence she gives to Wesley's methodology.

Wesley did not articulate an explicit theological method. He was concerned more for the practical relevance and applicability of theology than for its theory. But he was not unconcerned for coherence and consistency in formulating theological ideas. He accepted *sola Scriptura* (Scripture alone), which had become the watchword in the formation of a renewed and Reformed approach to Christian doctrine in the sixteenth century, He also accepted the spirit in which Anglican scholars approached theology in the seventeenth century. They were not concerned with developing systematic theologies; rather, they pursued a theological method that could integrate various sources of religious authority in a spirit of catholicity.

In this same spirit, Wesley's distinctiveness rests not in a systematic theology, but in a theological method — that is, the framework in which theological questions are handled. The synthetic work of the theologian pertains more to the quality of method or the means of approaching religious questions than to the quality of the system or the end result of theological research. Certainly Wesley recognized the value of both for Christians, but he saw greater value in the method by which one approached the immediate needs of people inside and outside the church. Wesley found wholeness more in the process of doing theology than in its perceived completion. Donald Dayton notes that the more magisterial Reformed traditions have found Wesley's approach puzzling due to its lack of emphasis on constructive theology and its failure to articulate creeds and confessions.[7]

Given the dual heritage from the Continent and Anglicanism, Wesley freely undertook a variety of theological enterprises ranging from writing monographs on Christian doctrine to sermons that served as the primary repository of his ideas. Wesley saw no point in questioning the Reformed and Anglican approaches to theology; he felt that their complementary insights provided a contemporary and relevant theological foundation for the Evangelical Revival.

Now, since there is no explicitly stated theological method, we must distill one from Wesley's writings, and his works do provide many clues to the nature of his approach. In the 1771 Preface to his collected works, Wesley writes "that in this edition I present to serious and candid men my last and maturest thoughts, agreeable, I hope, to Scripture, reason and Christian antiquity."[8] Here Wesley betrays both Reformed and Anglican influences on his approach to theology; namely, he maintains the primacy of scriptural authority in his writings by always listing it first. But he frequently mentions experience as a genuine source of religious authority that needs to be recognized along with tradition and reason as a means to confirming, illuminating, and vitalizing the truths of Scripture. In one notable example, Wesley includes it in the title of his longest theological monograph: *The Doctrine of Original Sin, according to Scripture, Reason, and Experience.*

One might question Wesley's reference to anything other than Scripture as a genuine source of religious authority. But that was not an issue for Wesley, who lived in the context of eighteenth–century Anglican theology. Anglicans had long appealed to tradition and reason as genuine sources of religious authority. These appeals did not contradict the Continental Reformation principle of *sola Scriptura*. Anglican theologians realized that the Reformers had integrated human experience, reason, and tradition as factors in their theological method. Anglicans, including Wesley, considered their approaches to theology complementary to *sola Scriptura*. Scripture remained the primary source of religious authority, but other sources were specifically named as essential — albeit secondary and contingent on the primacy of inspired Scripture — to theological reflection.

Wesley seldom referred to all four sources of religious authority at the same time, but when he did, it related to a particular doctrine or theological idea. For example, Wesley refers to the four sources in a pamphlet entitled "The Principles of a Methodist," which was his first controversial writing on behalf of the Methodist revival. In it Wesley defends his doctrine of sanctification:

> If there be anything unscriptural in these words, anything wild or extravagant, anything contrary to the analogy of faith, or the experience of adult Christians, let them "smite me friendly and reprove me;" let them impart to me of the clearer light God has given them.[9]

Here Wesley rejects believing anything contrary to Scripture or reason, affirming only what is reasonable in light of the Word. He also appeals to the analogy of faith, which Outler describes as "both the truths revealed in Scripture and solid inferences drawn from them, as in the creeds and biblically–grounded theology."[10]

Wesley's use of the analogy of faith implies his affirmation of the rich tradition of Christian attempts to interpret and understand scriptural truths. Although he looked most to Christian antiquity, he was not averse to considering many other sources of theological insight. The analogy of faith (*analogia fidei*) is a common concept in the history of biblical interpretation. It presupposes a sense of the theological meaning of Scripture that is needed beyond the analogy of Scripture (*analogia Scriptura*). (The latter has to do with interpreting unclear, difficult, or ambiguous passages of Scripture by comparing them with clear and unequivocal passages that refer to the same teaching or event.)[11] Wesley affirmed both as necessary analogues for rightly understanding Christian truths.

Finally, Wesley appealed to the experience of Spirit–filled Christians, particularly adults who have reached some degree of maturity in their understanding and commitment to such complex issues as the doctrine of sanctification. Although Wesley did not use experience to define Christian doctrine, he expected experience to corroborate what is affirmed by Scripture. Donald Dayton suggests that Wesley approached the topic of Christian experience with a great deal of subtlety and theological rigor, including a concern for "the organization of the life of the church for the cultivation of that experience, and the support of Christian life and mission in the world."[12]

By appealing to experience, Wesley heralded a subtle yet profound shift in the historical development of theological method. He did not intend to be innovative in his approach to theology. On the contrary, he sought to conform to the orthodox tradition of Christian beliefs handed down from the apostolic church. Therefore his appeal to experience reflected an explicit attempt to affirm what had always been assumed as a part of vital Christian living. To hold in tension the need for religion of the heart as well as of the mind, Wesley wanted to recognize the experiential dimension of all true, scriptural religion. He did not see this as new or revolutionary. But it did signal a shift in direction.

Herein lies a unique strength of Wesley's theological method, namely, the recognition, delineation, and application of the unconflicting sources of authority of tradition, reason, and experience in contribution to and in correlation with the primary religious authority of Scripture. Wesley accomplished this by introducing his progressive ideas, especially for the role of experience, in the context of orthodox Christian beliefs — a tension which later theologians were less successful in maintaining.

Wesley, like John Locke, was a germinal thinker in trying to apply a universal methodology in understanding our world — a world that consists of multiple dimensions of reality, including the religious. More than Locke, Wesley sought to incorporate into his theology what he considered a comprehensively experimental approach in the investigation of all experiences relevant to Christian beliefs. As such, Wesley's theology had a correlative structure that sought to reflect fully on the Christian experience in a way that was intelligible and relevant. Whether or not we agree with every point of Wesley's theology, we can appreciate his attempt to conceptualize Christianity within the parameters of a then–modern scientific and philosophical worldview, yet so as to do justice to both the form of orthodox Christian beliefs and the vitality of a personal relationship with God.

Thus Wesley approached theology from a self–conscious and consistent perspective that used what he described as an experimental method. This method consisted of a proper use of inductive and deductive reasoning and the investigation of appropriate evidence relevant to religion. Scripture continued to represent the primary source of religious authority; all others were secondary though complementary resources in the search for religious truth. These secondary sources served to confirm, evaluate, and apply what was found in Scripture. Wesley correlated each element into a gestalt–like understanding of religious truths that did justice both to the rational content of Christianity and to the vital, spiritual piety characteristic of a personal relationship with God. Throughout his writings Wesley sought to develop a dynamic biblical theology that focused on a holistic conception of salvation and issued in a vital Christian philosophy of life.

To accomplish these goals, Wesley realized that he needed to do more than just study Scripture. So his theological inquiries entailed a probing for facts relevant to religion to be found outside of Scripture. Because Wesley's synthesis has properties not easily deduced from the sum of its parts, we must apprehend rules or principles representative of his thought. We must remember that Wesley was not a systematic theologian in the usual sense of the term. Although he sought to be coherent and consistent in writing theology, he unapologetically followed the paradigm of Anglican theology, which was more concerned with the spirit and method in which one approached individual questions of doctrine and practical theology. Consequently, it makes sense to choose a paradigm that reflects Wesley's modification (by the addition of experience) of the threefold use of Scripture, tradition, and reason found in Anglican theology, which was itself grounded in the Reformation affirmation of the primacy of scriptural authority.

## The Wesleyan Quadrilateral

The "Wesleyan quadrilateral" is a paradigm, or model, of how Wesley conceived of the task of theology. Wesley neither coined the term nor used it; it represents a modern attempt to summarize the fourfold set of guidelines Wesley used in reflecting on theology. Outler first referred to the Wesleyan quadrilateral in the late 1960s while serving on the commission on doctrine and doctrinal standards of the United Methodist Church. He chose to use the quadrilateral as an analogue to the already familiar term used by Anglican and Episcopal churches, the "Lambeth Quadrilateral," which represented the essentials for a reunited Christian church.[13] The Lambeth Quadrilateral is a slight revision of the four Articles agreed on at the General Convention of the (Anglican) Protestant Episcopal Church held at Chicago in 1886. The quadrilateral affirms Scripture as the rule and ultimate standard of the Christian faith, the Apostles' and Nicene creeds as summaries of the faith, the sacraments of baptism and the Lord's Supper, and the historic episcopate.

The substance of the Wesleyan quadrilateral is different from the Lambeth Quadrilateral. But Outler thought the term would serve as a helpful way to refer to the complex interaction among the four sources of Wesley's theology. In this book the quadrilateral will serve as a model for investigating the way in which Wesley approached theology, holding in tension the primacy of scriptural authority with the complementary sources of authority found in tradition, reason, and experience.

Because Outler coined the term "Wesleyan. quadrilateral," it is necessary for us to refer extensively to his writings throughout our investigation. His extensive work on Wesley, particularly in the first four volumes of the scholarly edition of the *Works* (Bicentennial ed.), makes him an indispensable resource for understanding the quadrilateral and Wesley's approach to theological method.

Outler did not intend for the quadrilateral to be used as a geometric figure. Such figures appear static and may be drawn in ways that distort important emphases found in Wesley's theology. Rather, Outler chose to use the quadrilateral metaphorically.

> It was intended as a metaphor for a four–element syndrome, including the four–fold guidelines of authority in Wesley's theological method. In such a quaternity Holy Scripture is clearly unique. But this in turn is illuminated by the collective Christian wisdom of other ages and cultures between the Apostolic Age and our own. It also allows for the rescue of the Gospel from obscurantism by means of the disciplines of critical reason. But always, Biblical revelation must be received in the heart by faith: this is the requirement of "experience."[14]

Outler chose to use the term "quadrilateral" because of its historical significance as a complex and dynamic theological term in the Anglican and Episcopalian traditions. He thought the quadrilateral could be used as a convenient summary of Wesley's theology without losing the fundamental characteristics of his thought, including the primacy of scriptural authority. Unfortunately, the original intent of using the quadrilateral as a metaphor or model for Wesley's theology has foundered for a variety of reasons. One reason is that no one has sought to study the quadrilateral at length in the context of Wesley's understanding of theological method and religious authority.

Despite the possibility of misunderstanding, the term "quadrilateral" has become popular for referring to Wesley both within and outside Wesleyan circles. Outler publicly expressed regret that he had coined the term, since it has been so widely misconstrued.[15] But the term is so popular that it deserves extended treatment even though it is not the only model for studying Wesley's theology. Other models could be used, as for example, the models of Wesley as a practical, an ecumenical, or a systematic theologian that have been used in the past. But for studying the subjects at hand, the quadrilateral serves as the most helpful model.

This book intends neither to advocate repudiating the quadrilateral as a concept for describing Wesley's theology nor to rehabilitate the term to make it more acceptable or relevant for contemporary usage. Rather, the quadrilateral will serve as a heuristic tool, and consequently it will be used in a way that helps to do historical and theological justice to Wesley's use of Scripture, tradition, reason, and experience.

A need exists today for a genuinely catholic model of theology that considers the interdependent significance of all historic claimants of religious authority — namely, tradition, reason, and experience — in relation to Scripture. The Reformers' emphasis on *sola Scriptura* represented an important foil to abuses of church authority in sixteenth–century Roman Catholicism. But the Reformers themselves appealed to more than Scripture in formulating theology, recognizing the need to present their beliefs in a well–reasoned fashion that reflected the ecumenical creeds of the patristic church; yet emphasis on *sola Scriptura* served to uplift the Protestant concern to make Scripture the rule and ultimate standard of faith.

Later Anglican theologians such as Richard Hooker sought to develop a *via media* (middle way) between theological overemphases they perceived in Continental Protestantism and in Roman Catholicism. They hoped to avoid the episcopal strictures of Roman Catholicism and the system–building tendencies of Protestantism, both of which they viewed as hindering a comprehensive and vital understanding of Christian belief. In explicitly appealing to tradition and reason along with Scripture for religious authority, the Anglicans did not consider themselves particularly innovative, but instead believed they had brought greater integrity to their endeavors.

Using the quadrilateral as a model helps to communicate to us that Wesley shared that same concern for comprehensiveness and vitality as his Anglican forebears.[16] The quadrilateral allows us to maintain a gestalt–like understanding of Wesley's approach to theology without becoming overconcerned with trying to uncover a systematic theology, which for all practical purposes Wesley never intended or desired.

Wesley was concerned for hands–on involvement in ministry, and his theological work was written to serve that end. Just as learning and ministry do not occur in the abstract, Wesley approached theology with application in mind for problem–solving. Whether it was a matter of doctrine or ministerial expediency, Wesley tried to hold in tension all that he believed to be relevant to the immediate needs at hand. That is why he modeled his theology closely on what he considered the most authentic tradition of the Christian church passed down through the Protestant Reformation and the Church of England. His incorporation of experience into his theological method, while it may have initially affected only a small group, was a germinal idea that continues to be important to the historical development of theology.

## A Model of Evangelical Theology

The term *evangelical* has become an increasingly popular term with which Christians describe their religious beliefs. "Evangelical" derives from the Greek word *evangelium*, which refers to the gospel (literally, "good news") used throughout the New Testament to indicate the message of God's gracious offer of salvation. Because of its centrality to the New Testament message, Richard Muller notes that the term is favored by the orthodox as a reference to the promise of salvation offered in Christian preaching.[17] Historically the Reformation principle of justification by faith alone *(sola fide)* represented a reaffirmation of the evangelical gospel message.

Beyond these basic understandings of "evangelical" there is great diversity as to the historic and theological nuances of its meaning for contemporary Christianity. George Marsden identifies three distinct, though overlapping, senses in which "evangelical" or "evangelicalism" may be thought of as a unity. He sees two of the definitions as broad and inclusive, the other more narrow and specific.

First, evangelicalism is a conceptual unity that designates a grouping of Christians who fit a certain definition. Second, evangelicalism can designate a more organic movement. Religious groups with some common traditions and experiences, despite wide diversities and only meager institutional interconnections, may constitute a movement in the sense of moving or tending in some common directions. Third, within evangelicalism in these broader senses is a more narrow, consciously "evangelical" transdenominational community with complicated infrastructures of institutions and persons who identify with "evangelicalism."[18]

The first and third definitions tend toward the exclusiveness that occurs when individuals or groups, whether or not they are representative of various theologies or denominations, are left out due to differences in conceptualizing what it means to be evangelical. The second definition permits greater latitude in defining "evangelical." This openness to diversity of meaning need not be considered a liability, particularly when it comes to studying the theology of Wesley.

William Abraham argues that the term "evangelical" represents an "essentially contested concept" that can only be understood through an appreciation of its history.[19] Since that history appears diverse, we should refrain from imposing a definition on the term that is too precise or clear–cut. Such definitions as articulated by modern evangelicals potentially exclude historical figures such as Wesley or even Luther and Calvin. Instead, Abraham argues that

the term "evangelical" embraces at least three constellations of thought: the Reformation, led by Luther and Calvin, and the Evangelical Revival of the eighteenth century as found, say, in Methodism, and modern conservative evangelicalism. Within these historical movements, the meaning of the word "evangelical" is essentially contested.[20]

Abraham's definition of "evangelical" tends to be more catholic and inclusive than some others in its appreciation of those who seek to affirm an orthodox understanding of Christian beliefs. A similar concern is found in the works of Donald Bloesch, who explicitly seeks to establish a greater sense of "catholic evangelicalism."[21] Although there remains many ways to define evangelicalism, we contend that its theological and ecclesiastical boundaries need to be conceived more broadly. They need to include those who identify with evangelicalism, yet have been unwilling or unable to become a part of the "organic movement" to which Marsden alludes in his second definition.

Certainly Wesley considered himself to be in the orthodox tradition of Christianity. Although "evangelical" was not a catchword of eighteenth–century theology, Wesley would have felt comfortable with more inclusive understandings of the word. He distinguished between what he considered essentials of theology and mere personal opinions. Since the source of most tensions among Christians consisted of the latter, Wesley chose to emphasize unity and catholicity rather than diversity and exclusivity. He permitted a wide spectrum of theological opinions, preferring to avoid the static extremes of dogmatism.

Yet Wesley was not indifferent to the orthodox Christian understanding of Scripture. As Outler notes, "Wesley's theological pluralism was evangelical in substance (firm and clear in its Christocentric focus) and irenic in its temper ('Catholic spirit')."[22] Thus the catholic spirit in which Wesley claimed to approach theology incorporated Scripture, tradition, reason, and experience in the hope of presenting Christian beliefs in a way that affirmed a spiritually transformed life along with orthodox summaries of scriptural truth.

Gabriel Fackre writes that *catholicity* is a word and concept beginning to be heard in contemporary evangelicalism. He cites authors such as Bloesch and Robert Webber as proponents of an "evangelical catholicity" that has its roots in the Mercersburg theology.[23] Although Fackre fails to note deeper roots of evangelical catholicity in the theology of Wesley, he aptly points out, "Hermeneutical catholicity incorporates all historic authority claimants — Bible, church, world — according to the priorities and functions assigned to them by an evangelical doctrine of revelation."[24] In reference to the "world," Fackre includes the importance of experience (world) that is hermeneutically formative and also reason (world) that functions in a correlative role.

So Fackre unwittingly touches on the four sources of religious authority to which Wesley gave credence: Scripture, tradition (church), reason, and experience. He also describes evangelical catholicity in a way compatible with Wesley, particularly with regard to the priority of Scripture over other sources of religious authority.

> Scripture is the *source* of authority based on its unique prophetic–apostolic inspiration. The church (as the whole people of God) and its classical tradition constitute the authoritative *resource* for interpreting the Bible, warranted by the Spirit's gift to the church of "illumination," but always standing under Scripture. The world of general human experience — rational, moral, affective — comprises the *setting* in which Scripture and tradition are read, so legitimated by a common grace at work in "general revelation."[25]

Fackre states in a contemporary and sophisticated style the kinds of ideas already present in Wesley in eighteenth–century England. What Fackre sees as progressive and necessary in the development of evangelical thinking today, Wesley took to be normative for a spiritually vital and doctrinally orthodox approach to theology.

Another point Fackre makes that is vital to our thesis is that "Every evangelical hermeneutic, functionally if not formally, finds some place in its authority structure for church and world."[26] He recognizes that much more than Scripture is involved in evangelical hermeneutics and in theological method as a whole. The appeal to *sola Scriptura* is limited in articulating often unacknowledged or unrecognized forces shaping avowedly evangelical theology. To correct that deficiency, proponents of evangelical catholicity as described by Fackre argue "for a more self–conscious, and therefore more critical, appreciation of ecclesial and secular factors in hermeneutical theory and practice."[27] Thus a new paradigm of theology is needed — one in which more than Scripture is explicitly included as a genuine source of religious authority and in which the concept of catholicity becomes a part of the warp and woof of evangelicalism.

Bernard Ramm makes a similar plea in his book *After Fundamentalism.* He writes that evangelicals "have not developed a theological method that enables them to be consistently evangelical in their theology and to be people of modern learning. This is why a new paradigm is necessary."[28] Ramm argues for the theological method of Karl Barth as the solution to evangelical needs. Gordon Lewis and Bruce Demarest offer an alternative paradigm in *Integrative Theology,* attempting to set forth a theological method that "is biblically grounded, historically related, culturally sensitive, person–centered, and profoundly related to life."[29] But neither of these attempts succeeds in achieving a genuinely catholic approach to theology that recognizes the interdependent relationship between Scripture, tradition, reason, and experience. We argue that the Wesleyan quadrilateral meets the need for catholicity as a model of evangelical theology.

## An Overview of the Book

To discover Wesley's contribution to contemporary evangelical theology, we must grapple with his understanding of theological method and religious authority. Our intent is to investigate and define the theological method found in Wesley's writings. We will do this by examining his theology in light of his fourfold guidelines – the quadrilateral – and will begin by relating Wesley's theology to the seventeenth– and eighteenth–century debate concerning method and authority. When our study of Wesley's theology is completed, we will evaluate its contribution to his contemporary situation and to more recent debate on theological method and religious authority, particularly within the evangelical community.

Although the heart of our investigation of the Wesleyan quadrilateral begins in chapter 3, "Wesley's Theological Method," readers familiar with Wesley's theology and his sources will benefit from chapter 1, "The Background of Theological Method." That chapter traces the historical development of theology from the early church through Wesley. Readers less familiar with Wesley's theology may find it more worthwhile to begin with chapter 2, "An Overview of Wesley's Theology."

Chapters 4–7 expound in turn on Wesley's understanding and use of Scripture, tradition, reason, and experience. Chapter 8 brings the historical and theological investigation back to the question of the relevance of the Wesleyan quadrilateral today.

# 1

# The Background of Theological Method

The term *method* derives from the Greek word *methodos* (*meta*, "after," and *hodos*, "road" or "way"). A method is a procedure or principle used in any organized discipline or in organizing one.[1] The study of methods, or methodology (*methodos* plus *logos*, "the study of"), describes how we obtain knowledge about something. In philosophy, methodology "is applied both to the process or art of investigation and to the treatise or body of knowledge resulting from investigation."[2] In theology, methodology relates to "explorations of the conditions under which theological claims may be true," and in a more general sense, "it refers to an array of decisions every Christian theologian must make in the course of doing theology."[3]

Most people follow certain regular or methodical steps in thinking about and articulating what they believe. We do not usually think about those steps, however; we are more likely concerned with finding solutions to immediate problems. But when we do reflect on how we actually arrived at a particular solution, we are raising the question of method. J. J. Mueller says, "Method then reflects upon reflecting."[4] All Christians — not just the trained theologians — reflect on their beliefs methodologically, though each may do so with varying degrees of self–awareness and logical precision. The task of theological method, or methodology, involves making the steps explicit, evaluating and formulating them in a way that makes Christian belief as reasonable and compelling as possible.

To promote the Methodist revival, Wesley considered it essential to present the Christian message of salvation and holy living in just that way. This involved both practical and theological methods, though Wesley wrote more explicitly on the former than on the latter. The name "Methodist" refers, not to theological method, but to the practical methods — organizing small groups and encouraging spiritual self–discipline — that Wesley and his colleagues used in regard to evangelism and Christian nurture.[5] Wesley would not have associated the name "Methodist" with theological method any more than his contemporaries would. Despite scholastic concerns for methodology, it is not until the modern era that we find in Christianity a pervasive, specific concern for theological method. Nevertheless, the very fact that Wesley conceived of his ministry and theological ideas as being *methodical* in orientation reveals his predisposition toward having a method for everything he said or did.

Wesley claimed to have presented his principal theological doctrines with consistency over the course of his life and ministry. This claim assumes a self–conscious approach to formulating theology. Although Wesley may not have fully articulated his theological method, we may raise the method question and reflect on how he discovered the theological answers to the immediate problems he faced. First, however, we need to understand a little about the historical development of theological method and how that process supplied Wesley with sources for developing his own approach.

## A Survey of Theological Methodologies

Tracing the development of Christian theological method is not easy, and any attempt at a summary runs the risk of oversimplification or misrepresentation of individual theologians or theological traditions. Yet we must make such an attempt in order to place Wesley in a proper historical and cultural context and to determine his sources. We will rely on both primary and secondary sources, first, because it is not within the scope of this book to investigate the entire history of theological method, and second, because others have already done extensive work, especially in regard to Anglicanism in the century preceding Wesley.[6] Henry McAdoo's books *The Structure of Moral Caroline Theology* and *The Spirit of Anglicanism* are noteworthy examples.[7]

In this survey we will pay more attention to developments closer to Wesley's time than to ancient thought, more attention to questions of religious authority than to questions of biblical interpretation. Principles of interpretation are important for understanding Wesley, but here we must confine ourselves to the more general understanding of how theologians or theological traditions viewed sources of religious authority and used them in reflecting on and formulating theology.

### The Early Church through the Middle Ages

The early church gradually developed theological positions in response to conceptual challenges from paganism, heresies, and other doctrinal threats within the church. Individual Christians first responded to these challenges through apologetical writings. The Christian apologists who found the greatest acceptance in the early church affirmed the authority of both Scripture and the church to defend the faith. J. A. Fichtner comments, "Irenæus, Cyprian, Origen, Tertullian, and other ecclesiastical writers are emphatic in their teaching that the Scriptures should be read in the Church and that ecclesial tradition is 'the exposition of the Scripture.'"[8]

The first ecumenical councils were called to consider questions about doctrines of immediate importance to the stability of the church. But even then, attempts at becoming philosophically and theologically systematic did not arise all at once.[9] Gradually, after the canon became established, Scripture provided the material basis for establishing church doctrine, and patristic exegesis held itself subject to Scripture. The church, however, continued to serve as the guardian and authoritative interpreter of Scripture. The council of Chalcedon, for example, clearly affirmed "the unerring faith of the Fathers" in presenting the catholic, apostolic faith.[10]

The combination of scriptural and church authority proved effective for meeting doctrinal needs during the first millennium of Christianity, and it remained methodologically important to theology even after the Great Schism occurred in the eleventh century. Both the Eastern Orthodox and the Roman Catholic churches affirmed the approach to theology contained in the ancient Christian creeds.

As the Roman Catholic Church developed in the West, theologians such as Anselm articulated a growing concern that faith seek a rational understanding of Christian belief.

> I acknowledge, Lord, and I give thanks that You have created Your image in me.... But I desire to understand your truth a little, that truth that my heart believes and loves. For I do not seek to understand so that I may believe; but I believe so that I may understand.[11]

Because God created us as rational beings, we should seek to have rational integrity for what we believe. This search for a rational — or at least a reasonable — understanding of Christian belief culminated in the scholastic attempt of Thomas Aquinas to integrate faith and reason into a science that proceeds from philosophical as well as revealed principles. Aquinas stated that

> although the argument from authority based on human reason is the weakest, yet the argument from authority based on divine revelation is the strongest. But sacred doctrine also makes use of human reason, not, indeed, to prove faith... but to make clear other things that are set forth in this doctrine.[12]

Reason does not supplant or equal the authority of Scripture as the primary source of divine revelation, but it does play a critical role in Aquinas's theology. Regarding the Thomistic influence on Anglican theology, McAdoo notes that "Aquinas can be seen as the forerunner of an approach to reason and to the synthesis of faith and reason which left its mark on [Richard] Hooker and others."[13] Despite the growing concern to establish a reasonable understanding of Christian beliefs, the Roman Catholic Church maintained the preeminent authority of Scripture *and* of the church and its tradition in formulating theology.

## The Protestant Reformation

The Reformation, particularly in the person of Martin Luther, reacted against abuses of ecclesiastical authority occurring in the Roman Catholic Church. Luther applied an essentially coherent theological method based on *sola Scriptura* ("Scripture alone") to counter the ecclesiastical tyranny. He stated,

"Herein I follow the example of St. Augustine, who was, among other things, the first and almost the only one who determined to be subject to the Holy Scriptures alone, and independent of the books of all the fathers and saints."[14] Scripture was seen as the only sufficient and divine rule of faith and practice. Church tradition was no longer viewed as an unconditional authority, but rather as actually undermining the sole authority of Scripture. Luther thought that soon after the time of Jesus Christ there

> arose the sayings that the Scriptures were not sufficient, that we also needed the laws and the interpretations of the councils and the father.... Out of this finally developed the papacy, in which there is no authority but man–made laws and interpretations.[15]

To counter the systemic ecclesiastical abuses Luther perceived in the Roman Catholic Church, religious authority needed to be based solely on the most reliable and ancient source available: Scripture.

John Calvin sustained the theological foundation of solafideism (including *sola Scriptura)* by constructing a system of theology based on the transcendent glory of God. In this sense Calvin differed from Luther, who did not try to present Christian beliefs as a conceptually integrated and systematic whole. Calvin also did not see the Reformation in total opposition to "the ancient writers of a better age of the church,"[16] but he still emphasized the sole authority of Scripture.[17] Despite the Reformers' distrust of the Roman Catholic Church and the Scholastics' use of reason, Reformation theology preserved many principles of theological formation from the scholastic period. McAdoo comments that "the same method of appeal to authorities and of categorical assertions persisted."[18]

After the Reformation, church tradition progressively gained authority in the Roman Catholic Church. A more precise conception of the twofold authority of written Scripture and unwritten tradition was established at the Council of Trent (1545–1563). The decree of the council read: "The council is aware that this truth and teaching [of all saving truth and moral teaching] are contained in written books and in the unwritten traditions that the apostles received from Christ himself or that were handed on, as it were from hand to hand, from the apostles under the inspiration of the Holy Spirit, and so have come down to us."[19] Fichtner notes that the Roman Catholic Church still emphasized Scripture as the material source of doctrine, but also affirmed that the church "holds no truth on the basis of Scripture alone, independently of tradition."[20]

## The English Reformation

The Reformation in England took a distinctively different approach to theology from either the Continental Reformers or the Roman Catholic Church. The Church of England encountered religious controversy in trying to decide which theological traditions and sources of authority should prevail. Under the leadership of Thomas Cranmer, John Jewel, Hooker,. and others, the church intentionally constructed a theological *via media* between Protestantism and Roman

Catholicism.[21] Despite similarities with Continental Reformers, the early Anglican divines resisted Calvinist attempts to force a Presbyterian polity on England and to impose a literal interpretation of Scripture.[22] The Anglicans also resisted Roman Catholic extremes in asserting ecclesiastical authority.

Richard Hooker was perhaps the greatest defender and theoretician of the emerging theology distinctive of the Anglo–Protestant reform movement. He led the way in making the Church of England "an independent branch of the Church Universal. . . with a positive doctrine and discipline of its own and a definite mission in the wide economy of Grace."[23] Others followed in articulating the need to stand in the middle between the traditions of Roman Catholicism and Calvinism, most forcefully represented by Puritanism.

In the seventeenth century, Robert Sanderson echoed Hooker's attempt to forge an Anglican middle way. In the preface to his sermons, Sanderson stated in defense of the Thirty–nine Articles:

> This is the main hinge, upon which the whole dispute turneth, and whereunto all other differences are but appendages. The true belief, and right understanding of this great Article concerning the Scripture's sufficiency, being (to my apprehension) the most proper Characteristical note of the right English Protestant, as he standeth in the middle between, and distinguished from, the Papists on the one hand, and the (sometimes styled) Puritan on the other. I know not how we can be a Papist, that truly believeth it: or be a Puritan, that rightly understandeth it.[24]

Albert C. Outler relates Peter Heylyn's complaining of "how much truth was lost on both extremes and yet how easy to be found by those who went a middle way in search thereof," and how Thomas Fuller had prayed that "we may hit the golden mean and endeavour to avoid all extremes: the fanatic Anabaptists on the one side and the fiery zeal of the Jesuits on the other, so that we may be true Protestants or, which is far better, real Christians indeed."[25]

Steering this course throughout the seventeenth century, Anglicans in some instances saw themselves as ecumenical forces in the Christian world, uniting disparate approaches to theology. Edward Stillingfleet, who as a Latitudinarian advocated religious tolerance, summarized his ecumenical ideas in the *Irenicum* (1659).[26] He advocated a union between episcopalians and presbyterians, desiring to achieve a church model that would embrace everyone. In the preface to the *Irenicum,* Stillingfleet wrote:

> I conclude with the words of a late learned, pious and moderate prelate in his *Via media;* I have done, and now I make no other account, but that it will fall out with me, as it doth commonly with him that offers to part a quarrel, both parts will perhaps drive at me for wishing them no worse than peace. My ambition of the public tranquility shall willingly carry me through this hazard: let both beat me, so their quarrel may cease: I shall rejoice in those blows and scars which I shall take for the church's safety.[27]

Another Latitudinarian, John Tillotson, advocated liberality in Christian belief because "it is not necessary to the true nature of faith, that we should be infallibly secured of the means whereby the Christian doctrine is conveyed to us."[28]

What Anglicans perceived to be inadequate in the theological method of Continental Protestantism was its narrow approach to the principle of *sola Scriptura*. Anglicans rejected any scriptural authoritarianism fostered by a literal and exclusivistic hermeneutic. Hooker echoed the Roman Catholic heritage of the Anglican tradition by arguing that the universe is ordered by rational principles that may be discerned by reason unaided by Scripture. Thus Hooker conceived of reason as providing a degree of freedom and authority in knowing truth.

> There are but two waies whereby the spirit leadeth men into all truth: the one extraordinarie, the other common; the one belonging but unto some few, the other extending it selfe unto all that are of God; the one that which we call by a special divine excellency, Revelation, the other Reason.[29]

Hooker found reason especially helpful in establishing ecclesial laws that Scripture did not address, as he explained in his *Laws of Ecclesiastical Polity*.[30] The power of reason in formulating theology became a critical source of religious authority. One could not avoid its presence in methodological considerations. It required theologians to be more responsible in their work, because the use of reason allowed a greater degree of freedom in approaching theology.

This increased emphasis on responsible reasoning in theology led Hooker to develop what McAdoo describes as a "liberal method" in approaching theological questions.[31] Hooker's liberal method does not resemble the liberal theology of the nineteenth century; he still affirmed the primacy of scriptural authority and maintained a high regard for the doctrines of Christian antiquity. But he questioned the way in which interpretations of Scripture and sometimes church tradition came to have authoritative status.

So there evolved in Anglicanism a methodological approach to theology that drew from the best sources of Christian doctrine, including both the Roman Catholic and Protestant traditions. This integrative approach affirmed the authority of reason as well as Scripture and the best of Church tradition in treating theological questions. McAdoo notes that Hooker justified his theological positions "by the three–fold test of 'intrinsic reasonableness', by 'the judgment of antiquity, and by the long continued practice of the whole Church; from which unnecessarily to swerve, experience hath never as yet found safe,' and the 'authority of the Church itself.'"[32] Francis Paget summarizes Hooker's contribution to Anglican theology this way:

> Thus Hooker's appeal in things spiritual is to a threefold fount of guidance and authority — to reason, Scripture, and tradition all alike of God, alike emanating from Him, the one original Source of all light and power — each in certain matters bearing a special and prerogative sanction from Him, all in certain matters blending and co–operating.[33]

Hooker's emphasis on Scripture and reason in the theological context of church tradition was taken up with enthusiasm by other Anglican divines. Without expecting to redirect the course of theological method, Hooker, notes Alister McGrath, "indicated the direction in which Anglican theology would develop, without defining its final form."[34] Yet that direction became more developed in the writings of Anglicans in the following century.

Many followed Hooker's lead in combining the three elements of his theological method. For example, Sanderson claimed that no convincing arguments could be brought against him "either from reason or from authority of Holy Writ, or from the testimony either of the ancient Fathers or of other classical divines of later times."[35] In 1659 John Pearson wrote *An Exposition of the Creed,* which proved to be a buttress to orthodox Christianity, during the seventeenth and eighteenth centuries. Pearson not only affirmed the theological use of Scripture, tradition, and reason for himself, but confirmed that these three sources of religious authority were widely accepted even among those with heretical tendencies.

> Against these [heretics] I proceed upon such principles as they themselves allow, that is upon the Word of God delivered in the Old and New Testament, alleged according to the true sense, and applied by right reason; not urging the authority of the Church which they reject, but only giving in the margin the sense of the primitive Fathers, for the satisfaction of such as have any respect left for antiquity, and are persuaded that Christ had a true Church on the earth before these times.[36]

Jeremy Taylor, who had a profound effect on Wesley's theological development, reflected the same methodological concerns as Hooker, Sanderson, and Pearson. In *A Discourse of the Liberty of Prophesying,* Taylor said:

> For I am sure I have no other design but the prosecution and advantage of truth…but I have written this [discourse], because I thought it was necessary, and seasonable, and charitable, and agreeable to the great precepts and design of Christianity, consonant to the practice of the apostles, and the best ages of the church, most agreeable to Scripture and reason, to revelation and the nature of the thing; and it is such a doctrine, that, if there be variety in human affairs, if the event of things be not settled in a durable consistence, but is changeable, every one of us all may have need of it.[37]

William Law also made use of these three sources of religious authority. Of Law's writings, A. K. Walker states, "Though he appropriates the method oddly, giving more credit to mystical writers than other theologians, he is still concerned with Scripture, tradition, and reason."[38] Additional Anglican divines could be mentioned who reveal similar methodologies, but they only serve to show the pervasiveness of this threefold synthesis. McAdoo summarizes this Anglican consensus:

> To put it another way, there is no essential difference in the views of Hooker, Taylor, Sanderson, Hammond, Wilkins, Boyle, Stillingfleet and Patrick. Each

responds to his own situation by putting the main stress on the element or elements of theological method which answer to it, and this gives the work of each a distinctive colour and individuality.[39]

## The Spirit of Anglicanism

The Anglican attempt to devise a *via media* between historic approaches to Christian theology motivated theologians to focus on the subject of theological method. They wished to free themselves from the doctrinal strictures of other Christian traditions and the theological and ecclesiastical disorganization that continually plagued the Church of England. Because of a growing concern to articulate the complexity of theological reflection and doctrinal formulation, Anglicans produced a great deal of work dealing with theological method. As a result, McAdoo sees theological method as the most distinctive characteristic of seventeenth–century Anglican theology.[40] He describes this methodology as "the *spirit* of Anglicanism, including as it does the centrality of Scripture and the visibility and continuity of the Church, both confirmed by antiquity, and illuminated by the freedom of reason and liberality of viewpoint."[41]

Hooker's approach is representative of Anglican theological method in asserting the ability and freedom of theologians to assimilate diverse sources of theology. The resulting eclecticism made it possible for Anglicans to live with the tensions of a theologically pluralistic environment and at the same time facilitate their aim of developing the Church of England into a religious middle way in the Christian world. On the one hand, Anglicans felt the need for historic catholicity. They wished to remain in the mainstream — indeed the heart — of orthodox Christian beliefs. On the other hand, they asserted the theological freedom that they felt by virtue of their God–given powers of reason.

McAdoo contends that in the midst of this theological ferment, Anglicanism exhibited a dialectical characteristic in its theological method that answered the need for catholicity and freedom.[42] They did not feel constrained from seeking what they considered a faith that is more primitively catholic than either Roman Catholicism or Continental Protestantism. Through this eclecticism, Anglicanism progressively integrated these dialectical gleanings into a self–identity that adequately responded to what its thinkers saw as challenges to the growth of the Church of England.

The *practical* divinity of sixteenth– and seventeenth–century Anglicans is another distinctive trait of their theology. Wesley thought "that there is not in the world, a more complete body of Practical Divinity than is now extant in the English tongue, in the writings of the last and present century."[43] Many Anglicans did not gauge their success by whether they had devised a new or improved system of theology; rather, they based success on their finding solutions to immediate theological problems and the practical benefit of helping others find solutions. Jeremy Taylor summarized this practical outlook in *The Rule and Exercise of Holy Dying:*

So that in this affair I was almost forced to walk alone; only that I drew the rules and advices from the fountains of Scripture, and the purest channels of the primitive Church, and was helped by some experience in the cure of souls. I shall measure the success of my labors, not by popular noises or the sentences of curious persons, but by the advantage which good people may receive. My work here is not to please the speculative part of men, but to minister, to practice, to preach to the weary, to comfort the sick, to assist the penitent, to reprove the confident, to strengthen weak hands and feeble knees, having scarce any other possibilities left me of doing alms, or exercising that charity by which we shall be judged at doomsday.[44]

The Anglicans' refusal to develop systematic theologies reflects neither an intellectual inability to do so nor a poorly developed theological method. On the contrary, their methodological approach entailed a distrust of theological systems. McAdoo suggests several causes for this, among them the rising importance of reason. Although the authority of reason in religion varied in degree, depending on the individual theologian, the growing respect for reason "produced a consistent reaction against the identification of faith with assurance and an equally consistent reaction against systems and syllogisms."[45] Another cause was the desire to adhere to Scripture as a whole and to its sense. McAdoo comments, "This is noticeable in many writers and it is a factor which militated against the idea of theological systems which frequently interpreted the whole or sense of Scripture by some particular part."[46]

Either way, no easy or systematic answers were expected for the tough religious questions of life or for the controversial issue of religious authority. Cambridge Platonists such as Benjamin Whichcote and Ralph Cudworth thought that truth was not to be found in rationalistic systems; they had a more intuitive way of thinking about theology, derived from Platonic and Neoplatonic ideas. The Cambridge Platonists, like the Latitudinarians, typified by Tillotson and Joseph Glanvill, found conceptual unity in the powers of reason to work methodically through theological issues rather than working toward a completed, rationalistic system.[47] The devotional writings of Taylor and Law specifically denounced the kind of speculative thinking involved in systematic theologies and its negative effect on the practical duties of being a Christian.[48] Law went to the point of denouncing all doctrines in favor of only "the Scriptures and *first-rate* Saints of the Church."[49]

Paul More suggests that the Anglican theological method precluded any finality in systematic content. He says, "What we have to look for in the ecclesiastical literature of England is not so much finality as direction."[50] Theological interpretation and application surely seem more crucial to Anglican theology than systematic formulations. The guiding methodological principles can be credited with enabling the Church of England to steer the middle course it desired, avoiding extreme biblical interpretations and reflecting the essence of classical orthodoxy. At the turn of the eighteenth century an anonymous author wrote a book entitled *A Summary of Divine Truths Agreeable to the Faith Profess'd*

*by the Church of England, confirm'd by Scripture and Reason* (1711), which defended the essential orthodoxy of Anglicanism despite the absence of a single systematic theology.[51]

Of the Anglican indifference to theological systems, McAdoo comments,
"This is the genuine Anglicanism, not at all on the defensive or given to being
apologetical, but quite serenely convinced of the completeness of its heritage."[52]
A systematic theology was not considered essential either to intellectual integrity or to catholicity. On the contrary, the Anglicans intentionally instilled adapt-
ability in their theological method so as to avoid the strictures of systematization and to keep the Church of England centered on what Pearson described
as "the primitive Faith."[53]

Catholicity was a vital concern. Anglicanism saw itself as renewing true,
primitive, catholic faith. McAdoo writes, "The absence of an official theology in
Anglicanism is something deliberate which belongs to it[s] essential nature, for
it has always regarded the teaching and practice of the undivided Church of
the first five centuries as a criterion."[54]

Reason, the third component of the methodology, found a place with the
Anglican theologians because of their intention to speak relevantly to the many
human and intellectual needs of the culture in which they lived. The Anglicans'
concern to be contemporary took at least two forms: (1) they sought to stay
abreast of new developments relevant to theology, especially in the field of science, and (2) they tried to reach the people through the practical means of sermons and devotional literature. They commonly advocated plainness of writing,
though not without scholarship.

In science, Anglicans progressively incorporated the use of experimental
philosophy into their theology. This resulted first of all from specific books that
had great influence, according to McAdoo, including the *Usefulness of
Experimental Natural Philosophy* (1663, 1671; two vols.) by Robert Boyle and *The
Wisdom of God manifested in the works of Creation* (1691) by John Ray.
Professional scientists like Boyle and Ray sometimes crossed over to the writing
of theological treatises; even Isaac Newton wrote about theology.[55] But this
assimilation of experimental philosophy also reflected the cumulative effect of
studies in natural history and science. All these, McAdoo says, "influenced the
development of the new way of looking at theological problems."[56]

Just as scientists dabbled in theology, so theologians tried to incorporate science and the scientific method into theology, resulting in a renewed emphasis
on natural theology. Thus the renewal of natural law, typified by Hooker's theology, is reflected in Anglican writings in the seventeenth century.
Latitudinarians had so much confidence in the powers of scientific and human
reasoning that they encouraged natural theology, as McGrath comments, in the
"desire to establish contact and common ground between theological method
and the 'new philosophy' of British empiricism."[57]

## The Role of Experience

Although experience did not play an explicit role in early Anglican methodology as it did later in Wesley's, it nevertheless must be mentioned in setting the context for the Wesleyan quadrilateral. Despite the absence of any formal statement, the presence of experience in theological reflection and formulation was tacitly assumed in much that was written during the sixteenth and seventeenth centuries. Hooker, without explicitly intending to make it a part of his theological method, considered experience alongside the study of Scripture and nature in his discussion of ecclesiastical polity. For example:

> What successe God may give unto any such kind of conference or disputation, we cannot tell. But of this we are right sure, that nature, Scripture, and experience it selfe, have all taught the world to seeke for the ending of contentions by submitting it selfe unto some judiciall and definitive sentence, whereunto neither part that contendeth may under any pretence or coulor refuse to stand.[58]

Such an appeal to experience was not contested by subsequent Anglican theologians, for they too assumed that experience should confirm and elaborate Christian truths established by the generally accepted standards of Scripture, tradition, and reason. Reason was formally the newcomer to Anglican theological method, but informally experience played an important supportive role. In the century preceding Wesley, even that supportive role gets little mention from theologians; but appeals to experience seem more prevalent in the practical theology of devotional and sermonic literature. Jeremy Taylor, for example, described how his personal pastoral experience aided him in formulating *Holy Dying* (1651). He claimed that he "drew the rules and advices [of holy dying] from the fountains of Scripture, and the purest channels of the primitive Church, and was helped by some experience in the cure of souls."[59] Moreover, he measured the success of his labors "not by popular noises or the sentences of curious persons, but by the advantage which good people may receive."[60]

Taylor's appeal to experience should not be minimized because of the pastoral nature of these writings. The large amount of sermonic literature during the seventeenth century reveals the pervasive concern for both founding and confirming Christian beliefs in the crucible of day–to–day experience. The great number of preached and published sermons by necessity had to resonate with Christians' real experiences of salvation and moral living. (Wesley followed this noteworthy Anglican tradition by using his own sermons as the primary means of Christian instruction for the Methodist movement.)

The emergence of experimental philosophy at the end of the seventeenth century brought an interest in sense data, but not necessarily in the kind of experience that is more personal and distinctly religious. John Locke had undertaken an inwardly oriented analysis of human understanding to go along with the outward analysis of nature in the physical sciences. But most Anglicans, including Locke, who embraced reason as a source of religious authority became distrustful of individual religious experience. "Enthusiasm" was a charge often directed against those perceived as having a private inspiration or exhibiting extravagance in religious devotion. Locke dedicated an entire chapter to a definition of enthusiasm, and that definition eventually became normative for eighteenth–century usage.[61] (Wesley was often accused of being an enthusiast, but he vigorously rejected that label, largely on the grounds that his estimation of Christian beliefs was consonant with reason and Scripture and the best of Christian antiquity.)

An Anglican critic, Peter Browne, early on faulted Locke for his tendency toward deism. But he also considered Locke a great genius and endeavored to extend his ideas theologically so as to encompass a more complete understanding of the nature and extent of experience, including religious experience. In *The Procedure, Extent and Limits of Human Understanding,* Browne argued:

> I propose rightly to state the whole Extent and Limits of human Understanding; to trace out the several steps and degrees of its Procedure from our first and simple Perception of sensible Objects, thro' the several operations of the pure Intellect upon them, till it grows up to its full Proportion of Nature: And to shew, how all our Conceptions of things supernatural are then *grafted* on it by Analogy; and how from thence it extends it self immensely into all the Branches of Divine and Heavenly Knowledge.[62]

By means of "the true nature of *Divine* analogy," Browne maintained "that the things of another World are now the *Immediate* Objects of our *Knowledge* and *Faith.*"[63] Although he did not gain lasting recognition for his work, Browne articulated a growing interest among Anglicans to incorporate into their theological thinking a broadened understanding of what may be experienced as a part of their religious beliefs. Richard Brantley suggests that "Browne's spiritual theology, then, pivotal in Anglican thought, signals the Anglican emphasis on spiritual experience during the rest of the eighteenth century and into the nineteenth."[64]

### Later Developments in Anglican Methodology

The century preceding Wesley saw a ferment of theological ideas that had an effect on Anglican methodology. McAdoo comments, "The history of the seventeenth century is one of religious controversy and theological dispute, and it reveals Anglicanism as standing apart from Roman Catholicism, from Calvinism after an initial period of rapprochement, and from Puritanism and the various religious bodies in the latter half of the century."[65] In attempting to establish a *via media* between extreme positions perceived to be held by Roman Catholics and the Reformers, Anglicans incorporated reason with Scripture and tradition in order to present a truly catholic understanding of Christian beliefs.

Yet, after the Restoration under Charles II in 1660, according to Maximin Piette, Anglicans were no longer able to rely on the official confessions of faith, including the Thirty nine Articles, to provide stability in church doctrine.[66] The importance of tradition faltered in the "ancients–against–modern conflict" reflected in the writings of many Anglicans, resulting in the disequilibration of theological method.[67] Scripture also became suspect primarily through the rising use of experimental philosophy in theological inquiry, not among such defenders of orthodoxy as Locke, but among the deists and some Latitudinarians. The latter groups argued for the primary authority of reason rather than Scripture, and this led to a rational religion dependent on natural rather than revealed theology.

So the threefold cord of Scripture, tradition, and reason began to unravel. The ascendancy of the authority of reason had several strands: Cambridge Platonists exalted an intuitive knowledge that supplanted all others; Latitudinarians uplifted the freedom of human reason over traditional religious authorities; and eventually deism sought only to affirm a rational religion devoid of the supernatural.

None of these pockets of thought became dominant in the Church of England, but all definitely had an effect. William Cannon comments, "The point is that rationalism had penetrated the ranks of orthodoxy; Christianity was viewed as nothing more than a correct set of opinions, a group of propositions which offer themselves to man's reason for acceptance or rejection."[68] Piette observes that from this religious crisis a moral crisis arose as Christianity was reduced to a formalistic affirmation of orthodox doctrine.[69]

Despite significant differences among Anglican theologians, however, questions of method still included all three sources of religious authority, according to McAdoo. To maintain credibility, theologians had to demonstrate a sound methodological integration. So while the earlier Anglicans gave closer attention to the threefold approach, it remained the norm for theological inquiry through the turn of the eighteenth century.[70]

## Sources of Theological Method in Wesley

This was the complex theological milieu in which Wesley gave himself to theological reflection and formulation. Entire books have been written on the sources of Wesley's theology and theological method, and even an extensive survey lies beyond the scope of this book.[71] The fact is that Wesley did not explicitly align himself with a particular theologian or theological movement for the development of his thought, but instead generally sought to assimilate already existing and accepted approaches to theological method, particularly the Anglican.

We should not assume, however, that Wesley made no contribution to the Christian understanding of theological method. On the contrary, he sought through his eclecticism to provide a more holistic understanding of religious beliefs, and he gave a proper respect to experience in the bargain.

Many scholarly accounts of Wesley's life are available, for he seems to have been one of those religious figures in history whose private life inspires and even demands intentional study for a full understanding of his theology.[72] For our purposes we want to give only a brief overview of Wesley's personal theological development, noting especially the influences that contributed to his theological method and beyond them some of the more prominent aspects of Anglican influence. The survey should help us begin to see a coherent theological method emerging in Wesley's thought.

The earliest influences on Wesley came from his parents, who were devout in religion and theologically aware. Both Samuel and Susanna Wesley were converts to Anglicanism from early upbringings in Nonconformity (Protestant dissenters from the Church of England). Samuel became an Anglican minister who produced numerous writings defending the church against Nonconformity. He was appreciative of contemporary Anglican theologians, often defending such controversial men as Henry Sacheverell and Francis Atterbury and even writing an elegy on the Latitudinarian Tillotson entitled "John, late Archbishop of Canterbury." Many of Samuel's views were later shared by his son John, including his admiration for Tillotson.[73]

In *Advice to a Young Clergyman,* a practical guide to those entering the ministry, Samuel Wesley demonstrated his vast knowledge and his desire to inculcate that knowledge in others. Surely John benefited from his father's advice to study "logic, history, law, pharmacy, natural and experimental philosophy, chronology, geography, the mathematics, even poetry, music or any other parts of learning."[74]

From his mother, John learned the rigors of a disciplined spiritual life. Piette notes that Wesley's "fire of inward desire she fed with the reading of Pascal and the *Imitation.*"[75] Outler suggests that Susanna encouraged John's spiritual development by introducing him to the will–mysticism of Spanish Roman Catholics such as Juan de Castañiza and Lorenzo Scupoli and of the Scottish theologian Henry Scougal.[76] But Susanna was aware of more than devotional literature dealing with spiritual reflection and discipline. When he was grown, she corresponded with John on a number of topics ranging from the nature of faith, salvation, and the Christian life to the hypostatic union of Jesus. She also discussed with John a number of theologians and philosophers, including Richard Baxter, George Berkeley, William Beveridge, Richard Fiddes, Thomas á Kempis, Law, Locke, Pearson, and Taylor.[77]

## Awakening at Oxford

The real beginning of Wesley's self–conscious reflection on theological inquiry can be traced to his student days at Christ Church College in the University of Oxford. In the passage of time, he progressively injected various elements of his Anglican heritage into his theological writings.

At Oxford Wesley studied in a theological environment influenced by the deanships of John Fell, Henry Aldrich, and Francis Atterbury.[78] Later on, he repeatedly recommended Fell's work *On the Epistles* to his Methodist assistants as a serious source of study in preparation for the ministry. From Aldrich, Wesley learned of Aristotle and logic through the dean's well–known textbook on logic, *Artis Logicæ Compendium.* He taught logic at Oxford and later translated Aldrich's work into English to promote logical inquiry among his Methodist assistants. Atterbury followed the traditional Anglican theological method by appealing to all three sources of religious authority when explaining and defending his preaching — for which he was well-known in Britain.[79]

Wesley received a thorough education in Anglican historical theology through the influence of his Oxford deans and professors. Outler notes that not even poor lectures from such men as John Guyse and Philip Doddridge could have failed to orient Wesley toward either the breadth or the controversies of theology in Anglicanism.[80] Moreover, we know that Wesley became familiar with the history of Anglican theology through the reading of Thomas Fuller's renowned *Church History of Britain* (1656) and Peter Heylyn's *Historia Quinquarticularis* (1660). Outler thinks these works helped to confirm Wesley in his preference for the Anglican tradition over any other.[81]

Other contemporary Anglican influences on Wesley included such men as George Bull, Samuel Clarke, Robert Lowth, and others associated with Oxford and the clergy leadership of the Church of England. But perhaps more than any of these, Wesley fell under the spiritual and theological tutelage of William Law. This great controversialist and devotional writer grew as a mentor for both John and Charles Wesley as they occasionally consulted him at Putney on spiritual matters.[82] Law exhibited an intense concern for Christian holiness as evidenced by his books *On Christian Perfection* (1726) and *A Serious Call to a Devout and Holy Life* (1728), both of which strongly influenced Wesley's spiritual development.

Law was also concerned to preserve Scripture, tradition, and reason in methodology and in so doing to avoid excessive rationalism. To that end, he published his *Case of Reason* against the deist Matthew Tindal and the Latitudinarian position in general.[83] Reacting against the intellectualism of the deists, Law sometimes made inflammatory comments against reason — not unlike Luther; but he constantly made use of reason in his arguments and at least preserved a place for it in theological inquiry and disputation.[84] Moreover, Law's "Appeal" reveals a concern for a methodologically balanced presentation of Christian beliefs. He intended to accomplish this by upholding Scripture, tradition, and reason and also by reconciling Christianity and science. Thus he would formulate a theology unifying revelation and reason.

While still at Oxford, Wesley also fell under the influence of non–Anglican thought, such as the mystical writings of Castañiza and Scupoli (whom he had learned of, we recall, through his mother) and other Roman Catholics such as Gaston de Renty and Gregory Lopez.[85] Outler says that Wesley inherited from these men and from Law the "participation motif" of religious experience before discovering

> its primal sources in the Johannine Gospel and its patristic interpreters (under the stimulus of the patristic revival in Oxford that he joined in). Thus, "holy living" as a vision of Christian existence was his earliest orientation.[86]

The experiential realization of faith in one's heart and practice remained important in Wesley's personal life as well as in his understanding of theology and theological method.

### Patristic Influences

The patristic revival to which Outler refers undoubtedly relates to the work
of such scholars as George Bull, Henry Dodwell, William Cave, Claude Fleury,
and Laurence Echard. Bull is well–known for marshaling a massive amount of
evidence in defense of Christian antiquity. In the 1730 edition of *The Works of
George Bull,* the editor, F. Holland, criticizes those — possibly Conyers
Middleton, Richard Watson, or Benjamin Hoadly — who claim that the primacy of Scripture is in some way opposed to the use of antiquity.[87] Wesley's early
interest in patristic studies was encouraged by John Clayton, a colleague in the
Holy Club at Oxford. Wesley credits Clayton with introducing him and other
Holy Club members to theological ideas and worship practices from the
ancient church.[88] No doubt Wesley's interest in patristic studies was nourished
through the reading of William Cave's *Primitive Christianity* (1672), Laurence
Echard's *Ecclesiastical History* (1702), and Claude Fleury's *Discourses on
Ecclesiastical History* (1721), all of which Wesley recommended to his Methodist
assistants for serious study in preparation for the ministry.[89]

Wesley continued patristic and theological studies after he left for Georgia
on a missionary journey in 1735. For the voyage Wesley gathered a sizeable
library, which Outler describes as numbering "more than sixty titles, the bulk of
them by Anglican authors of the seventeenth and eighteenth century, a few by
Nonconformists, and still fewer by Continental Protestants."[90] Outler considers
it significant that Wesley's library included a massive two–volume folio of
William Beveridge's *Pandectæ,* a vast array of ancient Eastern texts that influenced Wesley's experimentation with Christian liturgy as well as his views on
the participation–motif in theology. But Outler notes that in spite of his familiarity with patristic studies, Wesley's clearest historical competence was in seventeenth–century Anglican theology, coupled with an appreciation for certain
Puritan sources.[91] George Cell, William Cannon, and Robert Monk have provided excellent research in revealing the influence of Calvinist theology on
Wesley, especially as communicated by Puritan pastors and theologians in
Britain.[92]

### Pietism and Moravianism

Wesley also came into significant contact with Lutheran pietistic theology
through the German Moravians, with whom he sailed to the New World and
near whom he later lived in Georgia. He was greatly impressed with their piety;
his interest in experience predisposed him to their message of the personal
assurance of salvation. The influence of Peter Böhler, a representative of
Zinzendorf's Moravians in England, particularly helped Wesley through a time
of self–doubt about his ministry and his salvation. Böhler helped to nurture

Wesley spiritually up to the time of the well–known Aldersgate experience, which served as the *terminus a quo* of an important transitional period in Wesley's life.[93] The Moravian influence regarding assurance continued to play a crucial role in Wesley's later life in England.[94]

Outler sees the period surrounding Wesley's Aldersgate experience as a theological watershed of several Christian sources. Outler writes, "The unique mixture of theological notions thus far accumulated was now to be smelted and forged into an integral and dynamic theology in which Eastern notions of *synelthesis* (dynamic interaction between God's will and man's) were fused with the classical Protestant *sola fide* and *sola Scriptura*, and with the Moravian stress upon 'inner feeling.'"[95]

## Continental Protestantism

The major contribution of Continental Protestantism to Wesley's theology consisted of the doctrine of justification by faith alone (*sola fide*). Despite initial affinities with both Luther and Calvin, Wesley progressively moved away from the dogmatics of Continental Protestantism. The influence of Puritan ideas, however, remained important throughout his life. For example, he preserved the legacy of Puritan spirituality and Jonathan Edwards's analysis of religious affections through the publication of extracts of representative works in the *Christian Library* — though, as Outler points out, he did so with the "high Calvinism carefully filtered out."[96] In addition, Wesley recommended Baxter's work on justification and even published "An Extract of Mr. Richard Baxter's Aphorisms of Justification."[97]

## Anglican Preeminence

The synergistic character of Anglican theology appealed to Wesley, but it eventually brought him into conflict with Moravian quietism and Calvinist predestinarianism. Soon after Aldersgate, Wesley rejected the quietistic bent of Moravianism and instead turned to Anglicanism for doctrinal support of his emerging theology. In November 1738 he wrote that he "began more narrowly to inquire what the doctrine of the Church of England is, concerning the much controverted point of justification by faith; and the sum of what I found in the *Homilies* I extracted and printed for the use of others."[98] Outler notes that at this time Wesley undertook a more conscious self–identification with the English reformers:

> It marked the final stage of Wesley's maturation as a theologian and it continued to serve as the basic datum–plane for all subsequent developments in his thought. His pragmatic temper was prepared, of course, for contextual modifications of various sorts for new situations. But now at last — with his "Moravian" conversion at Aldersgate, followed by his disenchantments with Moravianism in Germany and Fetter Lane, his encounter with Edwards and his vital reappropriation of his Anglican heritage — the frame of Wesley's theology was finally set, and would so remain thereafter.[99]

Outler may overstate the settledness of Wesley's theology, but he correctly points out the self–consciousness of his approach — a self–consciousness that may be investigated in terms of theological method.

We cannot delve here into the development of Christian doctrine in the Methodist movement, except to note the emerging preeminence of the Anglican influence on Wesley.

## Seventeenth–Century Writings

If theological method was a topic of debate throughout the seventeenth century, then certainly Wesley was aware of that debate and of the issues at stake. He saw that the primary authority of Scripture was slowly crumbling and that tradition as a source of religious authority had all but disappeared among some prominent theologians, who supplanted reason as the primary source. He felt that reason was to be affirmed as an ally of Christianity when used proper- ly, but great care had to be taken to avoid excesses found in narrowly conceived systems of Christian beliefs, particularly deism.

Wesley progressively fused various elements of his Anglican heritage into his theological writings. During the early years of the Evangelical Revival, he relied on the first five Edwardean *Homilies,* usually attributed to Cranmer, in formu- lating a theological charter for his new ministry. [100] He first turned to the *Homilies* when searching for a theological foundation on which to base his newfound assurance of salvation. Wesley may not have always quoted directly from the host of sixteenth– and seventeenth–century Anglican divines, but he often made use of the *Homilies,* as in his apologetical writings in "An Earnest Appeal to Men of Reason and Religion" and "A Farther Appeal to Men of Reason and Religion."

For his sense of liturgy and worship, Wesley owed much to such Nonjurors as George Hickes, John Kettlewell, and Robert Nelson. [101] From Robert Sanderson he gained an appreciation of the Church of England as "the middle way." [102] Sanderson is best–remembered for his preface to the new *Prayer Book* (1662), with which Wesley was well acquainted. But Wesley primarily knew of and made use of Sanderson's works through *Logicæ Artis Compendium,* which Wesley abridged for common use. Wesley used this book, not only in teaching logic at Oxford and in training Methodist ministers, but also as a logical struc- ture on which to develop several of his sermons.

Pearson's classical work, *An Exposition of the Creed,* cited earlier as upholding the threefold sources of Scripture, tradition, and reason, made a distinct impres- sion on Wesley. The twelfth edition of this work was printed in 1741, so its pop- ularity continued throughout Wesley's early theological development and revival movement. In the book Pearson argued for the revival of Christian antiq- uity as a source of religious authority. He upheld the primary authority of "the Scriptures, from whence it [the Creed] was at first deduced," and also the rele- vance of natural theology, from which we derive "such arguments and reasons as are most proper to oppose the Atheists, who deny there is a God to be worshipped, a religion to be professed."[103] Showing a remarkable knowledge of the early Christian writers, Pearson argued for the importance of tradition during a time when theologians increasingly questioned its religious authority. Wesley highly recommended Pearson's *Exposition* as second only to the Bible in acquainting people with the doctrines of Christianity.

> In order to be well acquainted with the doctrines of Christianity, you need but one book, (besides the Bible,) — Bishop Pearson on the Creed. This I advise you to read and master thoroughly: It is a library in one volume.[104]

Wesley also quoted from Pearson in his apologetical writings. In defense of his view of sanctification, he included in a letter to the Bishop of Gloucester a two–page quotation from Pearson, referring to him as being as "learned and orthodox a Divine as ever England bred."[105] In "A Farther Appeal" Wesley defended himself against accusations of enthusiasm by including a three–page quote from Pearson ("a man no ways inferior to Bishop Chrysostom"), concerning "the ordinary operations of the Holy Ghost."[106]

Jeremy Taylor's influence on Wesley stems primarily from his pastoral writings on the idea of the Christian life as devotion as found in *Holy Living* and *Holy Dying*.[107] But these writings also contain insights into Anglican theological method — a fact most scholars overlook. Taylor claimed to draw his theological "rules and advices from the fountains of Scripture, and the purest channels of the primitive Church."[108] Taylor also employed reason in his theological method.

> Whatsoever is against right reason, that no faith can oblige us to believe. For although reason is not the positive and affirmative measures of our faith…yet in all our Creed, there can be nothing against reason.[109]

Taylor was quick to set definite limits on the authority of reason, but he could not imagine true Christian religion being unreasonable.

Outler points out that for his views on ministerial order Wesley was largely dependent upon the Latitudinarians — Tillotson, Stillingfleet, and Burnet.[110] From the Cambridge Platonists, whom he knew largely through the writings of John Norris,[111] Wesley recognized the importance of addressing all three sources of religious authority, even if Cambridge Platonists referred to tradition only to denigrate its methodological usefulness.

## The Growth of Science

Most Anglicans, especially the Latitudinarians and the Cambridge Platonists, were influenced by the growth of science and of scientific method, though not always the same way. For Wesley, the interest in experimentation was hardly for mere scientific knowledge; it affected his approach to theology. He was intrigued by scientific experiments in electricity, especially those done by Benjamin Franklin and Richard Lovett,[112] and he even published a work entitled "The Desideratum: Or, Electricity made plain and useful. By a Lover of Mankind, and of Common Sense," which drew from numerous scientific articles.[113] In the preface to this work Wesley extolled the highly probable health benefits of electricity, even though hypotheses had not yet been developed that adequately explained the facts about electricity derived from experimentation.[114] Wesley did not think that a complete philosophical or conceptual understanding of electricity was necessary in order to undertake further experiments which might reveal immediate and practical benefits of electricity. This reflects his approach to theology: his experimental approach did not require complete theoretical understanding if useful results were already being achieved.

In his appeal to experience as a source of religious authority, Wesley drew upon that experimental idiom that was characteristic of both the practical divinity of Anglicanism and the British empirical tradition. Like many other Anglicans, Wesley came to appreciate the work of John Locke's experimental philosophy and Peter Browne's critical response to it. Without accepting all that Locke argued for in his experimental philosophy, Wesley had praise for his work and his general support for traditional Christian beliefs.[115] Hindley suggests that Wesley not only "imbibed" Lockean philosophy from his readings of Browne, but also derived from him the needed conceptual extrapolation of Locke's philosophy to include religious experience as a crucial part of one's theological method.[116] Thus Wesley developed his unique integration of experimental method and biblical theology. In the preface to his "Sermons on Several Occasions," Wesley claims he "endeavoured to describe the true, the scriptural, experimental religion."[117]

By "experimental" — today we would use the term "experiential" — Wesley meant more than the empirical investigation of religious and other experiences.[118] He was primarily concerned with the intuitive experience of the transcendent reality of the Holy Spirit in a person's life. But because such experiences are to a certain extent empirically understandable and observable, Wesley was willing to investigate seriously the relevance of religious experiences to the formulation of theology. He wished to present his theological work in a way that was consonant with the best in contemporary scientific investigation rather than contrary to it.[119] Thus he reflected the trend in Anglican theological thinking that sought to bridge rather than obliterate differences between theology, philosophy, and science.

## Summary

From the time of Hooker, Anglicans had sought to incorporate reason into a balanced understanding of theological method that gave proper respect to the religious authority of Scripture and tradition. In the words of Francis Paget, "For on equal loyalty to the unconflicting rights of reason, of Scripture, and of tradition rest the distinctive strength and hope of the English Church."[120]

Amid competing currents of theological thought, Anglicanism for the most part recognized the need to respect all three components. This recognition resulted in a generally consistent approach, and McAdoo in fact concludes that this overall consistency represents the real distinctiveness of Anglican theology.

> If the distinctiveness of Anglicanism lies not in a theology but in a theological method, the distinctiveness of the method lies in the conjunction of these elements in one theological instrument. The impression of basic unity in writers of the seventeenth century is accounted for by concurrence in the use of this common theological method. Party theology in the later sense did not exist until the latter part of the century but there were differing emphases in theology. These were minimized by means of a shared method, so that, on occasion, Hammond will take a characteristically Latitudinarian line while Stillingfleet will make use of ideas usually associated with the Laudian point of view.[121]

Biblical authority remained central, but a new sense of freedom emerged in the Anglicans' understanding of doctrinal beliefs. Reason brought with it a freedom to renew the study of natural theology, generally within the confines of orthodox Christians beliefs, in a way that Continental Protestantism had discouraged. But Anglicans did not want to slip back into a revised form of Roman Catholicism. They prided themselves on presenting a theological alternative or *via media*, which, as McAdoo comments,

> was not in its essence compromise or an intellectual expedient but a quality of thinking, an approach in which elements usually regarded as mutually exclusive were seen to be in fact complementary. These things were held in a living tension, not in order to walk the tight–rope of compromise, but because they were seen to be mutually illuminating and to fertilize each other.[122]

This tension embraced not only the primacy of scriptural authority and the necessary role of reason in theological method, but also the ongoing need to retain a historical, orthodox understanding of Christian beliefs. References to Christian antiquity were not to be arbitrarily evoked to stifle a reasonable understanding of Scripture, but rather used to identify central motifs of Scripture and thus affirm the catholicity of those beliefs. Consensual creedal formulations from the early church were to be understood, valued, and followed as closely as possible; nonessentials in Christian beliefs, both ancient and contemporary, were to be identified and tolerated, but not required for orthodoxy. One needed to consider antiquity just as much as new knowledge derived from the burgeoning scientific studies of nature and the philosophies of experimentation.

If reason was free to supplement studies of Scripture and tradition, it was also free to incorporate new knowledge that might confirm and illuminate Christian beliefs from intellectual disciplines other than theology. A sense of tension existed between reason and the other sources of religious authority, namely, Scripture and tradition. But, as McAdoo suggests, it was a healthy, living tension that accepted neither authoritarianism nor uncontrolled liberty.

> An over–all characteristic of Anglican theological method is then this polarity or quality of living tension, which goes far towards explaining how the element of

reason did not for the most part become over–weighted during the seventeenth century since it never existed in a vacuum, theologically speaking, but operated in conjunction with other elements such as the appeal to Scripture and antiqui-ty.[123]

Wesley came on the scene at a time when the questions of theological method and religious authority had been prominent topics of debate in England for over a century. Despite inevitable differences in theological emphases, Anglicans generally still affirmed their distinctive threefold method-ology. Wesley's Anglican environment and education provided fertile ground for theological reflection.

In the midst of these debates, Wesley sought to revive a vital understanding of Christian faith, particularly within the Church of England. He had experi-enced a spiritual revival in his own life; so he endeavored to provide the same opportunity for revival to others. Piette observes that Wesley had been pro-foundly affected through a kind of personal experimentation in spiritual growth and self–discipline. Perhaps the insights that resulted from his experience would be of benefit to others. Piette says, "Since practical experience and experimen-tation had been triumphant in the field of natural science, Wesley was led to transport it to the religious domain – to the field of the supernatural life."[124]

Piette emphasizes Wesley's use of practical experience and experimentation in regard to personal spirituality. Wesley understood his task in the more prac-tical terms of evangelism and church renewal. But experience and experimen-tation may also be found in his working knowledge of theological method, even though he was content not to articulate a new approach. Anglicanism already provided an established way of approaching theological and practical issues, and Wesley simply worked within the flow of that thought. He did not perceive himself as formulating anything distinctively new and certainly not innovative in the history of orthodox Christian thinking. Yet, working within the parameters of theological method that he inherited from Anglicanism, Wesley not only assumed, but in important ways surpassed, that distinguished heritage.

# 2

# An Overview of Wesley's Theology

There has been great diversity in the attempts to interpret the work of John Wesley. Some emphasize Wesley's work as a vital Christian evangelist and founder of the Methodist movement, at the cost of neglecting the theological insight found there. Others emphasize Wesley's work as a significant and innovative theologian, overlooking the dynamic, evangelistic thrust of his thought and ministry. One must strike a balance between seeing Wesley as a practically oriented evangelist and a methodically oriented theologian. Wesley knew that good theology informs the best practice of ministry and that good practice in ministry informs the best theology.

No one considers his theology as a system of the same rank as an Aquinas or a Calvin, but then Wesley never intended to write a systematic theology. He would neither have apologized for this fact nor have tried to defend his theology for not being systematic in the classical sense of the term.[1] Though Wesley was not indifferent to such enterprises, he considered it more important to focus on issues having a more immediate and holistic impact on the life of faith in his day. Thus his theological endeavors took a more modest approach in practically ministering to the immediate needs of evangelism and the Methodist renewal movement in the Anglican Church.

In writing about practical ministry, Wesley wrote a great deal of theology. His theology may be found in his sermons, tracts, letters, journals, biblical commentaries, and other theological treatises. As diverse as they are in form, his writings provide only piecemeal glimpses into his theology because Wesley generally addressed pressing issues related to ministry. As such, the form of Wesley's theological writings appears more akin to a Luther than to a Calvin in the sense that Wesley utilized no formal apparatus or system for organizing all of his theology. Although Wesley sometimes commented that the content of his theology came within a "hair's breadth" of Calvin,[2] constructive characteristics in Wesley's theology reflect the systemic growth of a plant or tree more than the systematic organization of botany. In this sense, Wesley not only resembles the theology of Luther but also the theology that we find in Scripture — theology that grew out of the context of lived experience.

All during his writing ministry, Wesley sought to unite the dynamic,

Spirit–filled reality of life in Christ with sound analytic and critical thinking. Borrowing the words of his brother, Charles, John sought to "Unite the pair so long disjoined, Knowledge and vital piety: Learning and holiness combined."[3] Critics often forget that Wesley never intended to write a systematic theology and wrongly caricature him by evaluating him with inappropriate criteria. Interpreters must evaluate Wesley's theology by criteria in line with the intent or spirit of his writings.

## The Spirit of Theology

As we have seen, Wesley owed much of his theological understanding to the Anglican tradition in which he was raised and educated. He generally felt no need to articulate or justify his approach to religious issues, because he aligned himself so closely with the distinctive approach to theological method characteristic of seventeenth–century Anglicanism.

In describing the "spirit" of the Anglican tradition of theology, McAdoo observes that "the absence of an official theology in Anglicanism is something deliberate which belongs to it[s) essential nature, for it has always regarded the teaching and practice of the undivided Church of the first five centuries as a criterion."[4] Thus one distinctive characteristic of Wesley's theology, as with the Anglican tradition, is that it proceeds not from a systematic theology, but from the spirit in which theological questions are handled. Therefore, the theology of Wesley and Anglicanism should not be viewed as something indeterminate or loosely defined, despite appearances. McAdoo points out that, rather than lacking critical or comprehensive reflection, this theology "is something real and ponderable expressing itself by a specific theological method."[5]

Wesley recognized, however, that Anglican theology had the tendency to encourage a formal, rationalistic understanding of religion. In the preface to his compilation of "Sermons on Several Occasions," Wesley sought to avoid rationalistic pitfalls by renouncing academic identifications in order to stress soteriology as the focus of his theology.

> Therefore of set purpose I abstain from all nice and philosophical speculations, from all perplexed and intricate reasonings, and as far as possible from even the show of learning, unless in sometimes citing the original Scriptures....I want to know one thing, the way to heaven how to land safe on that happy shore.[6]

Yet Wesley did not dismiss all analytical and critical thinking. On the contrary, he continued to employ careful logic throughout his pastoral and theological writings. Wesley may not have been a systematic theologian, but he did approach his writing methodically and thus considered his work substantially consistent throughout his life and ministry. He sought to unite sound learning with the existential force of Christian experience, which he generally understood as a soteriological category.

This evangelical spirit of Wesley is not an isolated eighteenth–century phenomenon. Scholars such as John Dillenberger and Claude Welch refer to the almost simultaneous emergence of Continental Pietism, British Methodism, and the American Great Awakening as a "revival of the evangelical spirit."[7] Thus Wesley represents something perennial, answering the dual need among people for "knowledge and vital piety."

## The Soteriological Focus

Wesley's interest in theological interpretation and application focuses on his central concern for salvation — a concern that permeates his writings. According to Wesley, the end or goal of true religion is "salvation: the means to attain it, faith."[8] He adds "that these two little words — I mean faith and salvation — include the substance of all the Bible, the marrow, as it were, of the whole Scripture."[9] Wesley intended to communicate the evangelistic gospel of salvation, free and full, to all who would believe. He held that God in Christ made salvation free to all who would respond in faith and full to all who would respond to the ongoing grace of God in their lives through the sanctifying work of the Holy Spirit. Salvation, therefore, represents a complex, progressive event in which believers receive the grace to live holy lives.

Some interpreters consider his emphasis on holiness as the essential doctrine of Wesley's theology. But Wesley saw no reason to separate salvation and holiness unnecessarily.[10] In "A Farther Appeal," Wesley responded to objections concerning his central doctrines, including "either the nature and condition of *justification,* the nature and. condition of *salvation,* the nature of justifying and saving *faith,* or the *Author* of faith and salvation."[11] In other words, Wesley considered salvation and concomitant doctrines to represent the heart and soul of his writings.

Mitsuru Fujimoto argues that Wesley "selected one vital area of Christian theology, and in its treatment demonstrated himself to be genuinely a *systematic* theologian, not merely a practical one."[12] Without arguing for Wesley as a systematic theologian, traditionally conceived, Fujimoto rightly emphasizes the consistency of focus Wesley brought to bear on his theological writings.

Because of his comprehensive understanding of salvation and his concern to communicate that understanding to others, Wesley began his theologically instructive collection of "Sermons on Several Occasions" with the sermon "Salvation by Faith."[13] The sermons that immediately follow this one elaborate that first and most essential theme: salvation.[14] Subsequent sermons continue to emphasize the freedom and fullness of salvation offered to all by the grace of God through the saving work of Jesus Christ. Luke Tyerman observes that most of Wesley's sermon texts have direct bearing on his overriding concern to explain the scriptural way of salvation.[15]

Although salvation may constitute a reality more easily received than we often realize, the nature and implications of salvation for our lives require extended theological elaboration. Wesley believed that good Christian theory must inform a healthy, comprehensive view of one's relationship with God in

Jesus Christ. All his writings, not just his sermons, served either to elaborate on this theme of salvation or to promote the ministry of the Methodist movement in bringing salvation to all the world.

## Consistency of Theology

In refusing to identify with academic approaches to Christian thought and in claiming to speak only "plain truth for plain people," Wesley simply wanted to call himself a "Bible Christian."[16] As far back as his student days at Oxford, Wesley gloried in calling himself *homo unius libri* — "a man of one book."[17] In appealing to "the law and the Testimony," Wesley claimed that "This is the general method of knowing what is 'the holy and acceptable will of God.'"[18] But throughout his writings he appealed to more than Scripture; his approach betrays greater complexity.

Unfortunately, Wesley compounds the complexity in that he never provided an explicit statement of theological method or a theological prolegomenon. As a result, we must seek to distill methodological or systematic elements implicitly from Wesley's writings.

Although Wesley focused more on practical, soteriological interests concerning the Christian life, he did write with the intention of being methodical or at least consistent. Discussing Christian perfection in 1777, Wesley claimed that he wrote with purity and simplicity of intention and that his views had not substantially changed for over thirty–eight years.[19] Moreover, he undertook several writing projects that required extensive work in consistently presenting his ideas and those of others. For example, he wrote and edited four volumes of sermons that served as a doctrinal canon for the Methodists along with the *Notes upon the New Testament*.[20] Outler describes these works as the "negative limits" of Methodist doctrine that in 1763 came to be known as "the Model Deed."[21]

From the beginning of his ministry, Wesley shied away from establishing a set creed or articles of religion. Instead, doctrinal formulations arose out of "conversations" dealing with "1. What to teach; 2. How to teach; and, 3. What to do; that is, how to regulate our doctrine, discipline, and practice."[22] In 1784 Wesley finally established the Twenty–five Articles of Religion (a variation of the Thirty–nine Articles of the Church of England), though Outler points out that these *doctrines* had been used long before in dialogue form.[23] Despite Wesley's hesitancy to formulate doctrinal standards and his refusal to define them too narrowly, Wesley retained a constancy in theological outlook. Outler notes,

> Wesley's refusal to define doctrinal standards too narrowly was a matter of principle: it was in no way the sign of an indecisive mind. Such a notion makes no sense when one considers how confident his own theological self–understanding was (as reflected in his controversial writings), and in his arbitrary decisions as an editor.[24]

In addition to statements related to doctrine, Wesley wrote numerous tracts, exegetical notes, the huge *Journal,* and even a full–length monograph entitled "The Doctrine of Original Sin, according to Scripture, Reason, and Experience."

Certainly Wesley could not have claimed to have written consistently on such numerous and varied materials for so many years without a relatively coherent conception of how he approached theology.

Other Wesley scholars besides Outler have argued for the consistency of Wesley's thought in numerous ways. The most impressive example, concerning Wesley's view of human understanding, includes the study by Richard Brantley in which he argues that Wesley drew largely from the philosophical method of Locke in developing his approach to theology. Brantley states, "During the 1740s, then, Wesley completed his philosophical formulation of method."[25] He says,

> Wesley's methodology, at once theological and philosophical, continued to operate throughout his mind's long history. After the 1740s, it is true, when his thought was formulated to his satisfaction and he hoped to the satisfaction of fair−minded readers at large, he wrote more and more with his followers in mind....the later words are more often sermons than not; but this does not mean that the later sermons, of which I shall discuss a number, are necessarily any less fully methodological; for the writings of the 1740s, of which the ones just discussed form a large sample, demonstrate the philosophically theological procedure of his homiletical as well as nonhomiletical genres.[26]

Brantley marshals an impressive amount of support for his thesis concerning the connection between Locke and Wesley. He further believes that Wesley has too seldom received due credit for his theological and philosophical sophistication *and* for his influence on subsequent British thought, including disciplines beyond theology and philosophy.[27]

It remains a moot question as to whether anyone can truly remain consistent in his theology without fully articulating a systematic theology. Even then, consistency does not automatically follow. Wesley did change the emphasis of his theology over the course of years. Yet the spirit of Wesley persisted − a spirit that sought to communicate the plain truth of salvation, free and full, to plain people, without the encumbrances of nonessential theological jargon and system building. If Wesley changed − and no doubt he did from time to time − it involved not so much the essential doctrines of Methodism as a willingness to recognize different expressions of those doctrines.[28]

## Systematic Characteristics of Theology

A few interpreters of Wesley have noticed methodical or systematic elements in Wesley's theology, and some have provided initial studies into his theological method.[29] Most studies, however, center in the relationship between Wesley's use of religious authorities. Umphrey Lee comments that most Wesley scholars "too easily assumed that Wesley simply reinstated orthodox theology and the letter of the Bible as Christian infallibilities, or that he set up Christian experience as the final authority."[30] Lee considers the issue more complex because Wesley recognized "how impossible it is to fit the manifold facts of human experience into anyone of the theological molds which were ready to his hand."[31]

Because he sees Wesley using a variety of religious authorities, Lee admires the outcome of Wesley's work, though he considers it inconsistent and inadequate because of its failure to provide a logical statement of theological convictions.

That observation brings us to the quadrilateral, which serves in this book as a model or paradigm with which to investigate Wesley's theological method and use of religious authorities, specifically the relationship between Scripture, tradition, reason, and experience. The term proves helpful in distinguishing the sources of religious authority to which Wesley appealed, in varying degrees, in his approach to theology.

As we discovered, the term "quadrilateral" has a relatively recent history, though its constituent parts have functioned at least tacitly throughout church history.[32] Thomas C. Oden argues that all four sources of religious authority were "implicitly employed by ancient ecumenical teachers, but we do not find an adequate, explicit clarification of the relation of experience and reason to Scripture and tradition until the Reformation and modern periods."[33]

Modern use of the term originated with the Protestant Episcopal (Anglican) Church in nineteenth–century America. The Lambeth Quadrilateral (1888) signified the four articles representing the essentials for a reunited Christian church from an Anglican perspective. However, the four articles differ greatly from what interpreters describe as the quadrilateral in Wesley.[34] Yet, though the term signifies something different today, "quadrilateral" suggests a historical tie with the greater Anglican tradition. Outler had all this in mind when he imitated references to the quadrilateral in discussion of Wesley's methodological use of Scripture, tradition, reason, and experience.

In practice the term has often distorted both the Lambeth understanding of the quadrilateral and Wesley's understanding of theological method and religious authority. The very nature of the geometric term implies an equality or homogenization of the four elements. Although it may not have been intended by those who coined the term, too often it has resulted in making all parts of the Wesleyan quadrilateral of equal worth or authority in theology. At worst, it has resulted in a kind of vote between the four sources of authority where two or more may override another, impugning potentially the primary authority of Scripture.

Of course, Wesley never intended for this to happen. For him, Scripture always represented the primary source of religious authority. Wesley believed that tradition, with proper discernment, reinforces the truth of Scripture, as do reason and experience. If one insists on choosing a geometric figure as a paradigm for Wesley, a tetrahedron — a tetrahedral pyramid would be more appropriate. Scripture would serve as the foundation of the pyramid, with the three sides labeled tradition, reason, and experience as complementary but not primary sources of religious authority.

One of the more helpful paradigms of the Wesleyan quadrilateral may be found in the writings of Richard Lovelace. Lovelace, a Presbyterian, argues that Wesley, like the Continental Reformers, kept in balance the four sources of truth that shape the quality of our faith.

> It is helpful to analyze our current situation using what has been called "the Wesleyan quadrilateral"....
>
> Imagine a baseball diamond. Home plate is *Scripture*. First base is *tradition*. Second base is *reason* and third base is *experience*....
>
> No modern movement has the radical courage to follow Scripture where it leads, tempered with the delicate correctives of traditional knowledge, reason and experience, which the Reformers and John Wesley displayed.[35]

Presumably one must begin theological reflection with home plate — Scripture. But to "score a run" one must cross the bases of tradition, reason, and experience before completing the return to Scripture — the start and finish of theological reflection.

Any paradigm or model, however, eventually breaks down when it comes to such matters. One could easily turn the pyramid on its head and diminish the authority of Scripture, or perhaps turn the pyramid on a side with reason or experience serving as the foundation. Likewise, Lovelace's paradigm could easily be distorted. The important thing is the primacy that Wesley placed in Scripture; other sources of authority supplemented but never surpassed the Word. Wesley could believe all this because he never expected tradition, reason, or experience to confute Scripture in any substantial way. Thus, in order to understand the Wesleyan quadrilateral, in relation to Wesley and its heritage in Anglican theology, we must understand it historically and theologically. and *not* geometrically. Despite temptations to do otherwise, we must conceive of the Wesleyan quadrilateral metaphorically rather than literally.

Any attempt to devise a geometric paradigm or analogy for Wesley's use of Scripture, tradition, reason, and experience diametrically opposes his approach to theology. Wesley had a more organic and practical approach. Scripture remained primary in its religious authority, but Wesley expected that at least reason and experience would readily support and illuminate scriptural truths. There was no need to articulate a precise hierarchical relationship between the various sources of authority because Wesley did not expect them to contradict and harm one another.

Wesley does not use any kind of model for describing his methodology, but if we wanted to illustrate the quadrilateral, an organic paradigm would better communicate the catholic, integrative character of Wesley's theological method.[36] Perhaps an analogy of the human body would do. Like Paul's description of the church as the "body of Christ,"[37] Scripture, tradition, reason, and experience function as an organic whole. Scripture may serve as the *head*, but we should not speak of a single part of the body without the others. The various parts are interdependent for living a healthy and productive life.

Wesley often mentions several of the sources of authority in the same breath. For example, in the preface to the third edition of his collected works, he claimed to "present to serious and candid men my last and maturest thoughts, agreeable, I hope, to Scripture, reason, and Christian antiquity."[38] He may have excluded an explicit reference to experience here, out of concern to appear within mainline Anglican theology. But appeals to experience occur throughout his writings and constitute an essential part of the fabric of his theological method. Similarly, the full title of his longest theological monograph is "The Doctrine of Original Sin, according to Scripture, Reason, and Experience" – again, mentioning three of the four elements, omitting tradition. But the very purpose of the monograph is to affirm the doctrine of original sin as an essential part of Christian tradition. In the preface to this treatise he cites the need to "advance the cause of true, primitive, scriptural Christianity; of solid, rational virtue; of the deep, holy, happy, spiritual religion, which is brought to light by the gospel."[39]

Although Wesley does not explicitly group all four sources of religious authority together in description of theological method, all four are inextricably bound up in his theology because each source remains essential to the complex of his methodology. Frequently all four coalesced in single passages. For example, the quadrilateral is embedded throughout "An Earnest Appeal" and the *Arminian Magazine*,[40] as well as in "A Farther Appeal,"[41] "Principles of a Methodist,"[42] "Principles of a Methodist Farther Explained,"[43] "A Letter to the Right Reverend the Lord Bishop of Gloucester,"[44] "To Dr. Conyers Middleton,"[45] and "Original Sin,"[46] and in sermons such as "On Sin in Believers,"[47] and "Means of Grace."[48] No single aspect of his approach to theology should be emphasized to the exclusion of another; Wesley took all four into consideration in his doctrinal concerns.

In giving primacy to Scripture, Wesley felt free to introduce extrabiblical authorities in theological reflection and formulation. These authorities serve to organize, illumine, and apply Scripture. For example, tradition dispels doubts because it contains historic insights from those, primarily from Christian antiquity, who were united in their conceptions of the things pertaining to God. Reflecting on the interpretation of Scripture in the preface to his "Sermons on Several Occasions," Wesley wrote,

> If any doubt still remains [concerning biblical interpretation], I consult those who are experienced in the things of God, and then the writings whereby, being dead, they yet speak. And what I thus learn, that I teach.[49]

Here Wesley readily admits his constructive use of tradition in aiding the understanding of Scripture.

Reason and experience play equally important roles in Wesley's approach to theology. Reason facilitates the whole reflective and formulative process of theological endeavors while attention to experience serves as a creative means by which to capture the dynamic reality of faith in a personal, ongoing relationship with Jesus Christ. Neither experience nor reason adds substance to biblical truth, but it confirms and vitalizes such truths in the life of the believer. Experience particularly contributes to a more holistic formulation of Christian theology that respects the vital, ongoing witness of the Holy Spirit.

Wesley did not consider this use of experience to be theologically innovative. Rather, he perceived that experience had always been tacitly employed in the formulation of Christian theology. His emphasis on experience also reflected the concern for practical divinity evident in seventeenth–century British theology, which had an important influence on Wesley's thought.

The dynamic interrelationship among these four sources of religious authority informed all of Wesley's writings. Wesley did not reflect on a doctrine for long without considering how it related to tradition, reason, and experience as well as Scripture. Together the four sources provided a more genuinely catholic, integrative, and contemporary understanding of Christian beliefs. Unfortunately, he did not fully articulate the implications of this interrelationship. Since he had neither the inclination nor the need to systematize such ideas, he may never have understood the full potential of his theological method. But one cannot deny that theological method was a concern of his or that he functioned with discernable working hypotheses in his theological writings. Thus we may profitably continue to refer to the Wesleyan quadrilateral in reference to Wesley because of the distinctive application of Scripture, tradition, reason, and experience in his approach to theology.

## General Characteristics of Wesley's Theology

Before turning to the theological method specifically, we should consider the *general* characteristics of Wesley's theology that reflect his methodology. Of course, because no theological apparatus or overarching system unifies the whole of Wesley's theology, we must resist the temptation to make Wesley appear more systematic than he really is. Nevertheless, we may distill a cluster of characteristics without expecting them to provide either an exhaustive or a systematic interpretation of his theological method and general thought. In other words, we may find a number of traits appearing in Wesley that describe his theology even though they may not all represent terms he used himself. They provide insights into his theology that are relevant to us. We will deal with these in a sequence that reflects their general order of importance to Wesley.

Wesley considered himself first and foremost a *biblical* Christian and theologian. So the quality of being biblical must begin any discussion of his theology.

Beyond the primary authority of Scripture, Wesley's concern to uplift the *orthodox tradition* of Christian antiquity seems to represent the second most important resource for understanding Christian truths. Wesley considered tradition important because it contributed to the actual content of Christian beliefs. For example, from Christian antiquity we receive the canon of the New Testament and the doctrinal summaries of the undivided, ecumenical church. We also receive insights into theological, ethical, and ecclesial matters not mentioned in Scripture. Wesley believed that the Holy Spirit continued to inspire the canonical and creedal decisions of the ancient church and thus begat an essential extension of the witness of Scripture. Certainly Wesley was always careful to weigh the church's teachings in the balance of Scripture, but he held high respect for their substantive contributions to Christian beliefs and practices.

After tradition, reason seems to play the next strongest supporting role in religious authority.[50] Therefore his theology is not only biblical and orthodox, but also *analytical and critical.*

Finally, Wesley had equally important concerns for the *experiential* (in his parlance, "experimental") and *practical* dimension of theology.

These characteristics were not always explicit in Wesley's theological writings, but he brought an awareness of each source of religious authority to bear on his work. Wesley kept them all in a healthy tension, and he did not make doctrinal decisions without considering each source. Similar to the interplay between Scripture, tradition, and reason held in tension within the Anglican tradition, Wesley used his sources of religious authority as a single methodological instrument. Their interdependent and correlative relationship informed Wesley's reflection on and formulation of responses to the immediate theological needs of his life and ministry.

We will discuss each trait of theology in the order suggested by Wesley's priorities.[51] Our discussion does not entail an analysis of Wesley's theological method and view of religious authority. We will say more about the former in chapter 3 and focus on the latter in chapters 4–7. The matter at hand is primarily to introduce readers to the breadth of theology — making concerns found in Wesley. Together the various characteristics help us to gain a comprehensive overview of Wesley's theology that will provide the necessary background for a more detailed study of his theological method and view of religious authority.

## A Biblical Approach to Theology

It bears repeating that Wesley considered Scripture the primary source of religious authority. He described Scripture as the "inviolable Word" of God and as the "words 'of the Spirit of God.'"[52] His concern to uphold this primacy has increasing importance today because of those who would make tradition, reason, and experience coequal with Scripture in his theological method.[53] Other sources of religious authority may confirm, enhance, or vitalize the truth of the Scripture for our lives, but Scripture alone remains Wesley's final source of religious authority.[54]

Wesley did not ignore critical questions about the inspiration and interpretation of Scripture. Indeed, he used a fourfold argument to affirm divine inspiration in "A Clear and Concise Demonstration for the Divine Inspiration of the Holy Scripture." Although he sensed the need to elaborate on his view, Wesley generally cared less about the theory of divine inspiration than he cared about the content of the gospel message concerning salvation and how that message might best be experienced and communicated. Thus the authority of Scripture stemmed more from its existential sufficiency for salvation and holy living than from a theoretic or syllogistic construct for biblical inspiration.

Wesley did not feel a slave to Scripture. Like Hooker, he did not take an authoritarian or obscurantist approach to biblical interpretation. Although Scripture was the fountainhead of Christian theology, other sources of religious authority could confirm or enhance the truth of the Word. Scripture alone remained the only authority sufficient for salvation, but Wesley also felt the freedom and necessity of appealing to tradition, reason, and experience. His holistic approach to the diversity of religious authorities resulted in a more genuinely catholic theology, which is open to every dimension of relationship with God.

## An Orthodox/Traditional Approach to Theology

Wesley never considered himself to be outside the longstanding tradition of biblically inspired beliefs held since Christian antiquity. To him, the creeds faithfully distilled the essence of Christian doctrines. Thus the creeds and writings of the early church fathers were an invaluable tool for understanding and establishing central motifs of basic biblical truths. While acknowledging the need to use great care in selecting what to hold on to, Wesley often looked to Christian traditions as a source of encouragement and insight for dealing with issues not discussed in Scripture.

He perceived himself and the Methodist movement directly in line with the most ancient, orthodox strand of Christian tradition. In the sermon "On Laying the Foundation of the New Chapel," Wesley traced the historical progression of Christianity from the time of Christ up through the Methodist revival.[55] He began his chronology with the *old religion* of love, which he first described in "An Earnest Appeal."[56] This old religion he characterized as *the religion of the Bible, the religion of the primitive church* ("of the whole church in the purest ages"), *the religion of the Church of England,* and finally, as ending "the progress and nature of this religion," with *the Methodist "revival of religion."*[57]

Although we may consider Wesley presumptuous in arguing for this succession of Methodism from the oldest and truest form of religion, we can at least appreciate his concern to present the most orthodox or traditional understanding of the Christian message that was possible.

*Catholic Spirit*

Throughout Wesley's writings, Christian love constitutes the irreducible point of similarity among all believers, past and present, and the source of motivation for future acceptance, appreciation, and cooperation.[58] The classic statement of Wesley's openness to fellowship among the diverse traditions of Christian belief may be found in the sermon entitled "Catholic Spirit." By a "catholic spirit" Wesley means universal love toward others.[59] Such love should be directed not only toward God and one's neighbor, but especially toward the Christian neighbor despite differences in theological opinion. Catholic or universal love should represent a bedrock of Christlike love shared among Protestants, Catholics, and other Christians.

Wesley's catholic concern was not the least bit naive. He saw that certain doctrinal positions would continue to separate Methodists from other Christian traditions. But his spirit or attitude was always one of openness rather than antagonism toward other believers.

*Theological Liberality/Toleration*

Rather than cavil over diverse theological opinions, Wesley tolerated a degree of flexibility or liberality without compromising what he considered essential to the gospel message as best attested by Christian antiquity. He thus endeavored to maintain a degree of liberality in what he considered nonessential matters of theology. Wesley distinguished between what is scripturally essential or fundamental and what is nonessential or a matter of conscience.

In "The Witness of Our Own Spirit," Wesley said, "Whatever the Scripture neither forbids nor enjoins (either directly or by plain consequence) he believes to be of an indifferent nature, to be in itself neither good nor evil: this being the whole and sole outward rule whereby his conscience is to be directed in all things."[60] Wesley considered his emphasis on liberality biblically based, but it also reflected a growing spirit of religious toleration that was characteristic of seventeenth- and eighteenth-century England.

Wesley knew that knowledge of orthodoxy alone does not fulfill the requirements of true, heart religion. People may hold many differing theological opinions not essential to classical Christian beliefs, yet Wesley said that "their experience may be as sound as ours" concerning salvation.[61] In areas of disagreement Wesley chose to remain tolerant of the diverse theological opinions that inevitably arise from people's religious experience.

Outler argues that this nondogmatic approach provides "a charter for a distinctive sort of doctrinal pluralism — one that stands at an equal distance from dogmatism on the one extreme and indifferentism on the other."[62] Many Christians today do not like the word *pluralism,* yet a degree of pluralism will follow any attempt at religious toleration or ecumenism. By allowing his Methodists "to think and let think,"[63] Wesley accepted some theological pluralism as a consequence of catholic or universal love. Yet he constantly took care to weigh everything "with regard to the knowledge of the things of God, the true, scriptural manner of worshipping him; and above all his union with a congregation fearing God and working righteousness."[64] These scriptural and ecclesiastical safeguards enabled one to "keep an even pace, rooted in the faith once delivered to the saints and grounded in love, in true, catholic love, till thou art swallowed up in love for ever and ever."[65]

*Ecumenical Character*

Wesley's willingness to consider ideas or opinions from widely divergent sources added a dimension of Christianity that he considered unique in the Methodist movement. In one of his last sermons he wrote that Methodists accept into their fellowship all who love God and live righteous lives in accordance with that love.

> And in order to their union with us, we require no unity in opinions, or in modes of worship, but barely that they "fear God and work righteousness," as was, observed. Now this is utterly a new thing, unheard of in any other Christian community. In what Church or congregation beside, throughout the Christian world,

can members be admitted upon these terms, without any other conditions....
This is the glory of the Methodists, and of them alone![66]

Wesley sought fellowship with a number of Christian groups outside the Methodist movement and the Anglican tradition. Most notably, he enjoyed a long fellowship and cooperative ministry with the Calvinistic evangelist George Whitefield. "A Letter to a Roman Catholic" is an example of Wesley's hope for ecumenical cooperation; he suggested that Protestants and Roman Catholics ought not to dispute over diverse theological opinions but provoke one another to love and good works.[67] He pursued fellowship and cooperation with believers in many ways, not merely unity in distinct areas such as doctrine, evangelism, or social action. Although Wesley did not fully articulate the extent of his ecumenical inclinations, he clearly demonstrated a spirit of openness to experiment with ways of Christian cooperation.

## An Analytical/Critical Approach to Theology

Wesley lived long before the modern historical–critical methods of biblical interpretation, but he felt he lived in an "enlightened age," whose supposed enlightenment he often derided.[68] He knew of contemporary challenges to biblical authority, yet he affirmed the reasonable content of Christian beliefs and the general trustworthiness of its sources, particularly Scripture. He did not shy away from opponents of traditional Christianity, but seriously and critically engaged them in theological dialogue.

This emphasis on rational inquiry clearly reflects similar concerns of Anglican theology in the seventeenth century. Wesley was simply agreeing with the longstanding belief in the ultimate reasonableness or logical coherence of Christian beliefs founded on Scripture. Having spent many years at Oxford University, Wesley knew well the current trends in philosophy, theology, and biblical studies. He was aware of the need to present one's position logically or methodically and to defend oneself in public or private debate.

### The Reasonableness of Christian Beliefs

Wesley believed in the ultimate reasonableness of Christianity. In this regard he agreed with the prevailing view of the times, reflecting the philosophical and theological trends reminiscent of such defenders of classical orthodoxy as John Locke. Wesley generally agreed with Locke's approach to Christianity and its compatibility with experimental philosophy and the growing scientific revolution. However, Wesley rejected some of the more extreme, skeptical tendencies of Locke and especially of David Hume. Wesley certainly did not shy away from debate with contemporary critics of Christianity.

In affirming the reasonableness of Christianity; Wesley was also affirming the freedom of reason to reflect on the many implications of basic beliefs. He saw a dynamic relationship between reason and revelation and between reason and faith. As people have a degree of freedom in responding to God's gracious offer of salvation and to God's subsequent command to live holy lives, they also have a degree of freedom in understanding and formulating their theological beliefs. Christians should not feel constrained from using the best reason possible in reflecting on Scripture. Moreover, Christians may feel free to draw on extrabiblical sources in reflecting on theology. Most notably they may draw on new knowledge and methods that come from such intellectual disciplines as science and philosophy. Since all truth ultimately reflects the beautifully designed and rational creation of God, new sources of knowledge — even non-biblical ones — may be considered relevant and constructive, rightly understood, in theology and theological method.

### A Systemic Understanding of Theology

Although we should not characterize him as a systematic theologian, Wesley did seek to use the whole of Scripture consistently and comprehensively. His theology grew out of his ongoing ministry like a tree rooted in Scripture and the entire history of Christian doctrine.[69] He had an organic, systemic view of the Methodist movement growing out of and fitting into the dynamic, living, orthodox tradition of Christianity. From the outset of the movement, he claimed that all were "orthodox in every point; firmly believing, not only the Three Creeds [i. e., the Apostles' Creed, the Nicene (Niceno–Constantinopolitan) Creed, and the Athanasian Creed], but whatsoever they judged to be the doctrine of the Church of England, as contained in her Articles and Homilies."[70] With this attitude Wesley believed that he avoided formal and static conceptions of doctrine that stifled other Christian traditions.

### A Concern for Comprehensiveness

Wesley maintained a high personal standard of learning for what could be described as a comprehensive or truly liberal education.[71] Wesley exhorted others, especially his Methodist assistants, to develop themselves as whole persons, intellectually as well as spiritually.[72] This involved making use of all available resources, from religious to scientific, from theoretical to practical, to become enriched and broaden their relevance in ministering to others.

Wesley was not a scholastic theologian, however. Although he appreciated the benefits of a classical education and the best academic scholarship offered to Christians, he never reverted to a rationalistic approach to theology. Wesley believed he could harness the best human disciplines of knowledge in presenting the gospel of Jesus Christ in a way that enhanced rather than thwarted the vitality of Christian faith.

## An Experimental/Practical Approach to Theology

His various references to experience or religious experience reflect Wesley's belief that scriptural truths have an immediate relationship to people's lives. He used the term *experimental* to capture the experiential potential of knowing God in everyday living. But Robert Cushman comments that by "experimental religion," Wesley meant religion confirmed by experience. Cushman writes: "By experience, Scripture and tradition are confirmed in 'living faith.'"[73]

Of course, Wesley's describing his work as "experimental" includes more than just religious experience. In substantial agreement with the British empirical thinking prevalent in his day, Wesley believed that there is an experiential dimension to all knowledge, both natural and supernatural. For example, Wesley drew striking analogies between how we gain knowledge through physical *and* spiritual senses. The pervasiveness of the experimental character of knowledge, including spiritual knowledge, was crucial to Wesley's theology — a part long recognized by Wesleyan scholars.[74] This knowledge relates to every part of our lives and thus has an immediate and practical effect on us.

*Experimental Method*

Applying the term "experimental" to methodology was an outgrowth of the scientific and philosophical ferment of the seventeenth and eighteenth centuries. Experimental method initially influenced only secular disciplines, but it slowly became a part of Anglican theological method also.[75] During the eighteenth century, Samuel Johnson defined "experimental" as "1. Pertaining to experiment. 2. Built upon experiment; formed by observation [and] 3. Known by experiment or trial."[76]

Wesley was influenced by the empirical applicability of the term, even though he used it primarily in reference to the felt experience of the Holy Spirit in the lives of believers. He did not use the term often, but he used it in crucial places for understanding his methodological approach to theology — as in the thesis paragraph of his preface to "Sermons on Several Occasions":

> I have accordingly set down in the following sermons what I find in the Bible concerning the way to heaven, with a view to distinguish this way of God from all those which are the inventions of men. I have endeavoured to describe the true, the scriptural, experimental religion, so as to omit nothing which is a real part thereof, and to add nothing thereto which is not.[77]

Here Wesley not only affirmed the primacy of Scripture in discovering that which is reasonably true concerning religious beliefs, but also introduced this methodologically potent phrase: "experimental religion." The phrase suggests that his sermons and the theology contained in them were somehow related to or based on experience. Although Wesley did not elaborate on what he meant by "the true, the scriptural, experimental religion," the phrase is pregnant with insights or clues to understanding his theological method.

By *true* religion or Christianity, Wesley meant inward religion — the essence of religion, namely, our spiritual relationship with God and all that this relationship implies for living.[78] In his sermon "Upon our Lord's Sermon on the Mount, X," Wesley wrote that

> our great Teacher [Jesus Christ] has fully described inward religion in its various branches. He has there laid before us those dispositions of should which constitute real Christianity; the tempers contained in that holiness 'without which no man shall see the Lord'; the affections which, when flowing from their proper fountain, from a living faith in God through Christ Jesus, are intrinsically and essentially good, and acceptable to God.[79]

By *scriptural* religion or Christianity, Wesley meant that the kind of religion described by Scripture best communicates the essence of true, inward religion. Wesley dedicated an entire sermon to the discussion of "Scriptural Christianity." In another sermon, while discussing with a deist the probability of scriptural truths, Wesley describes how God graciously demonstrates the truth of Scripture to all who believe:

> Considering these things we may well cry out, How great a thing it is to be a Christian, to be a real, inward, scriptural Christian! Conformed in heart and life to the will of God! Who is sufficient for these things? None, unless he be born of God. I do not wonder that one of the most sensible deists should say: "I think the bible is the finest book I ever read in my life, yet I have an insuperable objection to it. It is *too good*. It lays down such a plan of life, such a scheme of doctrine and practice, as is far too excellent for weak silly men to aim at, or attempt to copy after." All this is most true upon any other than the scriptural hypothesis. But this being allowed, all the difficulty vanishes into air. For if "all things are possible with *God*," then "all things are possible to him that believeth."[80]

By *experimental* religion or Christianity, Wesley meant that the stated truths of Scripture concerning inward religion become verified in the life of a believer and that people should test or experiment with the truths of Scripture for themselves. Not only the truths of salvation but also other biblical truths prove true in experience. So Wesley undertook the method of experimental philosophy, already prevalent throughout Britain, in fully investigating the truths of Scripture and of experience.

George Eayrs points out that

> Wesley's method had these features: observation, investigation, written record, comparison, and induction from experiment. He knew and acted upon Bacon's dictum *(Novum Organum,* Preface) "not to dispute upon the very point of the possibility of experience."[81]

Eayrs thus draws attention to the experimental or inductive character of reasoning that Wesley wove throughout his theological and practical writings. Brantley goes so far as to argue that as early as 1730 Wesley had in mind "if not a synthesis of revelation and rational empiricism then an intellectually as well as passionately experimental emphasis in religion both revealed and natural."[82]

### The Hypothetical Character of Experimental Method

Wesley's use of "experimental" also reflects a willingness to admit the hypothetical nature of human knowledge. We rely on provisional or tentative proposals for the explanation of phenomena, both religious and nonreligious, that have some degree of empirical substantiation or probability. This approach to knowledge again is reminiscent of Locke. Conceptually we must recognize the experiential (experimental) dimension in all human knowledge.[83] For example, Wesley refers to the hypothetical approach to Scripture in this passage:

> If you ask, "Why then have not all men this faith, all, at least, who conceive it to be so happy a thing? Why do they not believe immediately?" — we answer (on the Scripture hypothesis), "It is the gift of God." No man is able to work it in himself. It is a work of omnipotence.[84]

Of course, from Wesley's personal experience, the truth of Scripture represented no mere hypothesis. He believed Scripture with complete certainty. Because of the gracious experience of God speaking directly to him through Scripture, coupled with the confirming testimony of the Holy Spirit in his life, Wesley believed that all may hear God speak by listening to Scripture.[85] Yet, when it came to theological reflection, Wesley recognized the phenomenal process people follow in coming to faith and knowledge of God. Strictly speaking, faith is a hypothesis — at least initially.[86] From a human perspective, our knowledge is incomplete; it can only be completed by God.

Stanley Frost discusses the hypothetical nature of faith evident in Wesley in speaking of the authority of God.

> It means that even God's authority is only relatively final, that is, final only so long as we accept the hypothesis which we call the Christian Faith. But this limitation is more apparent than real, for never, except in abstract discussion, do we go beyond the scope of that hypothesis, and then it is always with a conscious effort, made possible only by the firm conviction at the back of our mind that our Faith is an accurate account of Reality. We live and move and have our being within the realm of the hypothesis, and this philosophical limitation of God's authority no more affects our attitude to him, than does our philosophical doubt concerning the existence of the physical universe affect our attitude to the shelf on which we have just knocked our head. In acknowledging that the basis of certainty lies in faith and not in knowledge, we in no way lessen the significance of God's authority, as Wesley himself shows, both by his words and his deeds.[87]

All people follow a hypothetical or experimental path in coming to faith — a faith that in turn comes to understand what is true, including what is scripturally or spiritually true.

Given the experimental nature of human knowledge, Wesley gave special attention to religious experience or the experimental knowledge of the divine presence we have personally. Wesley strongly emphasized the privilege Christians have in experiencing the reality of Jesus Christ in their lives.

> This experimental knowledge, and this alone, is true Christianity. He is a Christian who hath received the Spirit of Christ.[88]

Elsewhere Wesley said:

> For in the Scripture language to say, or to believe, implies an *experimental* assurance. The sum is, none have the Holy Spirit but Christians: all Christians have this Spirit.[89]

While this participatory experience of the Spirit of Jesus Christ adds nothing to the substance of biblical truth, it confirms and vitalizes these truths in the believer's life. Thus the experimental dimension contributes to a more holistic understanding and formulation of Christian theology that respects the ongoing witness of the Holy Spirit. This is why Brantley describes Wesley's methodology as serving "as the model for putting experience into words."[90] And so Wesley's writings could not help but reflect the sometimes nonsystematic character of our experiences, even our experiences of God. Truths about God and his relationship with believers should not and, in fact, cannot be compartmentalized or demystified by human theological endeavors.

In keeping with his Anglican heritage, it was a matter of principle for Wesley not to articulate theology so rigidly or systematically that it denied the participatory activity of God in the world. Without explicitly saying so, Wesley presented an asystematic theology that avoided the formalistic tendencies of system building; yet he did it in a way that allowed for coherence and consistency over years of theological writing.

*Synthetic Eclecticism*

With his broad exposure to classical and contemporary religious thought, Wesley gleaned insights from sources as diverse as Roman Catholic mystics, Eastern Orthodox divines, Moravian pietists from the Lutheran tradition, and Reformed Puritan preachers.

Wesley felt free to draw from a diversity of sources, always with purpose and within the bounds of classical Christian orthodoxy. His work often exhibits a polar quality of living in constructive tension with the diversity of theological insights available from the history of Christianity. Wesley's belief in the reasonableness of Christian beliefs gave him the means and authority to interact with the diversity of theological traditions and to integrate them, along with the experimental approach to theology. Wesley felt free to do this as long as he did not overweigh the powers of reason and experience compared with Scripture and the tradition of Christian antiquity.

Brantley comments that "the boldly mediating quality of his 'rationalist, traditionalist, and biblicist' (as well as simply 'pragmatist') intellect is guided (if not determined) by the Anglican *via media* that lies between 'the Scylla of Rome and the Charybdis of Wittenburg.'"[91]

Wesley's synthetic eclecticism coincided with and enriched the practically oriented intentions of his ministry and writings because it allowed him much freedom in responding to the immediate needs of his life and work in the Methodist revival.

It should be noted that the use of *synthesism* to describe the theology of Wesley does not imply the kind of complex, philosophical understanding of synthesis usually identified with the term. Wesley basically tried to bring together separate ideas or differing theologies into a consensus of beliefs. He did not generally try to combine ideas (or theologies) into more complex (or systematic) wholes from simple things, nor did he conceive of theology as a dialectical process of continued growth consisting of thesis, antithesis, and synthesis. He envisioned the more pragmatic task of holding in tension the various polarities or paradoxes of Christianity and, for that matter, life in general.

Wesley never achieved a final balance of such polarities, but then, he never conceived of theology as a closed system or mathematical set that could be finally determined. The vital activity of the Holy Spirit in the life of individual believers as well as the church precluded one — humanly speaking — from reducing matters of faith and practice to a finite whole.

In recognizing the value of insight contained in each Christian tradition, Wesley did not arbitrarily pick and choose as he pleased, simply pouring new wine into old wineskins. He sought to incorporate or integrate older views in line with the spirit of his theology, resulting, it was hoped, in a more holistic, relevant body of Christian beliefs. In many ways Wesley sought to provide a theological *via media* or middle way just as Anglicans had sought to accomplish in the previous century. But Wesley sought to do it in a way which reflected his personal and theological concerns for the full experience of salvation in a believer's life.

Perhaps the most prominent example of Wesley's efforts to provide a *via media* among the various theological approaches of his contemporary Christian world may be found in his central concern for salvation. As already mentioned, Wesley affirmed a complex conception of justification and sanctification. He appreciated the Reformation emphasis on justification by faith alone, yet he did not want to neglect the important Roman Catholic emphasis on sanctification. Thus, in his sermon entitled "On God's Vineyard," in which he presents a capsule history of Methodism, he offers the following theological synthesis:

> It has been frequently observed that very few were clear in their judgment both with regard to justification and sanctification....Who has wrote more ably than Martin Luther on justification by faith alone? And who was more ignorant of the doctrine of sanctification, or more confused in his conceptions of it....On the other hand, how many writers of the Romish Church (as Francis Sales and Juan de Castañiza in particular) have wrote strongly and scripturally on sanctification; who nevertheless were entirely unacquainted with the nature of justification. . .. But it has pleased God to give the Methodists a full and clear knowledge of each, and the wide difference between them.[92]

Because of his place in the timeline of church history, Wesley believed he had the prerogative of bringing a sense of unity to the unallied diversity that was characteristic of eighteenth–century Christianity. He believed that he could bring not only the ideas of justification by faith and holy living together, but also the people who affirmed such ideas.

### The Practical Character of Wesley's Theology

Throughout Wesley's writings we find an ongoing concern for ministering both to the spiritual needs of people and to the practical aspects of their personal and social needs. With regard to the former, Wesley sought to proclaim the gospel message and to spiritually nurture those who believe. It was his experience that people had extensive spiritual needs. He also saw that people had extensive practical needs that touched all aspects of personal and social life; he sought to meet those needs in any way possible. He was willing to try new methods to do so.

1. *A personal framework of theology.* As we have seen, Wesley exhibited a great concern that Christians not succumb to following a merely formal, scholastic kind of religion. Theology should promote rather than obstruct the liveliness of

the Holy Spirit's inspiring and guiding individual believers. Thus Wesley interpreted Scripture in the framework of the personal. That is, he cared about individuals, about their relationship with God, and about their living holy lives motivated by love. True religion was never to be only formal or outward.

True religion is what Wesley liked to called "heart–religion" or inward religion — religion that balances "knowledge and vital piety." His remedy was the religion that had both outward and inward effects on a person's life — effects experienced and not only believed. Only an inward form of heart — religion represents true religion — personal religion consisting of righteousness, peace, and joy in the Holy Spirit.[93]

The most important ingredient of Wesley's personalistic, participatory conception of heart–religion is his emphasis on love — divine love in the human heart that manifests itself in love for God *and* for one's neighbor. Wesley considered this accent on love "the more excellent way," a revival of Jesus Christ's and primitive Christianity's emphasis on love.[94] He believed that the Church of Rome, under the influence of the pope, was too scholastic and had "a natural tendency to hinder, if not utterly destroy, the love of God...[and] the love of our neighbor."[95] Moreover, the Protestant Reformation, especially under the influence of Calvin's doctrine of predestination, deemphasized the centrality of love by placing great stress on a legal–oriented (rather than love–oriented) conception of God's providence and election.[96]

Rejecting these approaches to religion as formalistic and thus contrary to the idea of love as the central gospel message, Wesley advocated love "as a unifying factor in theology and a humanizing factor in life."[97]

2. *Skills in organization and discipline.* Wesley brought to his personal, theological, and ecclesiastical endeavors an enormous amount of energy and organizational skills for installing religious discipline. Some regard Wesley's organizational skills and religious discipline as among his greatest contributions to the Christian church, especially in terms of small–group meetings.[98] Colin Williams refers to such groups as *"ecclesiolae in ecclesia,* small voluntary groups of believers living under the Word and seeking life under the life of discipline."[99] These meetings were designed both to help believers who sought more Christian nurture than was currently available in the established Church of England and to renew the church itself. Although the private and public standards set by Wesley were often rigorous, they generally achieved their purpose of generating genuine religious growth in individuals and in the church body.

Wesley would have wanted us to see the genius of his ministry as involving more than organizational skills and religious discipline. These characteristics reflect his greater concern to meet the practical needs of Christians, including methodical reflection on and formulation of theology; they also reveal his experimental approach to Christianity. He knew from the crucible of his own life experiences the importance of having a clear understanding of what one believes and believing it with a sense of intellectual integrity.

Overall, Wesley's practical skills in organization and religious discipline complement the approach he used in theology. Wesley may not have written a systematic theology, but his many volumes of theological writings, taken together, represent a vast resource of doctrine and practical divinity. The same skills produced a discernible theological method.

3. *Contemporary expression of beliefs.* Wesley sought to preach and teach in ways easily understood by ordinary people. In the preface to "Sermons on Several Occasions," he made quite clear his intent to speak "plain truth for plain people," that is, in a way that could be understood by all.

> I now write (as I generally speak) *ad populum* — to the bulk of humanity — to those who neither relish nor understand the art of speaking, but who notwithstanding are competent judges of those truths which are necessary to present and future happiness. I mention this that curious readers may spare themselves the labour of seeking for what they will not find.[100]

Although Wesley tried to use simple terms, he did not speak simplistically, nor was he unaware of his world. On the contrary, he read voraciously and encouraged his Methodist assistants to do the same so that they might become more effective communicators of the gospel. Wesley edited the fifty–volume *Christian Library* to help expand the knowledge of the average Christian, particularly in matters of practical divinity. Such efforts on Wesley's part reveal his intention of speaking to a broad–based society not necessarily familiar with basic ideas of Christian faith and practice. Wesley moved easily among all kinds of people, effectively communicating with them and ministering to their needs.

4. *Holistic and social concerns.* Wesley's writings are permeated with a concern to meet both spiritual and practical needs. Spiritually, Wesley sought to proclaim the gospel message and to nurture those who believe. To accomplish this he was willing to entertain what experience has to say in deciding on a course of action, even when such a course has no explicit warrant in Scripture or church tradition. Wesley's theological method influenced the way he applied that theology to life, and his awareness of those applications (or related experiences) conversely influenced his theology. So he was willing to experiment with the unorthodox practices of outdoor preaching, extended intrachurch group meetings, singing hymns to popular tunes, and appointing lay preachers.

Wesley's care for people extended beyond their spiritual well being. In his time he was in the forefront of helping to alleviate the social ills of eighteenth–century England. His care for souls extended to the whole person, especially among the poor, the uneducated, the sick, and the dispossessed — for example, slaves and prisoners.

The poor received special attention — those whom Outler describes as "Wesley's chosen constituency: 'Christ's poor.'"[101] Toward them Wesley directed his primary evangelistic thrusts and his social actions. For example, he provided basic medical care and wrote simple medical manuals to help those who could not afford professional care.[102] He founded what came to be known as "the Poor House" for people such as widows who could not care for themselves. He also started an orphanage.[103] He took it on himself to educate those who did not have the means to get an education — although "after several unsuccessful trials," he found better people "of sufficient knowledge, who had talents for, and their hearts in, the work."[104]

At the Kingswood School Wesley needed to make changes in structure after many years of trial and error in its development.[105] He set up a benevolent loan fund for people with immediate financial needs, the only stipulation being that they should repay the loan within three months.[106]

Wesley preached what he practiced. Many sermons were intended to instruct the Methodists on how to handle their money, both to help the work of the ministry and to meet the needs of the poor. His best–known sermon dealing with money is entitled "The Use of Money." In it Wesley exhorted Christians to gain all you can, save all you can, and give all you can.[107] Wesley soon discovered that his Methodist followers were good at the first two principles, but ignored the third principle against surplus accumulation, which he considered the leading sin of Christian praxis.[108] He was so concerned over the misuse of money and corresponding injustices against the poor that he published several sermons specifically warning about the spiritual danger (to the hoarder) and the social danger (to the would–be recipient) of failure to spread the wealth. Outler aptly recognizes that Wesley's sermons were

> in clear contrast to the notion, proffered by the Puritans, but approved by others, that honestly earned wealth is a sign and measure of divine favour. What is interesting is that Wesley's economic radicalism on this point has been ignored, not only by most Methodists, but by the economic historians as well.[109]

Most Wesley scholars assess Wesley's teachings on social holiness or social responsibility as focusing on the renewal of society rather than its reformation or transformation. Wesley lived in an era when the social consciousness shared by modern Christians was lacking, so we must not expect from Wesley the kind of theological sensitivity and praxis sought by Christians today. But in his religious and economic radicalism Wesley laid the conceptual framework for later political involvement by Methodists, especially in the growth of the British liberal party and in the rise of socialism. Vivian Green writes that Wesley's "Religious radicalism had acted as a midwife to political reform."[110] Williams finds in Wesley's abolitionist support of William Wilberforce a belief "that God appoints times *(kairoi)* when the complete obedience of his followers and the leaders he has appointed is required."[111]

# 3

# Theological Method in Wesley

## The Ground of Faith

John Wesley understood all people to live by faith of one sort or another. He did not call it all *true faith,* because even heathens who never heard of Jesus Christ and scientists who hold a materialistic worldview presuppose certain faith assumptions. For example, Wesley said, "The lowest sort of faith, if it be any faith at all, is that of a Materialist, — a man who, like the late Lord Kames, believes there is nothing but matter in the universe."[1] Whether we call them faith assumptions, basic beliefs, presuppositions, or preunderstandings, all people function with some kind of faith.

When Wesley spoke of true Christian faith, he did not simplistically refer to it as something God does to humans without recognizing a genuine human involvement in the act of believing. It is true that faith begins through the divine seed of the Holy Spirit, just as the special revelation of Scripture was inspired by God through the Holy Spirit. It is also true that the Holy Spirit must continue to illuminate people as they read Scripture and methodically attempt to reflect on and formulate their beliefs as Christians.[2] However, religious knowledge does not result from an arbitrary act of God that people experience passively. People must personally commit themselves in faith to a hidden and transcendent reality if they hope to discover further religious truths.

In "An Earnest Appeal," Wesley drew an analogy between faith and experimental observation: "[Faith] is with regard to the spiritual world what sense is with regard to the natural."[3] But Wesley did not limit the nature of faith to only rational or moral functions.[4] He operated with a dynamic understanding of faith that touches every part of life. In this sense, truth is the test of various life experiences, including distinctively religious experiences. Colin Williams comments that "in Wesley experience is not the test of truth, but truth the test of experience."[5] Wesley expected that one's experience of faith provides the occasion for anticipating new religious insights and for verifying their trustworthiness. Because religious belief is capable of rational assessment, it may then be established as being reasonable. Wesley avoided extreme approaches to establishing the reasonableness of faith, especially approaches that produced a rationalistic or mystical conception of religion.

Wesley recognized that some Christians begin their theology with the doctrine of God, appealing to a form of classical natural theology. Placing faith in rational or empirical investigations, theologians such as Anselm and Aquinas offered proofs for the existence of the Christian conception of God. Having established the existence of God, one could confirm and complete Christian knowledge of God through appeals to the special revelation of Scripture. Theologians such as the deists, who were contemporaries of Wesley, had a rationalistic approach to God. However, Wesley rejected the deistic approach because it discredited the special revelation of Scripture as necessary for true belief in God.[6]

Other theologians placed authority only in Scripture and were skeptical of appeals to reason and general revelation. However, Wesley saw the dangers in this approach much as Richard Hooker and other Anglicans had seen in Continental Reformation theology. Such an approach encouraged a theological formalism that overemphasized the propositional or informational dimension of God's revelation. It did not sufficiently consider the personal or dispositional dimension of knowledge that is inextricably bound up with true faith.[7] Too often a deductively oriented approach establishes the nature and formal authority of Scripture without fully examining what the whole of Scripture has to say for itself. In addition, Christians have the privilege of receiving from God the Holy Spirit's assurance of their intuitive judgments and consequently must reserve a methodological place for the experiential confirmation of their beliefs.

Wesley did not denigrate the theory of religion, that is, the conceptual or cognitive knowledge of religion. Rather, he uplifted the importance of the experience of religion that God promises to all who respond in faith. In a letter Wesley wrote of a friend, "The theory of religion he certainly has. May God give him the living experience of it."[8] On the one hand, assurance of religious knowledge does not result from a sheer act of faith in which no rational justification for it can be given and no rational assessment is possible. On the other hand, assurance of religious belief does not result from the approach of formal logic in which such belief is considered certain or persuasive from a rationalistic perspective.

Somewhere in between, Wesley would argue that people — Christians and non–Christians alike — must make a personal judgment as to which faith assumptions or presuppositions they affirm. All people must weigh the evidence for a particular worldview and then make a decision. Although such decisions can never be based on all the facts (since it is doubtful that we can humanly gather *all* the facts), we still consider such decisions reasonable or reliable.

Thus Wesley was correct in emphasizing the personal dimension of knowledge. This personal dimension becomes most apparent when we have to decide on a general worldview, which consists of a whole range of considerations and not simply classical arguments for the existence of God.

Wesley believed that theology must be written in the context of personal faith in God, that is, the true faith of "a believer (in the scriptural sense)."[9] Only this way may a person's folly concerning things of a spiritual nature be remedied. Faith represents a cognitive dimension reminiscent of the *assensus,* or intellectual assent, characteristic of Roman Catholic conceptions of faith. But faith for Wesley also included the *fiducia,* or personal trust, characteristic of Luther and the Continental Reformation.

By faith Wesley affirmed the primary religious authority of Scripture. He brought the interpretation of Scripture into relation with tradition, reason, and experience in a way that relieved him of the dangers of a static and mechanical literalism in biblical interpretation.[10] Although he affirmed the possibility of and need for direct or intuitive perceptions of truth in making personal judgments, he expected such truths to comply with Scripture. Therefore Scripture stands as an epistemological safeguard to irresponsible appeals to enthusiastic, mystical, or other subjective experiences. But by emphasizing the personal knowledge which we experience through a salvific relationship with God, Wesley deterred Christians from becoming overly formal or rationalistic in their religious affirmations.

Despite his strong affirmation of the primacy of scriptural authority, Wesley appeared willing to concede the hypothetical nature of that authority. In other words, he insisted on recognizing the tentative nature of that authority from a human perspective of knowledge. According to Wesley, the authority of Scripture is certain because of the authenticating testimony of the Holy Spirit's confirming that Scripture is true. But on a conceptual level of discussion, Wesley referred to Scripture on an almost hypothetical basis.

Of course, Wesley had no doubts about the certainty of Scripture. Experientially speaking, Scripture had proved true in his life and in the lives of others. Thus Wesley stood with the classical Protestant view of the primacy of Scripture based on the internal testimony of the Holy Spirit *(testimonium Spiritus Sancti internum).*[11] Nevertheless, he felt free to state his view of Scripture as a hypothetical view in need of reasonable confirmation.

This approach resonated with the prevailing intellectual climate sympathetic to the experimental philosophy characteristic of the scientific revolution. Wesley did not himself affirm a purely empirical approach to religion or to Scripture. But he did incorporate an inductive character into his theology that included the inductive study of Scripture along with extrabiblical sources of religious authority;

Wesley regarded truth as experimental — that is, beliefs must ultimately be capable of proof in one's life experiences.[12] And he believed that Scripture would ultimately be confirmed as entirely trustworthy. Also, because truth is of an experimental nature, one may not easily construct a system or philosophy that compartmentalizes the whole of Christian beliefs. In the practical matters of everyday life, including our religious experiences of sin, justification, regeneration, assurance, and perfection, Wesley was sure that God would confirm the truth of Christianity as attested by Scripture.

Conceptually Wesley presupposed both the doctrine of God and the doctrine of Scripture as part of a basic thesis from which further knowledge may be developed and whose truth may be assessed by experience. While Wesley did not expect to prove, privately or publicly, all biblical truths at once, he was convinced that God would speak to people through Scripture, tradition, reason, experience, or whatever means necessary to produce faith and a sense of assurance in those truths.

## Wesley's Contribution to Theological Method

Wesley did not see himself as an innovator in theological method. The question never arose explicitly in the course of his theological and ministerial reflections, and theological method was not an immediate concern of his in the Methodist revival. He seemed content to write within the bounds of the Anglican methodology, which was based on the threefold foundation of Scripture, tradition (especially that of Christian antiquity), and reason.

Among the myriad influences on Wesley's personal and conceptual development, the Anglican tradition was primary. Understanding Wesley's Anglican background illuminates why he felt no need to articulate his view of theological method explicitly. He intended to do nothing more than work for the spiritual renewal of the Church of England and of England as a whole in the context of the prevailing views of theological method and religious authority.

Wesley affirmed all three Anglican sources of religious authority. But as we have already seen, Wesley also appealed to the religious authority of experience. Wesleyan scholars such as Umphrey Lee interpret Wesley's emphasis on experience as anticipating a similar experiential approach by nineteenth–century liberal Protestantism.[13] Friedrich Schleiermacher and Samuel Taylor Coleridge would later recognize the methodological contribution religious experience makes in understanding the Christian life and in formulating Christian theology.[14] Of course, Wesley did not go to the same methodological extremes as Schleiermacher and Coleridge in their romanticized appeals to experience. Yet he did conceive of experience as functioning in a unique and vital way in theological reflection and formulation.

By including experience in his theological formulations, Wesley did not perceive himself as contributing something new and innovative to theology or to theological method. Experimental principles involved with understanding and living out the Christian life seemed to pervade all theological approaches since New Testament times. Usually experience functioned tacitly in theological formulations, so Wesley did not consider it innovative to make explicit what had always existed in a greater or lesser degree of self–consciousness. No theology made sense to Wesley if it did not in some way become vital and personally real to believers, so Christians must explicitly take account of it. If a theology did not take account of experience or if it was not relevant to the believer's life, then it would never capture the truth of scriptural Christianity and probably not last long as an aid to theology.

Yet Wesley's inclusion of experience did signify an advance in formulating theological doctrines, even if it was not entirely new.[15] Practically speaking, Wesley's appeals to experience resulted in innovative views of evangelism to people at all levels of society, of the nature and extent of the sanctified Christian life, and of the Christian role in social amelioration. They did not immediately affect Christian theology in terms of theological method, but they did influence the practical application of the gospel message to believers personally and corporately. And they continue to influence theological studies and discussion of the quadrilateral in our day. However Wesley viewed his contribution to theological discourse, his influence is still felt in modern approaches to theological reflection and formulation.[16]

## Its Inductive Character

Because Wesley was not explicit in regard to a theological method, we must seek to distill its character from his writings. That is difficult because of the diversity of his works — essays, sermons, treatises, dialogues, journals, and letters. The longer essays, sermons, and treatises provide the clearest clues for distilling a coherent approach, particularly in theological or doctrinal formulations. Yet the shorter, less systematic writings offer clues also.

Wesley lived during the burgeoning scientific revolution, and he respected and appreciated its achievements.[17] This revolution reflected the science of Francis Bacon and Isaac Newton, the philosophy of Locke, and the tradition of inductive and deductive logic extending back to Aristotle.[18] Wesley's *Natural Philosophy* as a whole attests to his admiration for the advancements of science. He did not fear what science had to offer religious self–understanding. While his era was not among the most anti–religious periods of scientific inquiry, not all scientific ideas were sympathetic with Christian teachings. Nevertheless, Wesley believed that rational people could distinguish between what is and is not useful in science and scientific method.

Wesley greatly praised the works of men like Bacon and Newton for their "revival of learning" in the making of so many beneficial experiments "that, having accurately observed the structure and properties of each body, they might the more safely judge of its nature."[19] This appeal to experimentation gained widespread acceptance and application in a variety of disciplines, including theology. No doubt the experimental method of science occurred implicitly, if not explicitly, in Wesley's mind when he described his "Sermons on Several Occasions" as an endeavor to describe the true, the scriptural, experimental religion.[20] At least in the overall structure of those sermons, he saw his ministerial and theological enterprise analogous to the experimental or inductive method of the scientific revolution. Moreover, he encouraged the same in others. For example, discussing the limitations of reason in producing faith in "The Case of Reason Impartially Considered," Wesley did not want others to accept what he said without experimenting for themselves. He said, "But in a point of so unspeakable importance do not depend on the word of another; but retire for a while from the busy world, and make the experiment yourself."[21]

In principle Wesley understood the organization of his sermons as a kind of experimental, almost scientific, endeavor that touched on all the important aspects of Christian life and practice. If Christianity proved to be what Wesley experienced, then others might discover it for themselves. Whether Wesley always and systematically used inductive method in his writings remains highly debatable. George Ears describes it as the overarching method of Wesley's theology.[22] But the diversity of styles, literary genres, and intentions found in Wesley's writings makes this problem especially difficult to resolve. For example, when we read Wesley's sermons, we do not find consistent use of the inductive method in his Bible studies or his theological investigations. Wesley often had a variety of other, more practical concerns at work in the development of his sermons. Despite their well–conceived organization by paragraph, subsection, and section, Wesley's sermons were evangelistic or pastoral in orientation and not primarily scientific or methodological. Nevertheless, in the overarching scheme of his writings, he often approached his theological investigations along the order of a scientific or experimental enterprise. We may take Ears description of Wesley's method as consisting of "observation, investigation, written record, comparison, and induction from experiments" as suggestive of the overall inductive character of Wesley's theology.[23]

Let us illustrate the presence of Wesley's inductive reasoning with perhaps his most mature and systematic theological work – the monograph entitled "The Doctrine of Original Sin, according to Scripture, Reason, and Experience."

## A Case Study: "The Doctrine of Original Sin"

John Wesley wrote his treatise on original sin in 1756 in response to another work written earlier by John Taylor entitled *The Scripture–Doctrine of Original Sin*.[24] Wesley considered the work to be very scholarly, surpassing his own skills especially in Greek and Hebrew. Nevertheless, Wesley could not remain silent in the face of so many teachings he considered to be false. He regarded Taylor's work as nothing more "than old Deism in a new dress; seeing it saps the very foundation of all revealed religion, whether Jewish or Christian."[25]

Wesley believed that more than temporal repercussions occurred as a result of Adam's sin. People became spiritually and morally corrupt and culpable for eternal as well as temporal punishments. According to Wesley, "The Christian system falls at once" if we eliminate the doctrine of original sin and the idea that people exist "by nature foolish and sinful, 'fallen short of the glorious image of God.'"[26]

Wesley objected to the clever arguments Taylor used to remove traditional beliefs about original sin. To defend this aspect of classical orthodoxy, Wesley undertook to present a comprehensive theological position on sin. The result is the most systematic treatise Wesley produced – a treatise that reveals much about his theological method. While the treatise does not indicate a systematic approach for Wesley's whole corpus, it does reveal that he had a self–conscious method of study when he undertook serious theological reflection on this essential Christian doctrine. Other writings by Wesley may not exhibit his theological method as explicitly, but such method informed the overall approach he took in dealing with the theological needs of the church and the world.

We will use the categories of observation, interpretation, evaluation and application, and correlation in trying to understand the flow of Wesley's inductive reasoning. These categories are implicit in the structure of the "Doctrine of Original Sin" and in arguments developed therein. Part 1 approximates the investigative process of observation; part 2 is comparable to interpretation; part 3, evaluation and application; and parts 4–7, correlation. Our aim will be to uncover both the strengths and weaknesses of his theological method, paying special attention to the rationale underlying his thought. In so doing we hope to distill principles that transcend his eighteenth–century context so as to provide insights that may continue to bear fruit for contemporary theology.

## The Observation of Relevant Facts

Wesley began his experimental study of the doctrine of original sin with the first logical step of any inductive process, namely, observation. Similar to scientific observation, Wesley understood the need to direct careful analytic attention toward noted facts or particulars related to the existence of sin. So he tried to become saturated with facts relevant to the occurrence of universal corruption — of personal immorality and social injustices — so that he could be sure about the nature and extent of its existence and the need for some kind of constructive explanation. He stated:

> Before we attempt to account for any fact, we should be well assured of the fact itself. First, therefore, let us inquire what is the real state of humankind; and, in the Second place, endeavor to account for it.[27]

Wesley opened his treatise with a section entitled "The Past and Present State of Mankind," wherein he inquired, "What is the real state, with regard to knowledge and virtue, wherein humankind have been from the earliest times? And what state are they in at this day?"[28] He began his theological investigation by observing the facts available in Scripture, treating Scripture as a reliable source of historical data. Only a handful of deistic scholars in the eighteenth–century refused to consider Scripture a reliable source of historical facts, so Wesley had little reason to question its trustworthiness. In Scripture he observed an abundance of facts concerning the wickedness of humanity.

He continued by observing additional facts of wickedness in history, including research done in church and secular sources of history. For example, he had no qualms about drawing facts from such classical authors as Cato, Cicero, Horace, Juvenal, Ovid, and Seneca. Wesley believed that every "fair and impartial survey" of sacred and secular history manifestly revealed the "universal corruption" of humanity.[29]

Besides historical data, Wesley observed the contemporary state of humanity. From the "Heathen" and "Mahometan" societies to those that claimed to be "Christian," he saw the pervasive individual and corporate wickedness of people. "Common sense," Wesley argued, reveals such sins as hypocrisy, idolatry, ignorance, injustice, and the overall lack of virtue.[30] He concluded that no one, including Taylor, could look at the facts of the world and, in good conscience and with common sense, speak of the *dignity* of our nature.

In his final observation, Wesley asked people to reflect on their own experience. He expected that most people would humbly admit their moral shortcomings. However, he observed that many people feel quite pleased with themselves and do not consider themselves the least bit immoral or corrupt. In response, he condemned all prideful self–deceptions by criticizing these people as "the most careless, inaccurate observer, who does not trouble [themselves] with any more than their outside."[31] Any truly experiential observation of the totality of human nature must — again, in good conscience and with common sense — lead them to admit their propensity toward wicked and corrupt behavior.

Wesley thought that his observations of the facts of sin provided a compelling starting point from which to develop the doctrine of original sin. He assumed the legitimacy of inductive reasoning in these theological reflections, but this assumption rested on the ultimate authority of God's revelation as recorded in Scripture — revelation affirmed by both reason and experience.

Because Wesley considered reason a creation of God, it remained a trustworthy source of religious authority despite limitations due to the sinfulness of humanity. Although the authority of reason may seem logically prior to Scripture in practice, Scripture remains methodologically prior to Wesley's theological understanding. Regardless of the necessary assumption of our reasoning faculties in theological reflection, Wesley considered Scripture the only reliable source of divine revelation. Because of the human limitations of reason, only Scripture may truly be considered the primary source of religious authority. Christians should revere Scripture as the supreme starting point for theological investigation, despite the presence of our reasoning faculties, which must be presupposed in the methodological process.

Wesley began his observations of sin with Scripture, but included a variety of other sacred and secular sources along with appeals to personal experience. In so doing, he offered a theological method that supplemented the Protestant principle of *sola Scriptura*. To Wesley — as to Hooker and other seventeenth–century Anglican divines — the principle lacks sufficient comprehensiveness for theological reflection. To a greater or lesser degree, all theologians draw on tradition (sacred and sometimes secular), reason (even if only common sense), and experience (which includes facts from the physical and social aspects of the world as well as from personal experiences). Granted, these sources play varying roles, explicitly or tacitly, in theologians' methodologies. But together they provided for Wesley the experimental material with which to develop theology.

In critique of Wesley's approach to the doctrine of sin, Mark Horst points out difficulties with Wesley's claims that sinfulness is immediately obvious from experience.[32] In practice, Horst suggests that Wesley used doctrine to shape a believer's experience rather than provide the foundation for doctrine.[33] Surely Wesley did not turn to experience as a primary source of Christian belief, but as a resource for properly interpreting primary sources. And it is true that from Wesley's perspective, he considered sin to be manifestly obvious in human experience. No doubt Wesley assumed more than he could prove in treatises such as this one. This is especially true from our modern awareness that no one can be a truly objective observer. We all work with certain faith assumptions, basic beliefs, presuppositions, or preunderstandings, and Wesley only recognized this to the limited degree that it was recognized during the Enlightenment. Maddox rightly points out that Ears description of Wesley's experimental religion may very adequately detail what Wesley *understood* his methodology to be, but that his supposed inductive approach seems incredulous.[34]

We may criticize Wesley for not having carried through with his experimental method in a manner as thoroughgoing as he could have, or for not having recognized the limitations of his inductive inquiry. But that should not prevent us from trying to *understand* Wesley on his terms and in his historical, intellectual, and theological context. Recognizing that context will at least help us to realize that Wesley was working with as much intellectual self–awareness and integrity as any theologian in his place and time. Despite notable limitations we may recognize in his thought, Wesley was attempting to be experimentally oriented in his approach to theology.

We also should not expect to hold up Wesley as any kind of contemporary model of theological method without some attempt at contemporization or transvaluation. His methodology cannot be taken without regard for subsequent developments in theology, philosophy, science, or other disciplines germane to the truths of Christianity. But part of the genius of Wesley's theological method is that it intentionally takes into account the ongoing need for and process of reforming our beliefs in light of modern concerns and insights.

## The Interpretation of the Facts

Obviously no theological method is complete in the mere observation and accumulation of facts. Facts need interpretation, and Wesley believed they could be truly explained only in light of Scripture. In part 2, "The Scriptural Method of Accounting for this, Defended," Wesley argues that only the scriptural and orthodox doctrine of original sin does justice to the facts of universal misery and wickedness observed in the world. He concludes, "And this [doctrine] easily accounts for the wickedness and misery of humankind in all ages and nations; whereby *experience* and *reason* do so strongly confirm this *scriptural* doctrine of original Sin."[35]

Thus Wesley's argumentation on behalf of the traditional doctrine of original sin proceeded in accordance with Scripture, reason, and experience as explicitly stated in the full title of the treatise. He countered Taylor by appealing to all three sources of religious authority in pointing out the unreasonableness of Taylor's interpretation based only on experience and Scripture. If Taylor wanted to overturn the doctrine of original sin, then he was going to have to present a more logical and existentially compelling interpretation of the facts of life and Scripture. But that was exactly the point at which Wesley thought Taylor failed, because Taylor had not dealt comprehensively with all the facts.

To begin with, Wesley did not think that Taylor had presented a reasonable alternative in explaining the universal presence of misery and wickedness in the world. Taylor had argued that ignorance reinforced by bad education had propagated ill customs among people, but that the traditional doctrine of original sin was not a part of communicating the gospel message of Scripture. However, Wesley did not think that Taylor had adequately dealt with the logical implications of his position. Wesley stated:

> These are questions which I conceive will not easily be answered to the satisfaction of any impartial inquirer. But, to bring the matter to a short issue: The first parents who educated their children in vice and folly, either were wise and virtuous themselves, or were not. If they were not, their vice did not proceed from education; so the supposition falls to the ground: Wickedness was antecedent to bad education. If they were wise and virtuous, it cannot be supposed but they would teach their children to tread in the same steps. In nowise, therefore, can we account for the present state of humankind from example or bad education.[36]

Wesley flatly disagreed with Taylor's hypothesis and felt it inadequate to deal with all the facts.[37] From the standpoint of reason and the experiences of life, Wesley did not see how the obvious facts of misery, guilt, and sin could be accounted for except by original sin.

Although reasonable reflection on the reality of sin is confirmed by experience, the doctrine is articulated explicitly in Scripture. After rejecting Taylor's treatment of the facts of sin, Wesley turned to the scriptural interpretation of sin and its consequences. To him, the doctrine of original sin was manifestly apparent in Scripture to all who interpreted its "plain, natural meaning."[38] Wesley often appealed to what he considered the "plain obvious sense" of Scripture, and he rejected Taylor's "unnatural interpretation" of the facts of Scripture and of experience.[39]

Wesley repeatedly questioned Taylor's use of inconsistent logic in the interpretation of Scripture, his failure to draw out the implications of ideas to their logical extremes, and his virtual deceit in misrepresenting Scripture.[40] He also thought that Taylor made incorrect use of biblical terms, had Scripture "flatly contradict other Scriptures," and used "persuasive speech" in order to circumvent Scripture.[41] Thus he found proof for the inadequacy of Taylor's hypothesis in an inductive study of Scripture. Wesley said, "Till this [proof] is produced, I must still believe, with the Christian Church of all ages, that all men are 'children of wrath by nature,' in the plain, proper sense of the word."[42]

## Evaluation and Application of Religious Ideas

In defending the orthodox doctrine of original sin against the alternative interpretation offered by Taylor, Wesley had already begun the evaluative step in the inductive process of methodically studying the facts. But he continued the evaluative process more explicitly in part 3, "An Answer to Dr. Taylor's Supplement." Here Wesley assessed the relevance and usefulness of the supplement Taylor added to the first edition of his book in response to criticisms by D. Jennings and Isaac Watts.

Wesley continued to question Taylor's arguments on the grounds of an inappropriate use of logic.[43] Moreover, he did not think that Taylor had satisfactorily responded to the criticisms by Jennings and Watts.[44] In fact, in part 4 of the treatise, Wesley appended a lengthy extract from Watts's book on original sin.[45] He did this in order to affirm the soundness of Watts's position on the doctrine and the appropriateness of his critique of Taylor's work.

In part 3 Wesley criticized Taylor for his failure to consider all that is said about sin in Scripture. He thought that Taylor's attempt to contravene the traditional doctrine of original sin avoided a thoroughly inductive study of Scripture. In contrast to Taylor, Wesley concluded that the distinction between personal sin and imputed guilt is a "sound and scriptural" distinction.[46] He also argued that Taylor could not subsequently account for the afflictions of children — presumably innocent of guilt, according to Taylor — and of mortality.[47] Wesley approached this line of argumentation as he had in previous times. He argued from the evidence of Scripture and then from the evidence of "the state of the world, as a proof of God's displeasure, and the natural corruption of man."[48]

Wesley noted that other consequences of failing to affirm the traditional doctrine of original sin included minimizing salvation by grace. Taylor argued that people have sufficient power to perform the duties of God.[49] But that assertion led Wesley to accuse Taylor of reintroducing deistic ideas that denigrate the soteriological focus of Scripture.[50]

Finally, Wesley objected to Taylor's position on the original righteousness with which humanity was created. Taylor argued that people were neither created holy nor manifested "personal, internal holiness" when they became Christians. [51] But Wesley would not tolerate an interpretation of Scripture or experience that failed to recognize "a real, inward change; a renewal of soul 'in righteousness and true holiness.'"[52] Evaluating the Scripture texts offered by Taylor, Wesley maintained, "These texts, therefore, do manifestly refer to personal, internal holiness; and clearly prove, that this is the chief part of that 'image of God' in which man was originally created."[53]

## The Correlation of Ideas in Theology

The process of correlation should pervade a theological enterprise. One continually needs to establish mutual or causal relations between materials and ideas appropriate to the subject at hand.[54] Wesley was concerned that he develop a vital biblical theology that reflected and stimulated the experience of

Christian faith in one's life and practice. He did not limit his studies exclusively to Scripture, but reflected on facts discovered apart from it. Only by appealing to all three sources of religious authority in their proper relationship and as a single methodological instrument did Wesley think that a truly integrated and vital treatment of the subject could be achieved.

Unfortunately, Wesley did not take the task of correlation as far as we might have hoped. This disappointment results, not from a lack of a methodology, however, but from a desire for a systematic treatment that takes the inductive process from observation to correlation so as to produce a whole system of theology that integrates all other Christian doctrines. To the extent that Wesley consistently sought to deal with the whole of Scripture and of related facts on the doctrine of original sin, he was systematic. But we should not impose standards of systematization on his works that he himself did not.

For example, Wesley did not consider it either a pastoral or a theological necessity to formulate "one uniform, connected scheme of the great doctrine," because it had already been capably done by others.[55] Therefore he appended to his defense of the doctrine of original sin extracts from the works of Watts, Samuel Hebden, and Thomas Boston.[56] In citing these extracts Wesley was not avoiding his responsibilities as a theologian; rather, he was humbly acknowledging existing work that fulfilled the practical need of supplying whole treatments of the doctrine in support of his defense against Taylor.

Although Wesley did "not present a traditional systematic treatment of the doctrine, his treatise reflects all the theological traits we mentioned earlier as characterizing his writings generally. Wesley was biblical, orthodox/traditional, analytical/critical, and experimental/practical in his investigation of facts and ideas pertaining to the doctrine of original sin.

### The Primacy of Biblical Orientation

Wesley maintained the primacy of scriptural authority throughout his discussion of the doctrine. He praised Taylor for not having raised "any difficulties or objections against the Christian Revelation" and for having "studied the original Scriptures for many years."[57] But he wanted Taylor "to advance the cause of true, primitive, scriptural Christianity; of solid rational virtue; of the deep, holy, happy, spiritual religion, which is brought to light by the gospel!"[58]

### Fidelity to Orthodox Tradition

Wesley did not explicitly mention tradition as one of the sources of religious authority to which he appealed in the "Doctrine of Original Sin." But part of the whole purpose in writing the treatise was to defend a crucially important doctrine of Christian tradition. Although he was primarily concerned about the soteriological or evangelistic aspects of original sin, Wesley also felt that Taylor had unfortunately ignored the history of classical orthodoxy.[59] In one place Wesley rejected Taylor's argument that we should ignore the doctrine of original sin because it was formulated by the Roman Catholic Church. Wesley pointed out that the doctrine was held by "the Greek Church also; and, so far as we can learn, in every Church under heaven; at least from the time that God spake by Moses."[60] Thus Taylor stood against "the whole body of Christians in all ages...after seventeen hundred years."[61] Overall, in his concern to "advance the cause of true, primitive, scriptural Christianity," Wesley considered himself fully orthodox as well as agreeable to reason and experience.[62]

### Analytical and Critical Reflection

Wesley took an analytical and critical approach to the doctrine of original sin throughout the treatise. We have already noted the many logical problems Wesley found in Taylor's writings. Wesley sought to avoid all emotional argumentation on the subject, though he strongly felt that a great deal of the Christian message of salvation is at stake in the doctrine of original sin. Consequently he approached the subject by claiming "to 'speak the truth in love,' (the only warmth which the gospel allows,) and to write with calmness, though not indifference."[63] He used this approach because of his belief in the ultimate reasonableness of Christianity, including this doctrine.

### Experimental and Practical Concerns

Wesley brought both his experimental and practical concerns to bear throughout his study on original sin. The inductive character of Wesley's experimental approach to theology is, in fact, most explicitly articulated in this treatise. He thought that Taylor had ignored both the facts of sin and importance of the inward experience of God in one's life — "the *interiora regni Dei!*"[64] Taylor thus was "*disserving* the cause of inward religion, labouring to destroy the inward kingdom of God, sapping the foundations of all true, spiritual worship, advancing morality on the ruins of piety."[65] Instead he left only the *form* of religion without the *vitality* of experiencing a personal and growing relationship with God. Wesley believed he could adequately treat the subject of original sin only in the context of a dynamic reliance on the power of the Holy Spirit, "done with continual prayer, that I may know 'the truth as it is in Jesus.'"[66]

### A Summary of Correlation

We find that Wesley correlated his ideas on original sin with a self–conscious concern to interact with and integrate Scripture, tradition, reason, and experience. In fact, in this treatise we find the most explicit and best developed methodology used by Wesley to treat a particular subject of theology. We find similar methodological principles at work in other Wesleyan writings, but not to the same degree.[67] We should not expect to find the same methodological rigor in his other writings, since they cover a wide range of literary genres, purposes, and intended audiences. Nevertheless, Wesley was aware of the inductive character of experimental method, and to the extent that it was practically necessary, he explicitly used it. Certainly he intended all his writings to conform to Scripture, tradition, reason, and experience. The "Doctrine of Original Sin" provides a paradigm for how he envisioned the sources of religious authority being integrated into a consistent and comprehensive understanding of Christian beliefs.

## An Analysis of Wesley's Methodological Reasoning

To gain a greater understanding and appreciation of the inductive character of Wesley's experimental approach to theology, we will need to investigate certain presuppositions contained in his logic. First we will examine the rational presuppositions that undergird his thinking. Then we will study how Wesley applies such reasoning to his theology. After that, we will investigate the completeness of Wesley's inductive approach to the study of Scripture and other sources of religious authority. Finally, we will examine the way Wesley deduced that soteriology should serve as the basic concern of Christianity.

### Rational Presuppositions

Everyone thinks with certain presuppositions or faith assumptions. This is true for science as well as religion, though each discipline uses different terms. Science operates with the presupposition — or, if you will, faith assumption — that it may eventually solve all questions about the nature of the universe in which we live. If questions arise that it cannot answer, it does not appeal to religion for help, but continues to pursue its research on its own. Of course, the degree of confidence in this expectation varies from one person to another, but scientific investigation must progress with the conscious or subconscious presupposition that at least initial answers may be discovered.

Likewise, religion functions with certain presuppositions or assumptions, and Wesley understood this. We cannot query every assumption present in Wesley's theology, since that would doubtless result in interminable debate. However, we can distill general assumptions that rationally facilitated his methodology. These assumptions may have only functioned on a subconscious or tacit level in Wesley's mind, for he does not enumerate them himself; but we need to draw them out explicitly to understand more fully his theological method.

Wesley sometimes referred to *commonsense* reasoning. He inherited this emphasis on commonsense thinking through the works of such seventeenth–century Anglicans as William Chillingworth, John Tillotson, and Edward Stillingfleet.[68] Wesley's references to common sense initially entailed the general trustworthiness of sense perceptions. If we could not rely on sense perceptions, we could not begin to make generalizations about empirical observations. Wesley believed that our natural senses could be trusted as much as our spiritual senses.[69] In "The Witness of the Spirit," Wesley affirmed both as trustworthy by arguing for the immediate and direct perception of our spiritual senses.

> How, I pray, do you distinguish day from night? How do you distinguish light from darkness; or the light of a star, or a glimmering taper, from the light of the noon–day sun? Is there not an inherent, obvious, essential difference between the one and the other? And do you not immediately and directly perceive that difference, provided your senses are right disposed? In like manner, there is an inherent, essential difference between spiritual light and spiritual darkness; and

between the light wherewith the Sun of righteousness shines upon our heart, and that glimmering light which arises only from "sparks of our own kindling:" and this difference also is immediately and directly perceived, if our spiritual senses are rightly disposed.[70]

Although our natural and spiritual senses may not always be "rightly disposed," such senses were generally considered trustworthy with the aid of reason to discern truth from error correctly.

Like Locke, who laid the philosophical groundwork for experimental method in early eighteenth–century British thinking, Wesley believed that in our experience of the world "we have no innate principles," but all ideas come from empirical sensation or rational reflection on sense data.[71] There occur no universal, necessary, or *a priori* innate ideas of our world independent of experience. This understanding on Wesley's part explicitly reveals the influence of the British empirical thinking, especially as found in Locke. Even then, Wesley usually stated that such sources only led him more to Scripture, which provided the only sufficient source of matters pertaining to religion.[72] Yet Wesley reveals a functional knowledge of Lockean philosophy that appears in many of his writings. Scholars such as Gifford Hindley and Richard Brantley have gone to great lengths in developing the Locke–Wesley connection. Brantley concludes that

> John Wesley's method, if not always self–conscious, is assuredly present throughout his writings; his defenses of faith are enhanced by Locke's experimental idiom, which, though hardly so pervasive in Wesley's works as, say, his scriptural reference, is nonetheless so clearly a major feature of them as to demonstrate that besides being syncretic and steeped in tradition his theology *articulates* his understanding or empiricism.[73]

Wesley developed his own empirical or experimental methodology, following the lead of Peter Browne's interpretation of Locke, by expanding the arena of acceptable sense experience to include spiritual knowledge of that which transcends mere empirical facts. Browne shared Locke's rejection of innate ideas, but desired to incorporate contemporary religious experience as "some extraordinary way of communication," which Locke and his followers were unwilling to recognize.[74] Brantley argues that scholars have failed to recognize that "Browne's most original contribution to Lockean thought, and to Anglicanism, is his by no means antirational and almost sense–like intimation that the Spirit continues to witness."[75] He concludes that "From the 1740s, when Wesley first formulated his thought, to the last year of his life, when he spoke Lockean language with the ease of exhalation, he more or less consciously followed the Brownean procedure for making Lockean method the method of theology."[76]

Wesley also presupposed the trustworthiness of people's mental operations. He did not think we could rightly understand Scripture without the critical processes of our minds. Without assuming the reliability of our mental processes and the ultimate rationality of the universe, we could neither perceive nor apprehend sense experiences; nor could we reflect on or judge those experiences by "discerning, comparing, compounding, [and] abstracting" among them.[77] These functions of reason safeguard the legitimacy of the entire theological endeavor. Without such functions it would be impossible to reason or to reason with others, yet obviously we do.

Further, Wesley strongly appealed to the general reasonableness of people and to the logical capabilities of the mind — a confidence in reason characteristic of seventeenth–century Anglican divines and the Enlightenment. He relied on the orderliness and ultimate rationality of God's creation. Creation he took to include those truths which occur in accordance with the orderly and reasonable governance of God, but which we may not learn from our natural experiences of the world. For example, we cannot empirically or rationally discern the cause–and–effect relationship of original sin. Like so many other aspects of theology, we must accept the *fact* of original sin although we may not comprehend the *manner* by which the initial cause produced the final effect.

No one philosophically challenged ideas such as cause and effect until David Hume, so practically all people tacitly shared this assumption with Wesley. In fact, most people continue to assume the general orderliness and reasonableness of reality, though no one, not even in science or philosophy, has finally explained the manner of it.

## Theological Application

Following the traditional view of theology extending back to the Middle Ages, Wesley saw no contradiction in having theology interact with other fields of knowledge. Theology was not a discipline with a rigid, esoteric methodology that could not relate to other philosophical and scientific disciplines. He considered theology superior in significance, but informed by other disciplines in both methodologies and findings. He did not fear what such disciplines might say; ultimately, any reasonable philosophical or scientific investigation, done in good conscience, would confirm rather than refute the efforts of theology. Because the universe is the creation of God, we should attend to what we might learn from it.

Given so much debate in our day regarding a proper Christian view of the theory of evolution, we find in Wesley a remarkable and genuine openness to the philosophical and scientific advances of his time. Of the "gradual progression" found in nature, Wesley said,

> It is wonderful to observe by what a gradual progression the world of life advances through an immense variety of species before a creature is found that is complete in all its senses....

> The whole process of nature is so gradual that the entire chasm from a plant to man is filled up with divers kind of creatures, rising one above another, but so gentle ascent that the transitions from one species to another are almost insensible.[78]

> By what degrees does nature raise herself up to man?
> How will she rectify this head that is always inclined towards the earth? How

change these paws into flexible arms? What method will she make us of to transform these crooked feet into supple and skillful hands? Or how will she widen and extend this contracted stomach? In what manner will she place the breasts, and give them a roundness suitable to them?

The ape is this rough draught of man: this rude sketch, an imperfect representation, which nevertheless bears resemblance to him, and is the last creature that serves to display the admirable progression of the works of God. [79]

In these statements Wesley appears quite progressive in his openness to new concepts and empirical discoveries. However, Wesley still possessed, as we all do, a certain resistance to critical and historical questions about cherished religious beliefs. Yet he purposed to use a similar inductive method in his theological studies.

## Complete Induction

Wesley made the collection of biblical and various extrabiblical facts the starting point of his methodology in writing theological treatises. We see this approach in many of his pastoral writings as well. The explicitness of such methodology depended on Wesley's theological intentions in writing a particular work. Predictably, his letters, journal entries, and many sermons do not betray so great a loyalty to this inductive method.

We cannot read far into any of Wesley's writings without recognizing the vast knowledge of Scripture he gathered and applied toward his work — a fact that reveals a lifetime of close, exhaustive investigation of the Word. So thoroughly did Wesley incorporate the words of the Bible that at times his sermons appear to be more a synthesis than an interpretation and exposition of Scripture. Yet his writings present a more complex understanding and communication of the gospel than the mere recitation of Scripture.

The Bible often required elaboration beyond what was available in its words alone. This elaboration came through the use of central interpretative motifs provided by tradition, facilitated through the operations of reason, and confirmed by knowledge gained from experience. So while Scripture remained the primary source of religious authority for Wesley, it never stood alone. One's experimental openness to truth had to extend beyond Scripture to include complementary means of insight. Thus Wesley allowed for modifications in his theological understanding based on insights from experience. This included insights he might receive from the experience of others.

The investigation of various kinds of religious experiences helped to inform Wesley's theology in other doctrines besides original sin. Take the doctrine of entire sanctification, for example. Aspects of this doctrine, such as Wesley's emphasis on a *second* moment or crisis experience, reveal conclusions based more on experiential — and perhaps logical — reflection than reflection on Scripture per se. Mildred Bangs Wynkoop observes that Wesley definitely relied on both experience and Scripture in developing his thoughts on the doctrine.[80]

Experience also provided the stimulus for Wesley to change some of his earlier views of entire sanctification. Harald Lindström's excellent work *Wesley and Sanctification* identifies some of the later developments in Wesley's thought due to his observations of Christians' experiences of entire sanctification in the Methodist revival.[81] Wesley did not enjoy having to modify any of his ideas about Christian perfection, but he felt constrained to do so. We do not have space here to review all the modifications that occurred in his thinking, but they range from his acceptance of the doubt and uncertainty that the totally sanctified may feel to the belief that even entirely sanctified people can fall from grace.[82]

In debates with theologians about other traditional Christian doctrines, Wesley constantly appealed to Scripture, reason, and experience. As Wesley had denounced Taylor's work on those three grounds, so he denounced Francis Hutcheson's "Essay on the Passions." Wesley argued "both from Scripture, reason, and experience that his [Hutcheson's] picture of man is not drawn from life."[83] Thus, arguing from facts "drawn from life," Wesley believed that Christians may gain — by means of inductive methods which extend beyond Scripture alone — a more comprehensive and holistic theological understanding of truth.

These examples of Christian doctrine help to show the extent to which Wesley used inductive method in his theological investigations. He did not strongly affirm any position even a biblical position — until it received thorough support from rational reflection on relevant experiences. Without this grounding Wesley did not expect to make his position either understandable or compelling to people "of reason and religion."[84]

Wesley encouraged others to use the same method he did: gathering all available and pertinent facts, first from Scripture, then from other sources. We may question the actual completeness or the criteria of completeness in Wesley's collection of facts, or the order of priority for the authority of sources from which those facts were drawn; but we cannot question his expectation that inductive reasoning should take place in the theological enterprise. Of course, Wesley began with Scripture, and he expected Scripture to provide a sufficient guide for beliefs pertaining to salvation. But he also believed that Scripture provides the starting point for an even richer, more comprehensive inductive search. One begins with Scripture, but does not end there. Wesley expected that if — as he believed — Scripture revealed truth, then intensive investigations beyond Scripture would only help to illuminate and vitalize the truths of the Word in one's life.

## Soteriological Organization

Wesley believed that he used *complete* induction in his theological thinking, though it seems impossible that anyone could actually observe and interpret every conceivable fact related to religion.[85] For that reason Wesley's inductive approach to the doctrine of original sin, for example, may more appropriately be called *practical* — or, using a technical philosophical term, *ampliative* — induction.[86] That is, Wesley reasoned from a limited number of observed instances, primarily having to do with the sinful predicament of humanity, the need for salvation, and a concomitant life of holy living.

It is inconceivable that Wesley could have undertaken a completely inductive approach. He undertook a more modest, yet *practically complete,* examination of select instances of sin. Reasoning from a limited number of observed instances of sin to a general causal relationship between those sins and original sin, Wesley argued that the traditional doctrine of original sin provides a reasonable and sufficient explanation for the fact of sin in the world. He demonstrated the significant scriptural relationship between the reality of sin and the need for salvation.

Wesley ultimately organized the facts about the doctrine of original sin for soteriological purposes. He deduced that salvation — in the complexity of understanding what the term means — should represent the overarching concern or principle for organizing biblical and theological studies. Did Wesley truly deduce soteriological principles from genuine inductive investigation, or did he simply assume soteriological principles from the outset, representing laws of thought rather than laws of fact (even spiritual fact)? We are not certain. A case can be made, however, for the presence of thoroughgoing inductive reasoning in his theological writings. He may have used different *species* of inductive reasoning, but each shared the same *genus* of induction. For example, he inductively reasoned from particular instances of human misery and wickedness to formulating general or universal statements about the reality of sin, especially original sin. Because he had neither the time nor the space to use induction by complete enumeration (*perfect,* or *formal,* induction), he relied on practical, or ampliative, induction, which means reasoning from a limited number of observed instances to a general causal relationship.

At times Wesley appealed to an indirect method of supporting or confirming his hypothesis of original sin by falsifying those hypotheses competing with it, most notably those of John Taylor. This *eliminative induction* further bolstered Wesley's position in positively stating the traditional doctrine of original sin. Finally, Wesley relied on intuitive induction by making experience a critical test of truth. According to intuitive induction, not all necessity is logical necessity. Wesley held the view that sometimes we can experience necessary truths about the world — that is, our experience rather than logical necessity may show us what *is* the truth. Thus Wesley considered any reasonable person capable of recognizing the truth of original sin. He also expected that every person was aware of their inherent sinfulness, regardless whether they had taken the time to calmly and impartially investigate the actual doctrine.

We cannot expect that Wesley knew or even conceived of every possible implication of his argumentation. Not being a systematic or professional theologian, he did not work out all the ramifications of his approach to theology. No doubt he assumed a great deal — as most of us do when we think about theology. However, he was sure of his own experience and felt he had discovered the importance of God's free offer of salvation and of the fullness of what that salvation could mean in perfecting oneself in holiness. Without fully articulating the method by which he deduced his conclusions, Wesley believed that his theology reflected a true, experimental understanding of the human situation and that only God could ultimately provide sufficient grace and knowledge in experiencing salvation.

Although he did not expect to find in Scripture all the facts of theology, Wesley did expect to find a sufficient source of God's self–revelation through which God chose to speak to humanity, especially about salvation. Because what God speaks to us through Scripture is reasonable — as is all true religion — it must be properly interpreted by rational skills and experiential resources also made available to us by the gracious provision of God. Wesley could allow more than just Scripture to provide data for one's theological conclusions. Scripture remained the primary religious authority, and Wesley did not expect tradition, reason, or experience to contradict the Word. But he did allow a place for more than Scripture to inform one's thinking, and thus provided a more realistic and comprehensive understanding of how people correlate theology. Accordingly, Wesley provided a theological method that may enable us to develop a more holistic and integrative theology.

# 4

# The Authority of Scripture

## An Introduction

Perhaps Wesley's most enduring contribution to theological method stems from his concern for catholicity in including experience along with Scripture, tradition, and reason as genuine sources of religious authority. While maintaining the primacy of Scripture, Wesley functioned with a dynamic interplay of sources in interpreting, illuminating, enriching, and communicating biblical truths. Wesley felt the theological freedom to seek truth pragmatically through understanding our experiences. But he did so without succumbing to the implications of a thoroughly pragmatic approach that reduces truth to what is relative to its practical value in our experiences of life.

Nevertheless, Wesley viewed his theological endeavors tentatively; that is, he remained open to new insights that might be uncovered by integrating and then interacting with Scripture, tradition, reason and experience. He explicitly stated this openness in the preface to his "Sermons on Several Occasions" — his primary theological reference work.

> But some may say I have mistaken the way myself, although I take upon me to teach it to others. It is probable many will think this; and it is very possible that I have. But I trust, whereinsoever I have mistaken, my mind is open to conviction. I sincerely desire to be better informed. I say to God and man, "What I know not, teach thou me."[1]

The humility demonstrated in this prefatory remark to his sermons reflects more than the quality of Wesley's inner character. It reflects his theological character as well — in particular, his methodological approach to biblical truth and other truths present in the world. Wesley recognized that one must humbly approach the experimental task of reflecting on theology. In other words, we must remain open to the wealth of insight that God may reveal to us through a variety of sources about ourselves, our world, and our relationship with him.

Each focus of religious authority makes a unique contribution to uncovering truth and formulating doctrinal ideas. To understand and appreciate the contributions Wesley expected from the various sources of religious authority, we need to investigate each of them individually. In so doing, we learn more of the theological gestalt that resulted from his integration of Scripture, tradition, reason, and experience.

We must begin by looking at Scripture. We could consider the other components in any order without obscuring their respective roles for his methodology, since Wesley never wrote anything specifically about the relationship between tradition, reason, and experience. In fact, there are good reasons for placing any of them after Scripture.[2] Yet our intuition suggests how Wesley might have wanted them ordered in a scholarly discussion. We do well to consider the formula most often invoked when referring to the popular conception of the Wesleyan quadrilateral: Scripture, tradition, reason, and experience.

The priority of scriptural authority goes without question. Yet the secondary placement of tradition behind Scripture possesses an intuitive order of importance in Wesley's theology. Especially as found in the classical orthodoxy of Christian antiquity, tradition provided genuine substance to our beliefs. Wesley hesitated to say either reason or experience adds substance to our beliefs, but tradition served to fill in doctrinal lacunae not specifically addressed in Scripture. The canonization of the New Testament and the doctrinal summaries of the ecumenical councils offer the best examples of substantive contributions to the teaching of Scripture. Thus tradition merits second place in our order of discussion of the four sources of religious authority.

It becomes less clear whether reason or experience should come next. The *Book of Discipline* for the United Methodist Church lists experience before reason, but it claims that "theological reflection may find its point of departure in tradition, 'experience,' or rational analysis."[3] From our perspective, either reason or experience could appropriately follow. But from our study of Wesley and the popular model of the quadrilateral, reason seems to be the source of religious authority to which Wesley appealed most often in the formulation and defense of his theology. Either because of his own regard for the importance of reason or because he knew his theology needed to be well conceived from the standpoint of reason, Wesley regarded reason as inextricably bound up with the truths of Scripture and thus deserving of special recognition. This does not diminish the importance of experience. The point is, no theological method is complete without a genuinely catholic consideration of all historic authority claimants in reflecting on and formulating theology.

## The Primacy of Scripture

Clearly, Scripture was to Wesley a source of religious authority unlike and superior to any other. His theology germinated from God's self–revelation as found in the Bible. All theology and all experiences "are to be tried by a farther rule to be brought to the only true test — the Law and the Testimony."[4] In a letter to James Hervey, Wesley wrote, "I allow no other rule, whether of faith or practice, than the Holy Scriptures."[5] Out of concern for the ongoing faith of the Methodists, he wrote,

What I nightly wish is that you all keep close to the Bible. Be not wise above what is written. Enjoin nothing that the Bible does not clearly enjoin. Forbid nothing that it does not clearly forbid.[6]

Although Wesley felt willing to learn from other people and even other religious traditions, they needed to demonstrate it "by plain proof of Scripture."[7] Not only did Scripture, as the "oracles of God," serve as the "foundation of true religion,"[8] it also functioned as a kind of epistemological safeguard for the boundaries of true, experimental religion.

Wesley agreed with the greater Reformation and Anglican emphasis on the primacy of scriptural authority. More specifically, he considered the Anglican Church "nearer the scriptural plan than any other" church either in England or Europe, which is largely the reason why he never wanted to separate from the Church of England. Scripture served as the only sufficient source commonly available to people for investigating the nature of God and of life. Because Scripture applies both to theology and to the whole of life, Wesley considered tradition, reason, and experience viable resources in helping to understand and communicate the truths of Scripture.

Along with his theological respect for Scripture, Wesley gave it a special role in his personal life. Modern attempts to find antecedents of nineteenth–century liberal Protestantism in Wesley fail to do justice to his intimate trust and confidence in Scripture to serve as God's chosen means of self–revelation to individuals and to humanity in general. Wesley did not merely read Scripture; he listened to God personally speaking to him in its pages. Scripture represented the *living* words of God:

> The foundation of true religion stands upon the oracles of God. It is built upon the prophets and apostles, Jesus Christ himself being the chief comer–stone. Now of what excellent use is reason if we would either understand ourselves, or explain to others, those living oracles![9]

Wesley believed that we may place ourselves in such a relationship to Scripture that God will to speak to us through it. Thus he became highly excited when speaking of Scripture: "O give me that book! At any price, give me the book of God!"[10] It was existentially important to Wesley that he have the Bible and hold it as the primary rule of his life. Reading and then existentially listening to Scripture functioned in the same way as listening to God. God not only inspired the writing of Scripture, but continues to illuminate those who read it. The mere study of Scripture, of course, does not produce the necessary insight or inspiration for becoming a Christian. To enter into a saving relationship with Jesus Christ, one must be aided by the inner working of the Holy Spirit.

Commenting on the inspiration of Scripture in the *Notes upon the New Testament,* Wesley spoke of the ongoing need for inspiration or illumination from the Holy Spirit who serves a guide for those who approach the reading of Scripture in the context of prayer.

> All Scripture is inspired of God — The Spirit *of* God not only once inspired those who wrote it, but continually inspires, supernaturally assists, those that read it with earnest prayer. Hence *it is* so *profitable for doctrine,* for instruction of the igno-

rant, *for* the *reproof* or conviction of them that are in error or sin, *for* the *correction* or amendment of whatever is amiss, and for instructing or training up the children of God *in* all righteousness.[11]

Some theologians might refer to this theological understanding as the double–inspiration theory, when divine inspiration occurs in both the author and the reader of Scripture. Wesley did not formally elaborate such a doctrine, but he firmly believed in the continual inspiration or illumination of the Holy Spirit available to those who seek divine assistance in listening to God.

Although we need the continued presence of the Holy Spirit to guide us, Scripture remains a reliable source of God's self–revelation. Scripture does not supplant the Holy Spirit, but God has chosen to make it a sufficient resource for matters of religious faith and practice. Thus Wesley considered Scripture serving as much to *rule* our lives as God's Spirit serves to *guide* our lives.

> For though the Spirit is our principal leader, yet He is not our rule at all; the Scriptures are the rule whereby He leads us into all truth. Therefore, only talk good English, call the Spirit our "guide," which signifies an intelligent being, and the Scriptures our "rule," which signifies something used by an intelligent being, and all is plain and clear.[12]

Scripture and the Holy Spirit are not in conflict. Instead they serve as perfect complements in communicating what Wesley liked to describe as heart–religion – religion in which knowledge and vital piety perfectly join in the life of a believer.

## The Inspiration of Scripture

Belief in Scripture flows from belief in God, and not vice versa. Wesley did not assume the inspiration of Scripture without first committing himself, at least provisionally, to belief in God. Yet the growth of theistic beliefs came through reading Scripture and discovering its trustworthiness as a source of divine revelation about God and salvation through Jesus Christ. An almost dialectical interplay occurs between the reading of Scripture, the substantiation of experience, and the reasonably conceived insight that results from having committed oneself to Scripture as the self–revelation of God. The dialectical process comprises an active comprehension of things known whereby a person gains objective knowledge about God and salvation that may appear hidden to those unwilling to commit themselves to God.

Wesley committed himself at least by the year 1730 – eight years before his well–known Aldersgate experience – to making the Bible the primary source of authority for his life.[13] Yet Wesley sometimes doubted the truth of Scripture, for example, concerning the *instantaneous* nature of conversion by faith. He had not experienced the assurance of a personal conversion and knew of few who had. Although he desired such an assurance, he seriously questioned whether he could ever experience it. Peter Böhler and others encouraged Wesley by introducing him to people who had experienced instantaneous conversions.[14] These witnesses, coupled with similar kinds of conversions described in

Scripture, led Wesley to a point of belief when he too experienced a sense of personal assurance of salvation. It also led him to greater depths of commitment and willingness to participate in other truths mentioned in Scripture, for example, the possibility of living a holy life through the sanctifying grace of God.

Earlier Wesley had appealed to Böhler as to whether he should continue to preach despite his feeling "fully convinced of unbelief, of the want of that faith whereby alone we are saved."[15] Böhler replied, "Preach faith *till* you have it; and then, *because* you have it, you *will* preach faith."[16] This somewhat paradoxical comment by Böhler reveals the participatory nature of how we come to both believe *and* know. Without personally committing ourselves to something or someone as true, we will not fully understand the depth of truth present, nor will we experience the assurance of its truthfulness.

Wesley knew of similar participation motifs from the Catholic mystics he had read, but it was his discovery of such truths in Scripture *and* his heart–warming experience of personal assurance that ultimately led him to the added assurance of the inspiration of Scripture.

Wesley believed that "all Scripture is given by the inspiration of God" — an affirmation found both in Scripture and in Anglican formularies.[17] This affirmation represented a faith commitment that Wesley used to distinguish himself and the Methodist movement from "Jews, Turks, and Infidels."[18] He also believed "the written word of God to be the only and sufficient rule both of Christian faith and practice; and herein we are fundamentally distinguished from those of the Romish Church."[19]

As we have seen, the confirmation of Wesley's belief in Scripture came at least in part from his personal experience of its truth for salvation and from the ongoing witness of the Holy Spirit. He fully expected God's Holy Spirit to witness to the inspiration of Scripture so that one would experience a personal sense of assurance of its truthworthiness. But beyond divine confirmation that we experience, Wesley appealed to several other arguments that he thought would further *induce* people to believe in the inspiration of Scripture. In "A clear and Concise Demonstration of the Divine Inspiration of the Holy Scriptures," Wesley used empirical and rational arguments. First, he argued that the empirical facts that surround Scripture compel us to believe in its inspiration.

> There are four grand and powerful arguments which strongly induce us to believe that the Bible must be from God; viz., miracles, prophecies, the goodness of the doctrine, and the moral character of the penmen. All the miracles flow from divine power; all the prophecies, from divine understanding; the goodness of the doctrine, from divine goodness; and the moral character of the penmen, from divine holiness.[20]

The four arguments — divine power, understanding, goodness, and holiness, which Wesley called "the four grand pillars" for God — presuppose an already existing conception of God, and Wesley recognized this logical limitation. Nevertheless, the arguments served to substantiate a fundamental belief in God and characteristics about him that make belief in the inspiration of Scripture plausible as well as possible. Only after we encounter the living God in faith can we grasp the essential truths of Christianity. In a sense these arguments provided a way in which a believing mind can form a rational understanding of inspiration.

A second rational argument used by Wesley comprised a logical problem on the necessary source of inspiration. Here he offered three propositions for possible motivations in writing Scripture and how it makes logical sense to believe that God inspired the Word.

> I beg leave to propose a short, clear, and strong argument to prove the divine inspiration of the holy Scriptures.
> The Bible must be the invention either of good men or angels, bad men or devils, or of God.
> 1. It could not be the invention of good men or angels; for they neither would nor could make a book, and tell lies all the time they were writing it, saying, "Thus saith the Lord," when it was their own invention.
> 2. It could not be the invention of bad men or devils; for they would not make a book which commands all duty, forbids all sin, and condemns their souls to hell to all eternity.
> 3. Therefore, I draw this conclusion, that the Bible must be given by divine inspiration.[21]

This argument resembles popular arguments still used by such contemporary authors as C. S. Lewis. In *Mere Christianity*, Lewis argued that we have three options in our view of Jesus Christ. We must either consider him a liar, a lunatic, or the Lord of the universe.[22]

Of course, the options provided both by Lewis and Wesley are too simple for us to consider all possible approaches to the topic. In this instance, Wesley's intention to speak *ad populum* becomes quite evident because his reasoned approach to the inspiration of Scripture only made sense to those who already believed. In the final analysis, Wesley required the affective dimension of the testimony of the Holy Spirit to assure one of the inspiration of Scripture. Yet we may view the foregoing arguments as ways to *think* about inspiration rather than ways to provide *rational proofs* of inspiration."

Wesley never argued for a rationalistic conception of religion, but he continually argued for a concept of religion that is reasonable. As such, the objective of Wesley's discussion was not to discover rational, objective proofs for inspiration that we must then believe in by faith. Inspiration was first known in experience through a personal encounter with God. The aim of Wesley's theological reflections was to understand the nature of this inspiration in depth. This reflection contributes to a Christian's sense of assurance about divine inspiration — an assurance experienced in both the head and the heart.

Colin Williams intimates that Wesley argued theoretically for the inspiration of Scripture from the standpoint of a static and mechanical, biblical literalism. For example, Williams contends that Wesley's "interpretation of 'Thus said the Lord'...[is] a mechanical view which fails to do justice to the dynamic of the divine–human encounter."[23] But he moderates his interpretation by noting that the view of inspiration Wesley held in *practice* reflected how "biblical interpretation was brought into relation with tradition, reason, and experience in such a way that he [Wesley] was relieved of the dangers of a static and mechanical literalism."[24] However, this modified interpretation gives Wesley very little credit as to the sophistication of his theology and his understanding of language. On the one hand, Wesley said:

> The language of his messengers, also, is exact in the highest degree: for the words which were given them accurately answered the impression made upon their minds; and hence Luther says, "Divinity is nothing but a grammar of the language of the Holy Ghost."[25]

On the other hand, Wesley did not work with a naive understanding of language referring .to the nature and work of God. In his sermon, "The Witness of the Spirit," he used the same kind of *impression* terminology that we read above in his speaking of assurance. Yet he recognized the limitations of all language in describing God and his self–revelation.

> It is hard to find words in the language of men to explain "the deep things of God." Indeed, there are none that will adequately express what the children of God experience. But perhaps one might say, (desiring any who are taught of God to correct, to soften, or strengthen the expression,) the testimony of the Spirit is an inward impression on the soul, whereby the Spirit of God directly witnesses to my spirit, that I am a child of God.[26]

Wesley showed great confidence in God's continuous spiritual presence and work in the lives of believers both past and present. But he did not have a naive or simplistic approach with regard to what that confidence involves. He considered religious experiences to provide objective knowledge of God, not merely subjective. But though it gives us objective impressions of the divine, our knowledge — because of our humanness — remains *in part*. This recalls the words of Paul in 1 Corinthians 13: "We know in part and we prophesy in part....Now we see but a poor reflection [of the way things are]."[27]

Although Wesley lived before the day of historical–critical questions about Scripture, he nevertheless had some sophistication concerning the limits of language and reason. We should not, even in theory, relegate his understanding to that of a static and mechanical literalism. He believed in the inspiration of Scripture because it proved sufficient for salvation and for growing in the Christian life. Scripture became functionally authoritative for Wesley *before* he formulated his doctrine of Scripture. In fact, from his perspective, all conceptual formulations retain a hypothetical or tentative quality that mitigates a merely static or mechanical view of the inspiration and authority of Scripture.

To the extent that he affirmed Scripture as the primary authority of the Christian religion, Wesley agreed with the classical Protestant view of biblical authority. In his sermon, "On Faith, Heb. 11:6," he explicitly aligned himself with the Protestant position on Scripture.

> The faith of Protestants, in general, embraces only those truths as necessary to

> salvation, which are clearly revealed in the oracles of God....They believe nei-
> ther more nor less than what is manifestly contained in, and. provable by, the
> Holy Scriptures....The written word is the whole and sole rule of their faith, as
> well as practice.[28]

Although Wesley fully aligned himself with Protestant Christianity, he was not
content to use the principle of *sola Scriptura* in a way that excluded other sources
of religious authority. In keeping with his Anglican heritage, he was not afraid
to introduce extrabiblical authorities into his method of approaching theology
*and* Scripture. The whole theological task was too complex and interrelated to
other sources of religious authority to ignore how they contributed to illuminating, vitalizing, and organizing the gospel message.

## The Purpose and Authority of Scripture

We discover in Wesley that the primary purpose of Scripture comprises communicating the full gospel message of salvation — salvation that produces both
justification and sanctification in believers. Scripture contains a trustworthy
record of how God provided a way of salvation, especially as revealed through
the person and work of Jesus Christ. Scripture thus presents the "way of salvation."

Wesley articulated this way in such sermons as "Scriptural Christianity," "The
Scripture Way of Salvation," and "On Working Out Our Own Salvation." If we
want to be saved but do not know how, Scripture shows us "the steps
which...direct us to take, in the working out of our own salvation."[29] Thus
Scripture was always believed by Wesley to remain existentially essential to finding the way of salvation.

Articulating the order of salvation (*ordo salutis*) found in Scripture facilitates
the Word's intended purpose. Wesley recognized this practical application of
theology and so attempted several times to delineate each stage in the way of
salvation. Some scholars suggest that Wesley's order is one of his most systematic theological enterprises.[30] Indeed, Wesley generally regarded the order of salvation as the core of his theology. Harald Lindström presents a comprehensive
study of Wesley's various attempts to articulate this order. Of those attempts,
Lindström considers the 1765 sermon entitled "The Scripture Way of Salvation"
to provide the predominant factors Wesley placed in the *ordo salutis*: "1) The
operation of prevenient grace. 2) Repentance previous to justification. 3)
Justification or forgiveness. 4) The New Birth. 5) Repentance after justification
and the gradually proceeding work of sanctification. 6) Entire sanctification."[31]

Larry Shelton notes that Scripture functions sacramentally for Wesley.[32] By
sacramental use, Shelton explains: "When the means of Scripture is focused on
the need for salvation, its purpose is fulfilled....God works infallibly through the
means of Scripture to bring salvation."[33] To Wesley, Scripture provided that
means whereby God performs an action of grace corresponding to the finished
and ongoing work of Christ in our lives for salvation. He described the *"means
of grace"* as "outward signs, words, or actions, ordained of God, and appointed

for this end, to be the ordinary channels whereby He might convey to men, preventing, justifying, or sanctifying grace."[34] He applied this sacramental principle to Scripture by saying, "All who desire the grace of God are to wait for it in 'searching the Scriptures.'"[35] Now, although Wesley did not formally describe the prayerful study of and meditation on Scripture as a sacrament, he certainly conceived of it as a channel of grace.

To the extent that Wesley claimed to be a man of one book, he affirmed the Reformation call to the authoritative principle of *sola Scriptura*.[36] But his affirmation of Scripture as primary appeared in the context of an overwhelming desire for salvation and not in the traditional mold, at least, of Continental Reformation thinking. Because the authority of Scripture ensued from its efficaciousness in bringing a person to the experience of personal salvation, it did not rest on proving the inspiration or dependability of it. Later in his ministry Wesley affirmed that Scripture contained no falsehood.[37] But earlier, he perceived the authority of Scripture resting more on its function in facilitating salvation than on its factual, historical, or theological dependability.[38]

No doubt Wesley affirmed the authority of Scripture with greater zeal after his famed heart–warming experience at Aldersgate. At that time Scripture asserted its supremacy as never before.[39] But he had to learn it experimentally from the context of his experience — even if at first he was only tacitly or subconsciously aware of the learning process. As mentioned earlier, Wesley had wondered pre–Aldersgate whether a person could be saved instantaneously. He knew that Scripture contained accounts of people who were converted thus, but he could not bring himself to believe it. After conferring with Peter Böhler and further reflecting on the words of Scripture, Wesley could only exclaim: "Here ended my disputing. I could now only cry out, 'Lord, help thou my unbelief!'"[40] Only later did Wesley develop a more complete understanding of Scripture that included an account of its authoritativeness.

What Wesley experienced as true, he expected to find confirmed under the experimental scrutiny of inductive investigation, which included the study of Scripture as well as the whole of life experiences. His articulation of the "four grand and powerful arguments" — miracles, prophecies, the goodness of the doctrine, and the moral character of the penmen — came many years after his conversion and after the revival movement had crested.

By this time Wesley had the leisure to reflect theologically on the nature and authority of Scripture. Similar to his treatise on "The Doctrine of Original Sin," he took an inductive approach, requiring empirical facts, logical argumentation, and a "clear and concise demonstration...which [would] strongly induce us to believe that the Bible must be from God."[41] Religious belief remained fundamental to establishing the authority of Scripture, but Wesley expected people to be persuaded of its authoritativeness by an accumulation of arguments.

On this subject, Albert Outler notes, "The great Protestant watchwords of *sola fide* and *sola Scriptura* were in fact fundamentals in Wesley's formulation of a doctrine of biblical authority. But early and late in his career, Wesley interpreted *solus* to mean 'primarily' rather than 'solely' or 'exclusively.'"[42] In support of this claim, Outler quotes from the "Minutes of Several Conversations," where Wesley said, in response to those who say they read only the Bible:

> This is rank enthusiasm. If you need no book but the Bible, you are got above St. Paul. He wanted others too. "Bring the books," says he, "but especially the parchments," those wrote on parchment. "But I have no taste. for reading." Contract a taste for it by use, or return to your trade.[43]

Wesley's affirmation of the authority of Scripture did not preclude his life-long interest in and use of many other books, particularly those of theological relevance.[44] The fifty–volume *Christian Library* that Wesley edited clearly attests to his concern to provide everyone with a diversity of intellectual and devotional resources for Christian belief — resources having a degree of authoritativeness, even of a derived and supplemental nature.

But nothing could ever take the place of Scripture as the primary religious source of authority in Wesley's writings. He never wanted to become anything other than a biblical theologian. In the words of Thomas Langford:

> Wesley intended to be a biblical theologian. Scripture was the fundamental source of his theological expression; every doctrine must be measured against the standard presented in Scripture....Hence the two principal resources Wesley left his followers for their theological guidance were his sermons and his *Notes Upon the New Testament.*[45]

Wesley's use of Scripture flowed naturally from his mouth and pen. He did not merely preach Scripture; it became a part of him. His words, thought patterns, and concerns lived out in action all reflected the way Scripture became internal. Outler states that Wesley knew Scripture "so nearly by heart that even his natural speech is biblical."[46] In his *Notes upon the Old Testament,* Wesley said, "'Tis not enough to have Bibles, but we must use them, yea, use them daily. Our souls must have constant meals of that manna, which if well digested, will afford them true nourishment and strength."[47]

## Principles of Interpretation

Wesley did not use Scripture glibly, nor did he use it in a legalistic or proof–texting way. His use of Scripture emanated from a holistic understanding of and trust in its sufficiency to "make you wise" for salvation and for living a holy life.[48] He may not have always exhibited the most exegetical skills, but he was able to capture a gestalt or holistic understanding of Christian truths that exceeded his scholarship. He seemed especially capable of conceptually grasping and communicating the vital, dynamic character of Christian faith as it impinged on every aspect of a believer's life. At the same time he sought to integrate its conceptual content into the warp and woof of his theology and ministry.

We must not expect to find in Wesley a highly developed and sophisticated understanding of the interpretation of Scripture. Although Christians have systematically reflected on hermeneutics since patristic times, and although early biblical criticism began in the century before Wesley, he preceded most of the historical–critical questions of the nineteenth century and onward. In Wesley's Anglican context there was no pressing need to develop an apologetic for one's doctrine of Scripture or biblical hermeneutics. As such, we cannot determine how Wesley might have responded to the many historical–critical issues that still dog us today.[49] For instance, Wesley did not deal with questions of authenticity, authorship, and so on. Yet he did not slide past difficult passages in Scripture as though no problems existed.[50] He recognized that all people struggle to understand the mysteries of revealed as well as natural religion because "of our ignorance and inability to fathom his [God's] counsels."[51]

Interestingly, Wesley considered the possibility that religious knowledge, passed down from Noah and his children and his children's children, may have been affected by the addition of numberless fables. .

> We may likewise reasonably suppose, that some traces of knowledge, both with regard to the invisible and the eternal world, were delivered down from Noah and his children, both to their immediate and remote descendants. And however these were obscured or disguised by the addition of numberless fables, yet something of truth was still mingled with them, and these streaks of light prevented utter darkness. [52]

Although Wesley did not speculate on how much such fables affected Scripture, he conceded that people may obscure and disguise even religious truths that have been handed down from ancestors.

As to the sometimes mysterious aspects of Scripture, Wesley said, "Even among us who are favoured far above these — to whom are entrusted the oracles of God, whose word is a lantern to our feet, and a light in all our paths — there are still many circumstances in his dispensations which are above our comprehension."[53] Possessing Scripture did not in itself safeguard complete understanding of God's truth, though it always remained sufficient for leading people to salvation and providing guidelines for holy living.

Thomas Langford holds that Wesley, in his *Notes upon the New Testament,* followed the lead of prominent scholars of his times such as Hugo Grotius and especially Johannes Albrecht Bengel whose writings largely served as the basis for Wesley's commentary.[54] Langford writes, "His [Wesley's] intention was not so much to make any interpretation final, as to make the biblical source central. He reflected this openness in all his works as he attempted to join genuine piety with sound learning."[55]

Scholars such as Mildred Bangs Wynkoop have described "love" as the theological hermeneutic behind Wesley's biblical interpretation.[56] Larry Shelton concedes that "love" motivates Wesley's examination of Scripture, but suggests that "his methodology is primarily inductive, historical–literal, and soteriologically motivated."[57]

## The Inductive Character

The inductive character of Wesley's theological method extends to his interpretation of Scripture, and Shelton provides helpful research into how Wesley approached hermeneutical questions. First, Shelton observes that in the preface to the *Notes upon the Old Testament,* Wesley developed the inductive character-istics of his approach to the study of Scripture.[58] At the end of his preface, Wesley summarized six devotional steps to the study of Scripture.

> If you desire to read the Scriptures in such a manner as may most effectually answer this end (to understand the things of God), would it not be advisable (1) to set apart a little time, if you can, every morning and evening for this purpose? (2) At each time, if you have leisure, to read a chapter out of the Old, and one out of the New Testament; if you cannot do this, to take a single chapter, or a part of one? (3) to read this with a single eye to know the whole will of God, and a fixed resolution to do it? In order to know His will, you should (4) have a constant eye to the analogy of faith, the connexion and harmony there is between those grand, fundamental doctrines, original sin, justification by faith, the new birth, inward and outward holiness. (5) Serious and earnest prayer should be constantly used before we consult the oracles of God, seeing "Scripture can only be understood through the same Spirit whereby it was given"....(6) It might also be of use, if while we read we were frequently to pause and examine ourselves by what we read.[59]

These suggestions were given as preparation for more serious study of Scripture. But even on a devotional level, Wesley was concerned that Christians inductively study Scripture for themselves.

Second, Shelton observes that Wesley emphasized the primacy of the liter-al sense of Scripture. He states that Wesley did not advocate literalism per se, but the method followed by Luther and the other Reformers whereby the alle-gorical sense of Scripture was corrected by "the plain grammar and syntax [that] give the meaning of any statement without recourse to any esoteric spiritualiza-tions."[60] As a corollary to historical and exegetical techniques, Shelton points out that Wesley used what he described as *the analogy of faith,* by which "he means the general themes of the Bible as they are correctly interpreted."[61] Similarly, Outler describes Wesley's use of the analogy of faith as "one's sense of the whole" by which an interpreter of Scripture is able to grasp a gestalt under-standing of the truths of Scripture that supersedes a slavish dependency on the literal words.[62]

On close examination we find that Wesley always began by emphasizing the literal sense of the text. Yet he did not approach it simplistically or without the careful use of reason and, where possible, the confirmation or clarification of experience. He always revealed an openness to reconsider his interpretation of Scripture when given insights from reason and experience.

Finally, Shelton notes the soteriological focus that is apparent throughout Wesley's writings — a focus motivated by what Wynkoop described as Wesley's hermeneutic of love. Shelton maintains that although he was motivated by love, "Wesley's basic approach to interpretation and to the authority of Scripture is solidly in the historical–literal, Patristic and Reformation interpretative tradi-tion."[63] Deeming faith and salvation to "include the substance of all the Bible, the marrow, as it were, of the whole Scripture,"[64] Wesley organized the whole of his theological investigations around the central focus of salvation, which was the *raison d'etre* for the Methodist movement.

In describing Wesley's approach to Scripture as inductive, we do not find him systematically or formally using such an approach in all his writings. In fact, it could be argued that a deductive approach predominates in his approach to biblical hermeneutics. For example, Edward Sugden calls attention to the fact that Wesley "first worked out his theology by strict logical deduction from the Scriptures; and then he corrected his conclusions by the test of actual experience. His class—meetings were a laboratory in which he verified or modified his hypotheses."[65] One may interpret Wesley as merely deducing theological ideas from Scripture, under whose authority he had thoroughly and unquestioningly placed himself. But not even Sugden would want to say this, for even he realized that Wesley functioned as though he used a scientific method of hypothetical investigation, especially when verifying the correctness of his theological conclusions. Admittedly, Wesley believed that Scripture is entirely trustworthy, but also that it established its authority through the crucible of rational and experimental testing.

True to the Aristotelian tradition of logic that he admired and appropriated, Wesley's ideal was a deductive science. A deductive science proceeds logically from general biblical truths to particular truths of life experiences, showing that the particulars follow from the general by necessity. But Wesley saw that even though premises are logically prior to conclusions, in reality we don't necessarily come to know things in that order. Our knowledge starts from sense experience (including both physical and spiritual senses) — that is, from particulars — and finds there the general. Thus we reason inductively, a process that has as its goal a deductive science, which includes both induction and deduction as methodological components.

This was Wesley's way of working toward the ideal of a demonstrative theological science. For example, if he seemed biblically deductive in sermons or other theological writings, this was the result of inductive investigations that confirmed his general ideas or of the belief that such ideas would stand up to the test of inductive investigation and confirmation.

### The Process of Interpretation

*Discerning the Context*

In interpreting Scripture, Wesley began by studying the texts themselves. Although he did not concern himself with higher critical questions that became the rage in the next century, Wesley saw the need to interpret Scripture beyond its plain, literal meaning. Biblical hermeneutics entailed investigation of the context. Wesley warned that

> any passage is easily perverted, by being recited singly, without any of the preceding or following verses. By this means it may often seem to have one sense, when it will be plain, by observing what goes before and what follows after, that it really has the direct contrary.[66]

Scripture passages must stand under the scrutiny of other Scripture passages to clarify the meaning of the whole. As Wesley said, "The best way, therefore, to understand it [Scripture], is carefully to compare Scripture with Scripture, and thereby learn the true meaning of it."[67] In "An Address to the Clergy," Wesley added, "No less necessary is a knowledge of the Scriptures, which teach us how to teach others; yea, a knowledge of all the Scriptures; seeing Scripture interprets Scripture; one part fixing the sense of another."[68]

The use of Scripture to interpret Scripture is an important, explicit principle of Wesley's hermeneutics, though we may wish that he had been more consistent in applying it. No doubt he allowed his experience of and concern for salvation and concomitant holy living to shape his interpretation and exposition of Scripture. But the weakness stemmed not so much from poor methodology as from the lack of rigorously applying his stated rules of biblical interpretation.

*Experience*

In addition to the analogy of faith, Wesley relied on experience to help interpret Scripture. He used experience to confirm truths found in Scripture. He claimed he would not even believe the literal interpretation of Scripture unless it was confirmed by experience. We may illustrate this through a conversation between Wesley and Peter Böhler:

> When I met Peter Böhler again, he consented to put the dispute upon the issue which I desired, namely, Scripture and experience. I first consulted the Scripture. But when I set aside the glosses of men, and simply considered the words of God, comparing them together, endeavouring to illustrate the obscure by the plainer passages, I found they all made against me, and was forced to retreat to my last hold, "that experience would never agree with the *literal interpretation* of those Scriptures." Nor could I therefore allow it to be true, till I found some living witnesses to it.[69]

Consequently Wesley insisted that debatable interpretations of Scripture and subsequent formulations of doctrine be "confirmed by *your* experience and *mine.*"[70]

Since he expected experience to confirm Scripture, Wesley also allowed for the possibility of experience to clarify the meaning of Scripture when it is unclear or, more properly, clarify our interpretation of it. William Arnett notes that this "correctional value" of experience indeed operated in Wesley's interpretation of Scripture.[71] An excellent example may be found in Wesley's biblical understanding of entire sanctification. Some Wesley scholars suggest that his doctrine of entire sanctification sprang primarily from observation of Christians' experience of God's sanctifying grace in their lives.[72] Of course, observation of these experiences confirmed what Wesley already found to be true in Scripture.

A related example involves Wesley's response to the question of whether sin remains in a person subsequent to his or her entire sanctification. At least hypothetically, Wesley allowed for the possibility of experience correcting what might appear to be the plain and obvious meaning of Scripture:

Q. But what does it signify, whether any have attained it or not, seeing so many Scriptures witness for it?

A. If I were convinced that one in England had attained what has been so clearly and strongly preached by such a number of Preachers, in so many places, and for so long a time, I should be clearly convinced that we had all mistaken the meaning of those Scriptures; and therefore, for the time to come, I too must teach that "sin will remain till death."[73]

Of course, Wesley did *not* expect experience ever to contradict Scripture. Nevertheless, he expected that evidence gleaned from life experiences would crucially enhance proper interpretation and subsequent exposition and application of the Word.

*Reason*

Along with experience, reason played a vital role in Wesley's interpretation of Scripture. For Wesley, reason facilitates the entire thinking process, without which one could not hope or even begin to interpret Scripture. Reason constitutes a "precious gift of God....[it is] 'the candle of the Lord,' which he hath fixed in our souls for. excellent purposes."[74] The sinfulness of humanity may have effaced the moral image of God in individuals, but it did not utterly efface their natural image.[75] Reason, or understanding, functions as a part of that natural image and is a God–given capacity on which we may rely in the important process of scriptural interpretation.

Further, through reason God "enables us in some measure to comprehend his method of dealing with the children of men."[76] Reason guides us in understanding and responding to the important Christian ideas about repentance, faith, justification, the new birth, and holiness. Emphasizing the trustworthiness of reason, Wesley said,

In all these respects, and in all the duties of common life, God has given us our reason for a guide. And it is only by acting up to the dictates of it, by using all the understanding which God hath given us, that we can have a conscience void of offence towards God and towards man.[77]

As such, Christians should not "despise or lightly esteem reason, knowledge, or human learning."[78] Rather, Christians may profitably employ reason in their biblical and theological investigations.

Wesley even considered the leadership of the Holy Spirit consistent with our rational capabilities.[79] To be sure, reason has its limits; it is not greater than Scripture as a source of religious authority. But reason remains essential in the entire hermeneutical process of exegesis, exposition, and application of Scripture.

## Summary of the Principles

All these sources of authority complement one another in the methodological approach Wesley used in his biblical and theological investigations. While not articulating a systematic approach, Wesley followed basic guidelines in his interpretation of Scripture, and those guidelines are discernible. Arnett distills six general rules of biblical interpretation characteristic of Wesley. While we have already seen the substance of these rules in our discussion, Arnett provides convenient summary:

> First, the literal sense is emphasized.
> Second, Wesley insists on the importance of the context.
> Third, comparing Scripture is important.
> Fourth, Wesley stresses the importance of Christian experience in interpreting the Scriptures....Christian experience has both confirmatory and correctional value.
> Fifth, reason is to be used as the "handmaid of faith, the servant of revelation."
> Finally, we observe the rule of "practicality." Wesley was in large measure an apostle to the plain, unlettered people. Therefore he sought to eliminate the elaborate, the elegant, and the oratorical.[80]

Outler offers a similar summary of Wesley's principles of interpretation in his introduction to the Bicentennial edition of the *Works*. He lists five principles.

> The first was that believers should accustom themselves to the biblical language and thus to the "general sense" of Scripture as a whole....This leads to a second rule, adapted from the ancient Fathers and from the Reformers as well: that the Scriptures are to be read as a whole, with the expectation that the clearer texts may be relied upon to illuminate the obscurer ones....This holistic sense of biblical inspiration suggested his third hermeneutical principle: that one's exegesis is to be guided, always in the first instance, by the literal sense, unless that appears to lead to consequenc[e]s that are either irrational or unworthy of God's moral character as "pure, unbounded love"....A fourth hermeneutical rule follows from his doctrine of grace and free will: that all moral commands in Scripture are also "covered promises," since God never commands the impossible and his grace is always efficacious in every faithful will. His last rule is actually a variation on the Anglican sense of the Old Vincentian canon that the historical experience of the church, though fallible, is the better judge overall of Scripture's meanings than later interpreters are like to be, especially on their own. Thus, radical novelty is to be eschewed on principle.[81]

The important thing to note about Wesley's rules or principles of biblical interpretation is his openness to investigating more than the plain, literal meaning of any text. Wesley showed a willingness to explore alternative interpretations when the text or evidence of Scripture appears "contrary to some other texts," "obscure," or "implies an absurdity."[82]

Gerald R. Cragg confirms that Wesley was not a slavish literalist because he "invoked reason, tradition and experience in order to clarify the meaning of obscure passages."[83] Other scholars agree. Sugden argues that "Wesley was a critic, both higher and lower, before those much misunderstood terms were invented."[84] In support Sugden cites the preface to the *Notes upon the New Testament*: "Those various readings which have a vast majority of ancient copies and translations on their side, I have without scruple incorporated with the text; which I have divided all along according to the matter it contains."[85] Sugden further suggests that in the preface to the book of Joshua, Wesley stated almost exactly the modern critical view. Wesley wrote,

> Indeed it is probable they [Joshua to Esther] were collections of the authentic records of the nation, which some of the prophets were divinely directed and assisted to put together. It seems the substance of the several histories was written under divine direction, when the events had just happened, and long after put into the form wherein they stand now, perhaps all by the same hand.[86]

Along the same line, George C. Cell argues that Wesley may not have adopted the contemporary critical position on Scripture in *theory,* but certainly adopted it in *practice.*[87] Colin Williams cites several examples of how Wesley accepted textual criticism, refusing to approach doctrinal studies simplistically.[88] Outler agrees that Wesley was no "proof–texter" even though he viewed the entire Scripture authoritatively as "a whole and integral revelation."[89]

Other scholars disagree on the sophistication of Wesley's hermeneutics.[90] Despite attempts by Wesley to incorporate critical scholarship in his writings, he did not approach biblical studies as a professional scholar. His principles of interpretation were neither innovative nor consistent. But since he never intended. to blaze new trails in biblical scholarship, we should not be too critical. Even critics of Wesley's hermeneutics such as Wilbur Mullen recognize that however one analyzes Wesley's methodology, "the end result of his exegesis was fantastically successful…whether or not it would stand the test of twentieth–century hermeneutical analysis."[91]

In conclusion, the catholicity of Wesley's openness to all historic claimants of religious authority demonstrates that the inductive character of his theological method extended beyond theology to include biblical hermeneutics. Of course, he did not explicitly articulate this inductive process either in his biblical studies or in his theology, nor was Wesley always as rigorous as we would like in following such methodology. Yet the inductive character of Wesley's work may be discerned in his biblical studies even though he may not have used the methodology in the manner of a professional scholar. By recognizing inductive characteristics in his biblical studies, we understand better the pervasiveness and consistency of Wesley's use of a similar methodology in his approach to theology as a whole.

# 5

# THE AUTHORITY OF TRADITION

John Wesley reserved a special place for Christian tradition in formulating his theological and practical writings. Despite living in an age of progressive distrust in the authority of Christian tradition, Wesley affirmed its necessity for theological method.[1] In the preface to the first collected edition of his works (1771–74), Wesley stated the purpose of the edition: "I present to serious and candid men my last and maturest thoughts, agreeable, I hope, to Scripture, reason and Christian antiquity."[2] By "Christian antiquity" Wesley referred primarily to *"the religion of the primitive church,* of the whole church in the purest ages."[3] He explained "the religion of the primitive church" this way:

> It is clearly expressed even in the small remains of Clemens Romanus, Ignatius, and Polycarp. It is seen more at large in the writings of Tertullian, Origen, Clemens Alexandrinus, and Cyprian. And even in the fourth century it was found in the works of Chrysostom, Basil, Ephrem Syrus, and Macarius. It would be easy to produce a cloud of witnesses testifying the same thing, were not this a point which no one will contest who has the least acquaintance with Christian antiquity.[4]

## The Orthodox Tradition of Methodism

Wesley was always concerned that his theology and the Methodist movement be seen in the context of that Christian tradition, that most nearly represented true, scriptural faith. In his sermon "On Laying the Foundation of the New Chapel," Wesley placed Methodism in the orthodox succession of true, or genuine, Christianity, reflecting the most elemental manifestations of religion. This primitive, or "old," religion predated the "religion of the Bible"; it consisted of "no other than love: the love of God and of all humankind; the loving God with all our heart, and soul, and strength, as having first loved *us,* as the fountain of all the good we have received, and of all we ever hope to enjoy; and the loving every soul which God hath made, every man on earth, as our own soul."[5]

Old religion — or what Wesley elsewhere referred to as "heart–religion" — may be summed up in this "one, comprehensive petition, 'Cleanse the thoughts of our hearts by the inspiration of thy Holy Spirit, that we may perfectly love thee, and worthily magnify thy holy name.'"[6] These words described the essence of the spiritual church history with which Wesley wanted to identify. It was for spiritual reasons rather than for theological or ecclesiastical continuity, which was generally the case with Christian appeals to tradition. Nevertheless, Wesley thought that true or genuine Christianity could be traced through history and that, in fact, Methodism was the most recent, authentic; manifestation of "old religion." He traced its "genealogy" as shown on the next page.[7]

Though Wesley's abridged version of orthodox church history was biased toward the Anglican tradition and the Methodist movement, it reveals the essence of his understanding of religion and his concern to identify with what he considered other manifestations of true, scriptural Christianity. He deemed learning church history helpful in the process of understanding, appreciating, and — finally — realizing scriptural truth in life. Moreover, such knowledge would lead us to return to the only sufficient authority for religious life, namely, Scripture — from which we may then learn in more depth the "religion of the Bible."

## "Old religion"

## Religion of the Bible

## Religion of the primitive church

## Religion of the Church of England

## Methodism

Wesley made it clear that the history of Christian or church tradition plays a vital role in both the interpretation of Scripture and in the development of central motifs of religious belief. To be sure, he always affirmed the primary religious authority of Scripture. Yet, in reading Scripture, Wesley saw that doubt may easily arise over "dark or intricate" passages. In such cases we must use several hermeneutical procedures toward correct interpretation, not the least of which is an appeal to traditional church understanding of the text. Wesley said,

> If any doubt still remains, I consult those who are experienced in the things of God, and then the writings whereby, being dead, they yet speak. And what I thus learn, that I teach.[8]

Some, though certainly not all, church tradition contains both the biblical knowledge and the practical wisdom of Christians who experienced the kind of genuine heart–religion Wesley hoped to revive throughout Britain. Carefully chosen historical writings supplied Wesley with an invaluable extrabiblical source of religious authority for theologically informing his personal life and ministry. These writings could confirm true Christianity and provide substantive teaching on issues not specifically addressed by Scripture. Albert Outler notes, "That Wesley took 'Christian antiquity' as a decisive guideline in theology and ethics may be seen, early and late, throughout the corpus."[9]

So we can see why Wesley highly regarded "the religion of the primitive church." It represented an "age of golden days,"[10] or as Ted A. Campbell describes it, "a period in which an ideal of Christian individual and. community life was realized."[11] Despite Wesley's great confidence in Scripture and in reason's role in correct interpretation, he still recognized that certain doctrines required investigation "by Scripture and reason; and, if need be, by antiquity."[12]

In summarizing the history of the Methodist movement in various writings, Wesley again asserted the necessary role of tradition in biblical interpretation and application to holy living. In 1777 Wesley described the earliest Methodists as "orthodox in every point; firmly believing, not only the Three Creeds, but whatsoever they judged to be the doctrine of the Church of England, as contained in her Articles and Homilies."[13] In 1787, Wesley went so far as to place the *Books of Homilies* in the Church of England as second only in importance to Scripture during the formative years of the Methodist movement.[14]

Despite tradition's importance, Wesley definitely did not consider tradition either inspired or infallible. For example, with his high regard for the early church fathers, Wesley felt they made "many mistakes, many weak suppositions, and many ill–drawn conclusions."[15] For this reason he was very careful in his selection and application of church tradition. He rejected Roman Catholicism's tendency to elevate tradition's authority to the level of scripture authority. In his treatise entitled "The Advantage of the Members of the Church of England, Over Those of the Church of Rome," Wesley traced the way in which

> at the beginning of the Reformation, the Church of Rome began to oppose this principle, that all articles of faith must be provable from Scripture, (till then received throughout the whole Christian world,) and to add, if not prefer, to Holy Scripture, tradition, or the doctrine of Fathers and Councils, with the decrees of Popes.[16]

Wesley was ever concerned to steer a middle course between the Scylla of Catholic elevation and the Charybdis of Reformed denigration. He believed that Christians had to think and live creatively within the context of church history rather than undervaluing its valid place and function. But in affirming tradition's place as a religious authority, Wesley then had to determine its relation to Scripture and how it best functioned in illuminating and bringing biblical truths to life.

## A Reverence for Tradition

Wesley considered his faith at once biblical and consistent with the elemental beliefs of Christian antiquity. No one can read Wesley without observing a great reverence for the church fathers. He said:

> I exceedingly reverence them as well as their writings, and esteem them very highly in love. I reverence them, because they were Christians.... And I reverence their writings, because they describe true, genuine Christianity, and direct us to the strongest evidence of the Christian doctrine.[17]

The doctrinal "evidence" of the "primitive Fathers" to which Wesley referred included "particularly Clemens Romanus, Ignatius, Polycarp, Justin Martyr, Irenæus, Origen, Clemens Alexandrinus, Cyprian; to whom I would add Macarius and Ephraim Syrus."[18] Elsewhere Wesley added Chrysostom, Basil, Jerome, and Austin (an older English form of Augustine).[19] Outler observes that Wesley's roster was typical of Anglican patrology in general.[20]

Overall, Wesley particularly accepted as profitable for one's life and theology the writings of the ante–Nicene church fathers. There is no better example of this than his lengthy rebuttal to Conyers Middleton's accusations that "there were no miracles wrought in the primitive Church" and "that all the primitive Fathers were fools or knaves, and most of them both one and the other."[21] Wesley could not tolerate what he considered uncritical and biased interpretations of the early fathers.[22] (Luke Keefer uses the term *primitivism* to describe Wesley's strong interest in the early church and his desire to make it "the standard by which to measure the faith and practice of Christians in every age.")[23]

Wesley's views on Christian antiquity were largely informed and stimulated by the renaissance of patristic studies in seventeenth- and eighteenth-century Anglicanism.[24] Anglican theologians as far back as Richard Hooker and John Bramhall emphasized the beliefs and practices of the undivided church of the first five centuries as a criterion for classical orthodoxy. Bramhall wrote that the "ground for unity of faith is the creed; and for unity of government, the same form of discipline, which was used in the Primitive Church, and is derived from them to us."[25] And as Francis Paget wrote in his *Introduction to the Fifth Book of Hooker's Ecclesiastical Polity*: "For on equal loyalty to the unconflicting rights of reason, of Scripture, and of tradition rest the distinctive strength and hope of the English Church."[26]

Anglicans saw themselves in a unique situation compared with the Continental Reformers. They sought to recover and preserve the conciliar truths of Christian antiquity while avoiding the potential extremes of Roman Catholic authoritarianism and the doctrinal anarchy of Protestantism.[27] By introducing reason into the process of theological method, Anglicans sought to preserve traditional Christianity along with a renewed emphasis on the priority of Scripture.

Influenced by this Anglican renaissance of patristic studies, Wesley did not glibly refer to or use the writings of the church fathers. He made early Christian writings, doctrines, and creeds a lifelong subject of theological study and methodological import for himself and the Methodist preachers.[28] He considered early Christian writings "the most authentic commentators on Scripture, as being both nearest the foundation, and eminently endued with that Spirit by whom all Scripture was given."[29] He affirmed the general reliability of such writers, not only because of their helping to define the canon of the New Testament and their faithful transmission of both Testaments, but also because of the heart–religion he discovered in their personal testimonies.[30] Their writings provided tutelage both for a proper intellectual understanding about Christian doctrine and for nurturing believers in how to live vital, holy lives in Jesus Christ.

Wesley always defended his orthodoxy not only in relation to primitive Christianity, but also by emphasizing his lifelong allegiance to the Church of England in his doctrine and in his refusal to separate from the church.[31] The "religion of the Church of England," inasmuch as it reflected true Christianity, along with the primitive church was for Wesley a part of that ideal of religious belief found in the New Testament. He regarded Anglican teachings on doctrines such as justification by faith to be the most authoritative statement on the subject apart from Scripture. Wesley wrote, "The book which, next to the Holy Scripture, was of the greatest use to them in settling their judgment as to the grand point of justification by faith was the *Book of Homilies*."[32] The "Doctrine of Salvation, Faith and Good Works," Wesley's first doctrinal compendium, was an abridgment of Thomas Cranmer's work in the *Homilies*. The "Appeals" frequently used quotations from these Anglican formularies.

Even though he had been raised and educated in the Anglican tradition, Wesley considered his allegiance to the church to be based on the soundest of theological foundations, namely, Scripture. In a letter to Sir Harry Trelawny, Wesley emphasized his allegiance to the church: "Having had an opportunity of seeing several of the Churches abroad, and having deeply considered the several sorts of Dissenters at home, I am fully convinced that our own Church, with all her blemishes, is nearer the scriptural plan than any other in Europe."[33] He refused to separate from it because of his belief that the church substantially affirmed the truths of Scripture. In a letter to "John Smith," Wesley claimed always to "teach the doctrines of the Church of England.... I teach the doctrines which are comprised in those Articles and Homilies to which all the clergy of the Church of England solemnly profess to assent, and that in their plain, unforced, grammatical meaning."[34]

Wesley's strongest statement of affirmation appeared in an address entitled "The Advantage of the Members of the Church of England, Over Those of the Church of Rome." Here Wesley articulated the essence of his support for Anglicanism.

> Now, it is a known principle of the Church of England, that nothing is to
> be received as an article of faith, which is not read in the Holy Scripture, or
> to be inferred therefrom by just and plain consequence....
>
> On the contrary, at the very beginning of the Reformation, the Church of
> Rome began to oppose this principle....
>
> Seeing, therefore, the Church of England contends for the word of God,
> and the Church of Rome against it, it is easy to discern on which side the
> advantage lies, with regard to the grand principle of Christianity.[35]

Wesley's refusal to separate from the Church of England in the latter part of his
life and ministry testifies to his loyalty to a denomination that at least in doctrine sought to maintain its biblical foundation.[36]

Still, Wesley did not hesitate to disagree with either Christian antiquity or the
Church of England when he considered it necessary. For example, he exercised
the freedom to amend Anglican customs, but he did so without rejecting the
Anglican heritage as a whole.[37] But by and large, he felt justified in accepting
the fathers and the Church of England as being the most representative of
those teachings "common to all Christians in all ages"[38] — a requirement of
orthodoxy not unlike that of Vincent of Lérins, who defined orthodoxy, or what
"is truly and in the strictest sense 'Catholic,'" as that "which has been believed
everywhere, always, by all."[39]

Wesley was familiar not only with Anglican divinity, but with the Protestant
Reformers and the Reformed tradition as a whole. His interest in and knowledge of a broad range of theological and pastoral writings is manifestly evident
in the *Christian Library*. Although entries in the *Christian Library* are chiefly writings from Christian antiquity, they include extracts from Puritans, Baptists,
Quakers, and Roman Catholics. Mildred Bangs Wynkoop considers Wesley's
"open–mindedness" and sense of history his greatest theological strengths. She
states:

> We could well observe that Wesley's was not a closed thought system, unchange-
> able and static. A clue to his approach to life and religion which gives direction
> to his theological pilgrimage can be found in the fact of his searching spirit.[40]

## The Spirit of Toleration

Wesley's open "Letter to a Roman Catholic" proves that he had a spirit of religious toleration and ecumenism uncommon in his time. He allowed a great
deal of theological flexibility and chose not to quibble over diverse opinions on
nonessential aspects of the Christian faith. In the letter he sought to achieve a
degree of reconciliation with Roman Catholics, calling for mutual understanding and acceptance without compromising on essential, orthodox beliefs.

> Are we not thus far agreed [concerning "true, primitive Christianity"]? Let us
> thank God for this, and receive it as a fresh token of his love. But if God still
> loveth us, we ought also to love one another. We ought, without this endless jan-
> gling about opinions, to provoke one another to love and to good works. Let the
> points wherein we differ stand aside; here are enough wherein we agree, enough

to be the ground of every Christian temper, and of every Christian action.[41]

To be sure, Wesley objected to much contained in Roman Catholic doctrine, and expressed this, for example, in such writings as "A Roman Catechism, Faithfully Drawn Out of the Allowed Writings of the Church of Rome, With a Reply" and "The Advantage of the Members of the Church of England, Over Those of the Church of Rome." But he promised to overlook such objections so long as people accepted the essential doctrines established by the ecumenical councils of antiquity and would then "provoke one another to love and to good works."[42] He outlined the minimum beliefs essential to Christianity both in "A Letter to a Roman Catholic" and in other writings such as "The Character of a Methodist." Then, given this doctrinal foundation, he sought to embrace all Christians as fellow believers.[43]

Wesley proudly referred to the doctrinal liberality of Methodist discipline as something unique among Christians. Near the end of his life, he declared that love required Methodists to accept into their fellowship others who also loved God, regardless of their Christian affiliation, as long as they sought to "fear God and work righteousness."

> And in order to their union with us, we require no unity in opinions, or in modes of worship, but barely that they "fear God and work righteousness," as was observed. Now, this is utterly a new thing, unheard of in any other Christian community. In what Church or congregation beside, throughout the Christian world, can members be admitted upon these terms, without conditions? Point any such out, whoever can: I know none in Europe, Asia, Africa, or America! This is the glory of the Methodists, and of them alone![44]

Wesley considered this liberality not only unique, but also essential to his hopes for greater Christian cooperation and unity. The statement "We think, and let think" is a phrase Wesley used often from 1745 onward to describe the theological liberality of Methodists.[45] This early concern for religious tolerance continued throughout Wesley's life and ministry.

Unfortunately, the phrase "We think, and let think" is often misunderstood and misused by contemporary interpreters of Wesley. Wesley applied these words to *opinions* – that is, religious beliefs that may be considered nonessential for Christian orthodoxy. He distinguished what he considered essential and nonessential doctrines, similar to the way in which Martin Luther and Philip Melanchthon had permitted *adiaphora* — things neither commanded nor forbidden by Scripture that could therefore be decided in the church by the mutual agreement of the members.[46] Having differentiated the essential and nonessential, Wesley then advocated toleration for nonessential doctrines.[47]

Wesley's unusual degree of freedom to accept diversity or plurality in the nonessentials arose, he felt, from the divine infusion of a "catholic spirit" and "universal love" toward all Christians.[48] He illustrated this love with the story of Jehu, who greeted Jehonadab with the words, "Are you in accord with me, as I am with you?" to which Jehonadab replied, "I am." Jehu then said, "If so, give me your hand." And Jehonadab did so (2 Kings 10:15). Wesley sought to be one who "gives his hand" to all whose "hearts are right with his heart."

> "If it be, give me thine hand." I do not mean, "Be of my opinion." You need not.
> I do not expect nor desire it. Neither do I mean, "I will be of your opinion." I can-
> not. It does not depend on my choice. I can no more think than I can see or
> hear as I will. Keep you your opinion, I mine; and that as steadily as ever. You
> need not even endeavour to come over to me, or bring me over to you. I do not
> desire you to dispute those points, or to hear or speak one word concerning
> them. Let all opinions alone on one side and the other. Only "give me thine
> hand."[49]

To Wesley, a unity of doctrinal opinions was less important than a clear conscience with regard to a unity of love as a basis for ecumenism. Of course, we
cannot always determine how liberal Wesley allowed Christians' opinions to be.
But we can see a person who was less concerned with conceptual unity than
with practical Christian unity — a unity consisting of universal love and moti-
vating evangelistic fervor, personal piety, and social responsibility.

Yet Wesley strongly defended his historic and Anglican heritage and warned
those whom he thought had transformed rather than translated the substance
of classical Christian orthodoxy. Outler notes:

> To conclude from all this, however, that Wesley was indifferent to the issues
> involved in sound doctrine is to misunderstand him. He had a clear view of
> heresy as deviation from the core of "standing revelation"; and had no hesitation
> in denouncing views that threatened this core....If Methodism may rightly be
> charged with theological indifferentism, this has no valid grounds in Wesley him-
> self.[50]

## Discerning among Traditions

A number of factors contribute to discerning the *true* tradition among the many
strands of tradition in church history. But Wesley primarily used what he called
the *grand principle* of Christianity.

> I lay this down as an undoubted truth: — The more the doctrine of any Church
> agrees with the Scripture, the more readily ought it to be received. And, on the
> other hand, the more the doctrine of any Church differs from Scripture, the
> greater cause we have to doubt it.[51]

Scripture remained the primary source of religious authority to discern among
ideas, beliefs, doctrines, and traditions. Wesley never considered tradition to be
of equal authority with Scripture. Tradition proved useful to the extent it gave
evidence to the authority of the Old and New Testaments and to the way it
faithfully interpreted, communicated, and applied the content of the gospel
message.

The priority of Scripture over tradition becomes most apparent in Wesley's
writings to Roman Catholics, where he explicitly argued for the sufficiency of
Scripture as opposed to tradition as the primary source of religious authority.
For example, in the "Roman Catechism, and Reply," Wesley wrote, "The
Scripture, therefore, is a rule sufficient in itself, and was by men divinely inspired

at once delivered to the world; and so neither needs, nor is capable of, any further addition."[52]

In the preface to the same work, Wesley explained that Protestants also appealed to tradition, most notably Christian antiquity, in formulating their doctrines. However, such sources did not have the same degree of inspiration or infallibility as Scripture.

Wesley viewed tradition as an uneven pool of reliable religious authority — and this unevenness explains why Scripture must always remain primary. He did not consider Scripture to be uneven; it was uniformly authoritative throughout. Wesley had no "canon within a canon." By using Scripture as "the general principle," or measuring stick, with which to evaluate the reliability of tradition, one could appeal to tradition with confidence.

When the meaning of an idea derived from Scripture seemed unclear, Wesley believed using tradition may profitably help in "the explication of a doctrine that is not sufficiently explained, or for confirmation of a doctrine generally received."[53] Tradition provides, he said, a plenary sense or meaning to Christian beliefs that Scripture alone does not provide. It offers more mature and developed conceptions of scriptural truths that can only arise through lived experiences and extended reflection on those experiences. A plenary sense of scriptural interpretation enriches and illumines the meaning of a text as long as it does not contradict the original intent of Scripture. After all, classical orthodoxy is thought to lead people back to the Bible — in the fullness of its message — rather than away from it.

## Learning from Other Traditions

Wesley often drew eclectically from other sources of tradition besides the favored Christian antiquity and the Church of England. As long as those sources met his *general principle* of biblical orthodoxy, he felt free to draw on any writer or any religious tradition that gave insight to one's theological understanding and Christian lifestyle. In practice, Wesley deemed a variety of religious traditions valuable and helpful in creating a coherent and consistent view of Christian beliefs, even though, as we have seen, he did not set about to build theological systems per se.

The point is, Wesley did not pick and choose at random. He carefully interwove the many sources from which he drew into the warp and woof of his own theological principles. He focused as always on his understanding of salvation as consisting of justification by faith and a concomitant life of holy living. Keefer notes that Wesley emphasized soteriology rather than ecclesiology, that is, establishing an ecclesiastical succession with the ancient church.[54] The motivation for Wesley's eclecticism was his commitment "To reform the nation, and in particular the church; to spread scriptural holiness over the land."[55]

Wesley's synthesizing of apparently conflicting traditions into a cooperative and harmonious theological relationship reflects his confidence in the overall coherency and consistency of his theology. He saw no contradiction in drawing on diverse religious traditions as long as they fundamentally reflected Scripture. From Wesley's perspective, a greater theological gestalt could be achieved through the refusal to be provincial or biased in terms of which religious sources one found acceptable or even worthy of consideration.

One may consider Wesley the consummate theological synthesizer of the eighteenth century. Fully within the Anglican heritage of wanting to provide a *via media* among competing theologies, Wesley found himself, two centuries after the Reformation, in a historically strategic place to bring together the best of Roman Catholic and Protestant theologies. He could not only bring together Scripture, tradition, and reason in keeping with Anglican methodology, but also appeal to Christian experience as found, for example, in the catholic spirit of "universal love" as a thread that tied and had always tied believers together. It seemed both feasible and necessary to Wesley to combine the various traditions of Christianity into a complex whole.

In understanding Wesley, we can liken the growth of Christianity to the systemic growth of a tree. The tree of faith draws from various roots or sources of nourishment, including Scripture, tradition, reason, and experience. As the tree grows, it branches out into variations of the essential core of Christian beliefs — the primitive church, the earliest and most basic form of the faith — which is its trunk. The growth of the tree, however, is not static. As branches continually shoot out from the trunk, so the trunk continues to grow and enlarge as time passes. The tree's growth depends not only on continuous nourishment from the roots, but also on energy derived from the branches. Consequently, those branches are not to be ignored simply because one does not like their configuration. As long as a branch does not become diseased and poison the rest of the tree, the branch should be considered a part of the tree and its contributions accepted toward the growth of the tree as a whole. God is the sun, the ultimate power source for growth.

This metaphor is not Wesley's, but has a biblical origin. The apostle Paul said, "I planted the seed, Apollos watered it, but God made it grow" (1 Cor. 3:6). I believe the image helps us to understand Wesley's conception of Christianity accurately.[56]

To accomplish a theological *via media* Wesley refused to set overly strict doctrinal standards that might become too elaborate to integrate and interact with the genuine insights available from the various branches of the Christian tradition.[57] Seeking to avoid appearing to be a traditional systematic theologian, Wesley attempted to provide a theological and ecclesiastical context in which to unite all true, scriptural Christians. The benefit of Wesley's endeavors is an ecumenical spirit that allows for cooperation among diverse religious traditions. The liability is theological pluralism if the primacy of Scripture is not retained as an epistemological safeguard for Christian orthodoxy.

To be sure, Wesley welcomed a degree of theological pluralism as both possible and helpful to the overall health of Christianity. Faith flourishes in a rich matrix of religious experience and theological reflection. However, faith also needs the parenting of Scripture and of an orthodox Christian tradition that is nurtured by Scripture. Wesley would never have accepted the kind of theological pluralism that is based primarily on religious experience and that formally emerged in nineteenth– and twentieth–century liberal Protestantism. He would have firmly rejected any misuse of his references to Scripture, tradition, reason, and experience to substantiate a kind of theological pluralism that does not accept Scripture as the primary religious authority.

For Wesley, theological pluralism may be permitted to continue due to the presence of Christian love and tolerance within the community of believers, but it must be a wise pluralism that knows the parameters of biblical orthodoxy. It may not be a pluralism that refuses to heed Scripture and set boundaries. Wesley believed that all Christians could and should live in harmony with one another. Members of different theological or denominational traditions may feel free to develop their particular religious beliefs or special interests, but they should seek to stay within the parameters of true, scriptural Christianity.[58]

Wesley did not believe that theology should ever be pluralistic in the sense of being indeterminate in form, with neither harmonious unity nor continuity nor a fundamentally rational and coherent order. God is an infinitely rational being who created a world order that ultimately makes sense, though for now we may not fully understand everything about that world order because of our finite and fallen state. And so our attempts to understand or systematize the world fully will ultimately fall short of the task.

In principle, a systematic theology cannot do justice to the religious experiences of each and every Christian in every social and historical context. We may speculate on the truth of God's creation and purposes for humanity, but we should not presume to know too much. A degree of theological pluralism will inevitably persist as long as the human race, yet this fact should not cause anxiety or despair. The revelation of Scripture provides sufficient knowledge of God, of salvation, and of the holy lives God intends for people. As long as Christians keep Scripture the fountainhead of their beliefs, they may enjoy the liberality of theological opinions as an expression of the diversity and richness of religious experience.

## Ministering with Other Traditions

Motivated by the need he saw for Christian unity and cooperation, Wesley actively participated in ministry with Christians outside the Church of England and outside the British Isles. Though at times he hotly debated theological differences with Christians outside the Anglo–Catholic–Methodist milieu, he still expected to work toward common goals of evangelism, holy living, and social betterment as required by love for one's neighbor. He did not naively expect denominational barriers to disappear, but he did expect that Christians could avoid contention on the one hand and "provoke one another to love and good works" on the other.[59]

Since God loves all Christians, Wesley reasoned that we should love one another as well by accepting and tolerating differing opinions while working to promote and communicate the essential truths of the gospel message contained in Scripture. He did not advocate theological indifference, which he sometimes characterized as "speculative latitudinarianism" and "practical latitudinarianism,"[60] but he encouraged Christians to set aside such opinions for the work of Jesus Christ. He still required that Christians affirm a predominantly orthodox view of the faith as he understood it from Scripture and Christian antiquity. But beyond basic doctrines having to do with God, Jesus Christ, the Holy Spirit, the church, and salvation, Wesley was surprisingly tolerant of his co-workers in Jesus Christ.[61]

We can cite several examples of the kind of cooperative ministry that Wesley shared with other Christian groups. Perhaps the most noteworthy is his longstanding friendship and ministry with George Whitefield, an avowed Calvinist. For years Wesley cooperated in very successful evangelistic efforts with Whitefield. To be sure, Wesley and Whitefield had their differences of opinion, and at times those differences caused controversy.[62] But Wesley's overarching concern was to continue in a relationship of mutual understanding and appreciation, even when he did not agree with all of Whitefield's theology. Wesley and Whitefield preached occasionally in each other's pulpits, and before Whitefield died, he requested that Wesley preach his funeral sermon, which Wesley did in 1770.[63]

Another example of Wesley's concern for catholic Christian cooperation is his several contacts with Roman Catholics. Wesley overcame Protestant biases against Catholics and subsequently sought to bring about at least a functional reconciliation for the purpose of shared ministries. To accomplish this, he first tried to obliterate incorrect stereotypes from both Protestant and Roman Catholic sides, and then he positively sought to enunciate points of agreement.[64] The culmination of Wesley's efforts was that both Protestants and Roman Catholics should "endeavour to help each other on in whatever we are agreed leads to the kingdom."[65] Again, Wesley did not naively expect total reconciliation and cooperation, but he considered it his duty as a Christian to seek out fellow believers for the sake of the love that Christ has for believers and wants shared with others.

In conclusion, Wesley considered tradition second only to Scripture as a source of religious authority, to the degree that it reflected both the intellectual content and the spiritual vitality of Christian faith. Tradition, especially as found in the ecumenical creeds and patristic writings of Christian antiquity, supplemented church doctrine in matters where Scripture was silent. To the extent that the Holy Spirit continued to direct decisions in the early church, Wesley believed tradition was an essential extension of the witness of Scripture. Sensing the need to be critical in evaluating tradition, Wesley believed that Christians are capable of separating the wheat from the chaff (cf. Matt. 3:12; Luke 3:17). Having sifted the wheat, Christians should learn from and appreciate the truth regardless which tradition it springs from.

Using Scripture and Christian antiquity as guidelines for distinguishing essential beliefs from nonessential opinions, Wesley embraced those traditions that shared his evangelical zeal for the gospel message of salvation. In a catholic spirit of universal love for Christian believers, Wesley tolerated a wide range of theological and ecclesiastical opinions. All along his motive was to further the proclamation and lifestyle of the gospel through progressive, cooperation in ministry.

# 6

# The Authority of Reason

John Wesley set a high value on the role of reason in religion. He said, "It is a fundamental principle with us [Methodists] that to renounce reason is to renounce religion, that religion and reason go hand in hand, and that all irrational religion is false religion."[1] In "An Earnest Appeal," Wesley claimed to join "men of reason" in "desiring a religion founded on reason, and every way agreeable thereto."[2] He said, "Passion and prejudice govern the world, only under the name of reason. It is our part, by religion and reason joined, to counteract them all we can."[3] He deeply believed in the ultimate rationality of true religion and in the immediate reasonableness and need of the Christian message for the world.[4] Wesley's appeal to reason often followed appeals to Scripture.[5] He liked to use the phrase "the plain scriptural rational way" in presenting the plan of salvation; any other way seemed an overly enthusiastic mysticism or a spiritless form of rationalistic religion.[6]

## The Prominence of Reason

Wesley believed that people were created in God's own image. God created humankind

> not barely in His *natural image*, a picture of His own *immortality*; a spiritual being, indued with understanding, freedom of will, and various affections; — nor merely in His political *image*, the governor of this lower world,... — but chiefly in His *moral image*; which, according to the Apostle, is "righteousness and true holiness" (Eph. 4:24).[7]

Wesley maintained that the image of God persisted in the human race after its moral corruption, though people no longer lived righteously before God.

> The Scriptures do say, "God created man in his own image" (Gen. 1:27). But whatever that phrase means the same in Genesis 9:6: "Whoso sheddeth man's blood, by man shall his blood be shed: For in the image of God made he man." Certainly it has the same meaning in both places; for the latter plainly refers to the former. And this much we may fairly infer from hence, that "the image of God," whereinsoever it consisted, was not utterly effaced in the time of Noah.[8]

Due to human sin, the image of God became effaced, but not obliterated. The original constitution of people, which made them different from animals, remained.

Wesley considered human reasoning an essential part of that original constitution along with humankind's political and moral capabilities. Reason is a unique gift from God, and God graciously continues to permit reason to function in significant ways even though sin reigns in the moral character of people. Our rational capabilities fall short of God's infinite reasoning, yet they remain largely intact despite this.

Wesley's great confidence in the power of people to think logically, especially in spiritual matters, falls perfectly in line with his Anglican theological background. The Church of England considered reason the synthesizing medium between Scripture and tradition, Continental Protestantism and Roman Catholicism, and so on. Robert G. Tuttle suggests that this high regard for reason extends back to the Aristotelian tradition.

> The Church of England, although denying (at least by virtue of its Articles of Religion) that natural theology was the only route to faith, was nonetheless basically Aristotelian in its approach to God. Through its Arminian doctrine it taught that man (since original sin affected him only from the neck down, corrupting his heart but not his intellect) had the freedom to reason his way to faith. Although his heart was prone to evil, his mind was left free to reason with the heart and respond to God by faith once the call was understood.[9]

Wesley shared this Anglican regard for Aristotle's having had "an universal genius, applicable to everything."[10] The Aristotelian tradition of logic at Oxford was transmitted to Wesley through the work of Henry Aldrich's *Artis Logicæ Compendium*. Wesley used Aristotelian logic throughout his theology and ministry, and he exhorted others to do the same.[11]

No doubt Wesley's confidence in reason reflected the larger intellectual milieu in which he lived. In contrast to Reformers such as Luther, who disparaged the theological use of reason, Wesley easily affirmed eighteenth–century England's and Anglicanism's confidence in reason.[12] Living during the Enlightenment, Wesley was certain of the dependability of reason and of the ultimate harmony between Scripture and reason. Of course, he saw the limitations of rational inquiry. Yet reason remained a trustworthy aid to interpreting Scripture and a reliable adviser for the searching pilgrim.

Wesley's familiarity with Enlightenment philosophy is evident in his affirming much of the empirical philosophy of John Locke, who dominated the intellectual climate of early eighteenth–century England.[13] Wesley read Locke's *Essay Concerning Human Understanding* in Oxford in 1725, more than ten years before his Aldersgate experience and the beginning of his evangelistic and publishing career.[14] He later published a digest of Locke's work, with critical comments, in the *Arminian Magazine* in 1782–84 (vols. 5–7).

The development of British empiricism clearly had an important impact on Wesley's thought, although scholars disagree on the extent of that impact. That Locke's experimental philosophy influenced Wesley's thinking throughout his life cannot be dismissed and needs to be pursued in unraveling characteristics of Wesley's theological method. We also need to keep in mind that Locke was an Anglican who had theological as well as philosophical interests. His writings reflected the tradition of Anglican concern to incorporate reason into a balanced and universal understanding of religion.

As we have seen, Locke's influence on Wesley's theology was stimulated and broadened by the writings of Peter Browne. Wesley studied Browne's *Procedure, Extent, and Limits of Human Knowledge* (1728) and later abridged it for his multivolume work *Natural Philosophy.* Clifford Hindley points out that Wesley learned from Browne how empiricist principles could "be applied directly to theology, and the importance attached by Wesley to experience reflects very largely the presuppositions he had imbibed from his study of Browne's essay."[15] Richard Brantley concurs with Hindley and also offers excellent research in uncovering the extent to which Wesley's "Methodism derived from the method of [Locke's] *Essay.*"[16]

Wesley's evaluation of reason's relevance to Christianity evolved as he matured in his theological reflections. In contrast to his views on Scripture and tradition, which remained relatively the same throughout his writings, Wesley's ideas on reason underwent change and development. Scholars disagree, however, as to the degree of change. Tuttle suggests that Wesley's faith and thought–development occurred between the dialectical poles of Aristotelian rationalism (and asceticism) and Platonic intuitionism (and mysticism).[17] Umphrey Lee observes, "The young Wesley spoke the language of this [Enlightenment] time when he wrote his mother that faith is 'an assent to any truth upon rational grounds.'"[18]

But the young Wesley also came into contact with mystical aspects of Christianity, possibly encouraging his experimentation with bibliomancy as late as the early 1740s.[19] Later he shunned bibliomancy along with what he considered extreme tendencies in mysticism. So there was an evolution of thought, and we can expect to trace a course of development of reason in terms of specific emphases in Wesley's thought.

For example, when Wesley wrote his sermon "The Circumcision of the Heart" in 1733, he defined faith as "an unshaken assent to all that God has revealed in Scripture."[20] After his conversion in 1738, Wesley still included references to the rationality of true Christian faith in his religious discussions, though in fact his conception of faith had been enriched to include much more than reason alone.[21] The most notable references to the power of reason to persuade people religiously may be found in Wesley's bold and confident appeals to "men of reason and religion" in his early apologetical writings. In later reflection Wesley described the development of the Methodist movement as allowing "no method of bringing any to the knowledge of the truth, except the methods of reason and persuasion."[22]

By the 1780s Wesley still reserved a prominent place for reason in his theology, but he had become more modest in his assessment of its powers. In his old age he wrote his most explicit sermons on the nature and role of reason in religion in "The Case of Reason Impartially Considered" and "The Imperfection of Human Knowledge." Perhaps, Albert C. Outler suggests, Wesley intended these two sermons to serve as "antidotes and alternatives to what Wesley regarded as *false* rationalism" among Methodists who were no longer as *plain* as they had been in their earlier, humbler beginnings.[23] Perhaps Wesley had reflected on England's growing disillusionment with the powers of reason in the waning decades of the eighteenth century. By that time the skeptical ideas of David Hume were gaining greater popularity, and this only increased with the respect paid to him in the philosophy of Immanuel Kant. Or perhaps Wesley's own mature reflections on religious belief wanted a more balanced, public statement that avoided the extreme positions he had in practice tried to avoid throughout his life.

Whatever the reasons, Wesley became more explicit in defining reason and more earnest in describing its limitations. Reason was still important, but only with equally important qualifications. These qualifications signaled not so much a radical change in the substance of Wesley's thinking, but rather a shift in theological emphasis.

## The Reasonableness of Christianity

Most thoughtful people in the early eighteenth century considered religion compatible with reason. Thus Wesley found an accepting audience when he affirmed the reasonableness of Christianity. We may not understand that mind–set as readily today, when many people view religion as nonrational or irrational. But in the eighteenth century the idea of religion as compatible with reason was made commonplace by such books as Locke's *Reasonableness of Christianity* and the deistic John Toland's *Christianity not Mysterious*.

The prevailing philosophy of empiricism undoubtedly had an effect on Wesley's idea concerning the reasonableness of Christianity, but he was already predisposed by the Anglican tradition toward. reason, the Aristotelian tradition of logic, and the validity of reason as a source of religious authority. To Anglicans, reason served as a reliable mediating force between Scripture and tradition and as a creative force in addressing issues neither commanded nor forbidden by Scripture and tradition. Therefore reason contributed to matters that could be decided in the church by the mutual agreement of the members.

Despite some development in his thought, Wesley consistently affirmed the reasonableness of Christianity, which he referred to as "the highest reason."[24] In "An Earnest Appeal" he described how he sought in vain for authors who might enlighten him on a proper understanding of reason. His lament over not finding a single theologian or philosopher who could provide an adequate conceptual framework for his beliefs indicates how self–conscious he was about his theology. He rejected those who sought to prove "that Christianity is contrary to reason" or "that no man acting according to the principles of reason can possibly be a Christian."[25] Nor did he receive any help from the deists, who sought to ground Scripture on reason but failed to unite knowledge and vital piety.[26]

Wesley paid due respect to individual philosophers and theologians from whom he gained insight in the use of reason, such as Aristotle and Locke. But he found no one tutor sufficient in and of himself for his theological needs and questions.

Nevertheless, he found Scripture and the religious truths contained therein to be exceedingly reasonable. He did not feel the need to appeal to anything other than Scripture, because it was the only resource necessary for developing a Christian concept of reason and epistemology. For example, in a letter to his mother, Wesley spoke of biblical truth as something that "commands" our intellectual assent against our free will and asserted that it is "impossible for us to disbelieve."[27] On this, Mitsuo Shimizu states that for Wesley it is impossible for us to disbelieve "a proposition once the mind clearly and distinctly perceives it to be true; distinct perception of a proposition's truth 'extort[s] our assent' and our judgment on this 'is not free.'"[28]

Clearly, Wesley's confidence in reason to help a person infer truth from Scripture and other sources of religious authority persisted throughout his life and ministry. In "An Earnest Appeal" he exhorted people "to use all reason" when seeking God, though they must reason "justly" and with "true judgments," by which he meant that people must reason carefully and with integrity.[29] In 1745 Wesley responded to a critic by asserting that "a rational assent to the truth of the Bible is one ingredient of Christian faith."[30] And in 1753 Wesley still referred to faith, in the "Compendium of Logic," as a rational form of knowledge: "To assent to testimony is the same as to believe; and such an assent is termed faith."[31]

Finally, Shimizu notes that as late as 1788, in the sermon "On Faith, Heb. 11:6," Wesley still spoke of faith as a form of rational knowledge. Shimizu states,

> Wesley again talks about several sorts of faith which depend upon rational evidence; the faiths of Materialists, Deists, and Heathen are based upon a rational assent to truths such as the divine being and attributes, the future state of rewards and punishments, or the immortality of the soul; the faith of the Roman Catholic rests upon the truths deduced from the tradition which goes beyond Scripture; the faith of the Protestant is built upon the truths such as Incarnation, Trinity, or miracles inferred from Scripture.[32]

Although faith as a form of rational knowledge encompasses only a portion of Wesley's full understanding, he always conceived of faith as reasonable.

For Wesley, there remained no doubt that reason serves "in laying the foundation of true religion, under the guidance of the Spirit of God, and in raising the whole superstructure."[33] Reason directs us in matters of "faith and practice" because "the whole of our religion is a 'reasonable service' [Rom. 12:1]."[34] For Wesley, reason functioned as a basis for theological and ecclesiological apologetics, a discovery he valued while facing ongoing opposition to his theology and to the Methodist movement generally. But most crucial to this book is Wesley's use of reason as an integral part of his theological method. To understand more about how Wesley used reason, we must turn to a discussion of his theory of knowledge and its relation to theological method.

# A Theory of Knowledge

If Wesley did not write a systematic theology, we could hardly expect that he would present a developed theory of knowledge. But just as he addressed many methodological questions in theology, so he also addressed the nature and extent of our capacity to know about the natural world in which we live and about the supernatural world of which Christians speak.

## Intuitive Versus Empirical Knowledge

We have already noted several of the philosophical influences on Wesley such as Aristotle and Locke, but it lies beyond the scope of this book to investigate the breadth of sources from which Wesley developed his philosophical and theological worldview. Wesley was aware of and drew upon a number of philosophical writers. For our purposes we will focus primarily on the two most prominent philosophical trends vying for ascendancy during the eighteenth century: (1) Continental rationalism, as reflected in the thought of Descartes, Nicholas Malebranche, John Norris, and the Cambridge Platonists, and (2) British empiricism, as reflected in the thought of Locke, Browne, and a growing number of Anglican theologians.[35]

Wesley was influenced by the tradition of rational, intuitive knowledge extending beyond the Cambridge Platonists and Descartes to Plato. In his sermon "The End of Christ's Coming," Wesley made reference to a kind of intuitive knowledge we may have, for example, of salvation.

> And we then see, not by a chain of reasoning, but by a kind of intuition, by a direct view, that "God was in Christ, reconciling the world to himself, not imputing to them their former trespasses," not imputing them to me.[36]

In the sermon "Scriptural Christianity," Wesley referred to "opening a window into their breast," implying that divine light or knowledge may shine directly into us, illuminating or enlightening our understanding.[37] This language reflects the kind of participation–motif found in illuminist mysticism, with which Wesley was familiar early in life. Outler suggests that Wesley inherited these mystic tendencies from such writers as "Castañiza, Scupoli, de Renty, Gregory Lopez, Samuel Clarke, John Norris — even William Law — before he discovered its primal sources in the Johannine Gospel and its patristic interpreters (under the patristic revival in Oxford that he joined in)."[38] Wesley eventually turned from these intuitionist or mystic traditions because of their excesses, but Wesley scholars such as Outler, Shimizu, John C. English, and Roderick T. Leupp feel they nevertheless had a lasting effect on his thought.[39] Wesley saw the apparent intuitionist and mystical elements as reminiscent of all the great mysteries of Christian belief.

There also appears in Wesley an analogy between physical senses and spiritual senses — an analogy that has been interpreted as revealing either the intuitionist or the empirical orientation of his theology. Describing people in a pre–Christian situation, Wesley said, "While a man is in a mere natural state, before he is born of God, he has, in a spiritual sense, eyes and sees not; a thick impenetrable veil lies upon them."[40] Wesley thought that all people have certain latent spiritual senses that appear inoperative; we cannot use them in the way we were originally created because of the moral corruptness of our nature. In Outler's explanation of this, the "human spirit is a 'spiritual sensorium,' analogical to our physical sense, and thus the capacity for intuitions of spiritual reality is comparable to sight and sound."[41]

Outler describes this *latency metaphor* as one of Wesley's favorites, and interprets it in line with ideas derived from Descartes through Malebranche, Norris, and the Cambridge Platonists.[42] Such ideas reinforce the intuitive strain of Wesley's thought, but we must not interpret Wesley too quickly as an intuitive or mystical thinker. We must keep in mind the analogous nature of Wesley's thought on the subject.

More than most Wesleyan scholars, Outler emphasizes the Platonic characteristics of intuitive knowledge in Wesley, reflecting more of the deep sense *impression* of religious knowledge (rather than *discovery)* that people experience. Outler refers to "impressions" described by Wesley, such as the natural reverence for parents, as "transempirical intuition."[43] However, when Wesley used the term "intuition" (and he did so sparingly), he conceived of the spiritual sense as fitting into a broader understanding of the noetic sensorium that people possess. Our sensorium consists of both physical and spiritual senses, though the effective functions of our spiritual sense requires a quickening that only God can provide. So people naturally possess some degree of spiritual sense, but they only exist and function due to God's prevenient grace.

Wesley felt no compunction in referring to such senses as "natural." Otherwise, it could not justly be said that all people are without excuse with regard to knowledge of God and knowledge of good and evil (cf. Rom. 1:18–23; 2:12–15).

Because he saw the breadth of theology in terms of this extended analogy of spiritual and physical senses, Wesley felt justified in referring to his work as a description of "the true, the scriptural, experimental religion." It was the true religion, first, in that it is neither false nor erroneous, in relation either to Scripture or to Christian antiquity, and in that it agrees with the facts of experience with regard to both the general nature of things and a personal, vital relationship with God. It was scriptural religion because Wesley believed that nothing contained in his theology would disagree with biblical revelation. Finally, it was experimental religion because, besides its agreeing with the facts of experience, Wesley felt it left him free to use experimental method in investigating the entire range of our God–given senses.

## The Influence of Experimental Philosophy

Despite the presence of intuitive tendencies in Wesley's theology, there appears an even stronger identification with the empirical or experimental thinking and language reminiscent of Locke's philosophical attempt to combine

Christian rationalism and empiricism.[44] Both in the way Wesley conceptualized theology and in the specific terms he chose to express himself, the British empirical tradition was the dominant philosophical worldview affecting his theological ideas. Wesley synthesized characteristics of experimental method with what he considered a truer — that is, traditional or scriptural — understanding of religion. But Wesley did it in a way that be believed would prove to be manifestly reasonable to all "men of reason and religion."

We must remember that Locke does not represent the extreme skeptical positions of later empiricists. Later empiricists such as Hume criticized Locke for not taking his empirical psychology to its logical conclusion of subjectivism.[45] If we think of Locke as a radical empiricist, we will forget that he made room for God to communicate with people through the extraordinary means of revelation and miracles.[46] Locke rejected Descartes's Platonic conception of "innate ideas," a notion Wesley repeatedly affirmed.[47]

Instead Locke stated that knowledge through reason consists primarily of a natural revelation. He said,

> *Reason* is *natural revelation,* whereby the eternal Father of light and fountain of all knowledge, communicates to humankind that portion of truth which he has laid within the reach of their natural faculties: *revelation* is *natural reason enlarged* by a new set of discoveries communicated by God immediately; which reason vouches the truth of, by the testimony and proofs it gives that they come from God.[48]

Locke retained a degree of Christian rationalism by accepting the idea of immediate divine revelation while emphasizing that reason is the final criterion in ascertaining the truth of revelation.[49] In contrast to deists, Locke insisted that we should not dispense with Scripture just because it contains divine revelation.[50] Reason could then *extort* for us, as Wesley said, not the absolute or final truth of Christianity, but truth that we may consider sufficiently reasonable or probable. Such truth provides the greatest degree of certainty that is rationally possible, given the fact that all human knowledge begins with sense experience and reflection on that experience.

No doubt Wesley felt drawn to the empirical worldview of Locke's philosophy because Locke rejected the excessively rationalistic philosophies of both Cartesianism and deism. Locke provided what seemed to Wesley to be a mediating position between the historical philosophical traditions of Platonic intuition, characteristic of Cartesianism, and strict Aristotelian logic, all too characteristic of deism. Scholars such as Tuttle argue that one cannot be both Platonic and Aristotelian. Quoting Samuel Coleridge, Tuttle states, "Everyone is born either an Aristotelian or a Platonist; one or the other, but no one can be both simultaneously."[51]

Tuttle goes on to suggest that Wesley struggled during the first thirteen years of his ministry trying to solve the dilemma of whether reason leads to faith, or faith leads to reason.[52] While he struggled with this philosophical conundrum, embodied to a certain extent in theological debates between Roman Catholics and Protestants, Wesley did not feel the need to side exclusively with either

Platonism or Aristotelianism. In Locke, Wesley found one who provisionally combined a seemingly necessary form of Christian rationalism with the experimentally persuasive philosophy of British empiricism.[53] Moreover, Locke accomplished this task with the intent of remaining faithful to the Church of England and to historical Christian orthodoxy.

Yet Wesley had reservations. To Wesley, Locke tended to overemphasize reason and thus did not adequately provide a "medium between these extremes, undervaluing and overvaluing reason."[54] Consequently, he differed with Locke at crucial intellectual points.[55] Outler rightly observes Wesley's dissatisfaction with some aspects of Locke's empiricism.[56] Leupp affirms Outler's intellectual analysis of Wesley as being both empirical and intuitive, especially because of Wesley's inclination toward the Platonizing tendencies of the Eastern Orthodox tradition.[57] But Outler, Leupp, and others overlook the fact that Locke does not fit the modern conception of empiricism, particularly in its skepticism regarding religion. Thus they tend to understate the empiricist and Aristotelian influence on Wesley.

Rex D. Matthews suggests that in places where Outler argues for the intuitive aspects of Wesley's writings, those same writings manifest proportionally greater indebtedness to Locke an empirical thinking.[58] Matthews disagrees with Outler's view that Wesley's epistemology is "not 'empirical' but intuitive" and is influenced most strongly by "Descartes, Malebranche, Norris, and the Platonist tradition in general."[59] As to Wesley's understanding of faith — seemingly the most intuitive aspect of Christian belief — Matthews concludes:

> While this position [concerning faith] may owe something to the Platonist tradition, especially as represented in the Cambridge Platonists and John Norris, as English and Outler have maintained, and more particularly in the works of Nicholas Malebranche, as Shimizu has argued, it finds expression most directly in the language of Hebrews 11:1 — faith as "the evidence of things hoped for, the conviction of things not seen. "[60]

In Locke, especially as his thought was transmitted through the mediation of Browne, Wesley found an approach to theology that affirmed the importance of Aristotelian logic, yet provided room for a traditional understanding of belief in God and in the extraordinary means he uses to communicate to humankind, such as miracles and the revelation of Scripture.[61]

## A New Class of Senses

For our basic knowledge of the natural world around us, Wesley generally accepted the British empirical interpretation of the senses as formulated by Locke. In contrast to the Cartesian or intuitive approach, Wesley believed that all human knowledge comes from some kind of sense perception or from reflection on our sense perception. This makes Wesley appear to be quite the empiricist in terms of understanding the physical world.

> For many ages it has been allowed by sensible men, *Nihil est is intellectu quod non fuit prius in sensu:* that is, "There is nothing in the understanding which was not

first perceived by some of the senses." All the knowledge which we naturally have is originally derived from our senses. And therefore those who want [lack] any sense, cannot have the least knowledge or idea of the objects of that sense; as they that never had sight, have not the least conception of light or colours. Some indeed have, of late years, endeavoured to prove that we have innate ideas, not derived from any of the senses, but coeval with the understanding. But this point has been now thoroughly discussed by men of the most eminent sense and learning; and it is agreed by all impartial persons, that although some things are so plain and obvious, that we can very hardly avoid knowing them as soon as we come to the use of our understanding; yet the knowledge. even of those is not innate, but derived from some of our senses.[62]

Wesley affirmed the descriptive method of science and did not expect to attain knowledge of things beyond experience, that is, beyond our various capacities for sense–experience or reflection on that experience. However, our physical senses are limited in terms of what they may know beyond our experience of the empirical world. Wesley emphasized these limitations in order to make way for his interpretation of faith.[63]

Wesley argued by analogy from our empirical senses and knowledge toward new, spiritual senses of faith. Wesley contended that Christian believers are able to experience spiritual knowledge, and he argued as follows:

And seeing our ideas are not innate, but must all originally come from our senses, it is certainly necessary that you have senses capable of discerning objects of this kind — not those only which are called "natural senses," which in this respect profit nothing, as being altogether incapable of discerning objects of a spiritual kind, but *spiritual* senses, exercised to discern spiritual good and evil. It is necessary that you have a new class of senses opened in your soul, not depending on organs of flesh and blood, to be "the *evidence* of things not seen" as your bodily senses are of visible things, to be the avenues to the invisible world, to discern spiritual objects, and to furnish you with ideas of what the outward "eye hath not seen, neither the ear heard."[64]

Wesley was wise enough to see that this analogy of the spiritual senses might be misunderstood or misconstrued in an intellectual environment dominated by British empiricism. Some of Wesley's earliest critics such as "John Smith" charged him with having inconsistencies in his religious epistemological ideas. But Wesley believed that he had a gestalt–like understanding of the nature of faith that transcended an immediate human capacity for complete, logical articulation. As with many other Christian truths, Wesley believed that we can know the *fact* of God's self–revelation, though we may not fully understand the *manner* of it. God, creation, and God's ongoing relations with people remain ultimately reasonable, though for the moment we may not fully comprehend all that there is to know. Nevertheless, Christian believers have the privilege of experiencing spiritual truths that transcend their mundane existence.

For this reason, George Cell aptly describes Wesley's religious epistemology as a kind of "transcendental empiricism."[65] In support of this, Rex Matthews contends that transcendental empiricism is "'empiricism' because of his [Wesley's] insistence that there are no innate ideas of any sort, and that everything in the mind must first come via the senses; 'transcendental' because of his argument for the existence of the 'spiritual senses' of faith, which are the avenues to perception of spiritual reality."[66]

### The Fact Versus the Manner of the Senses

Without denying the genuine, self–conscious consistency that Wesley claimed for his theological writings, certain unresolvable tensions persist in them. The problem of apparent inconsistency arises in part from his concern to present the essential *facts* of theology without feeling compelled to present the *manner*, or explication, of those facts. For example, Wesley thought it more important to believe in the fact of original sin than in the manner it succeeds from one person to another, or in the fact of the Trinity than in the manner in which we may rationally conceptualize it.[67] Since our human understanding cannot comprehend all of the *means* by which God accomplishes things, we need not bother to try to figure out every last detail.[68] Nor did Wesley generally concern himself with such details.

This practical approach to theology steered Wesley away from spending time on what he considered the nonessential minutiae or *opinions* of theology.[69] He was often critical of Locke's tendency to become overly complex, vis–a–vis Aristotle, in describing epistemology.[70] Thus, we do not expect Wesley to be especially concerned to clarify all the implications of his analogy of spiritual senses. From his writings we cannot be sure if such senses represent intuitive gifts from God that we cannot personally obtain, or if they represent a latent property that is partially distorted by the human condition of sin and is in need of God's regenerative grace.

Some scholars such as Hindley argue that Wesley was simply confused in attempting to develop his analogy between physical and spiritual senses.[71] Others such as Outler, Shimizu, Leupp, and English argue that Wesley pursued and achieved — to an appreciable degree — a synthesis of empirical and intuitive traditions that produced an epistemology that intuitively transcends mere empiricism.[72] Still others such as Brantley and Matthews argue that the philosophy of Locke, as interpreted by both Browne and then Wesley, offers sufficient epistemological background for understanding how intuitive ideas fit into an empirical — or, as Wesley said it, "experimental" — presentation of Christian beliefs.[73]

Wesley's use of the term *experimental* rather than *empirical* reveals more about the completeness with which he sought to employ inductive method than the settledness of any epistemological foundation on which to devise a systematic theology. To be sure, Wesley wanted to draw an analogy between his theology and experimental philosophy, but the analogy pertains more to his method than to a particular empirical worldview. Wesley did not hesitate to point out limitations in empirical philosophy, but his criticisms reflected a belief that experimental method had not always been sufficiently comprehensive. We should also pay attention, according to Wesley, to the investigation of transcendent dimensions of reality not easily discernible, but nonetheless real and essential to our humanity.

We must keep in mind that the very nature of Wesley's use of analogy — or of any analogy for that matter — resists the kind of analysis that seeks to categorize and interrelate every detail involved. To this extent, Wesley's use of the analogy between the physical and spiritual senses served more as a heuristic clue or tool for our religious understanding than a final statement concerning the nature of things. For Wesley, reference to spiritual senses provided a model or useful hypothesis that proved successful as an investigative tool for theology.

Although Wesley's ideas are not developed as systematically as we might like, they suggest a theological understanding that surpassed that of his contemporaries. Perhaps we should be satisfied to say that Wesley anticipated a needed synthesis between the verities of religious faith and those derived from scientific, experimental method. He left it to the initiative of others more qualified to work out the systematic implications of his germinal ideas.

Certainly Wesley believed that people need "a new class of senses opened in [their] soul, not depending on organs of flesh and blood."[74] Such people become Christians who "live by faith, and not by sight" (2 Cor. 5:7); their faith comes from God who is the "Author of faith and salvation....It is he that works in us both to will and to do,"[75] who illumines spiritual sight by "the intellectual Sun...the Sun of Righteousness,"[76] and who gives the Holy Spirit, "the Spirit of truth" (John 14:17, 15:26), as a witness "with their spirits that they are the sons of God."[77]

Matthews points out that Wesley was definitely not the first thinker to speak of spiritual senses, but the first to wed the notion of the spiritual senses with an empirical worldview.[78]

### The Relationship to Scripture and Experience

Wesley argued vigorously for the truth of his analogy between the physical and spiritual senses because he ultimately believed it was established by Scripture and confirmed by experience. In his view, these new, spiritual senses provided the direct witness of the Spirit, which Christian believers experienced in common. He wrote that "no man is a partaker of Christ until he can clearly testify, 'The life which I now live...I live by faith in the Son of God,' in him who is now *revealed* in my heart."[79] This felt experience originated in the *"direct testimony* of the Spirit,*"* for which Wesley primarily argued from "the plain meaning of the text" of Scripture and from Christian experience.[80]

This concept of direct, divine illumination appeared often in Wesley's writings. The imperfection of the physical senses left us with "an universal blank" regarding the invisible things of the world,[81] and our only hope rests in God's gracious activity in a person's life. Further, ideas derived from the natural senses provide us with different "species" of knowledge, but ideas derived from spiritual senses provide knowledge of an entirely different "genre."[82] We receive from God an ability to *see* what transcends human limitations of sense experience; God empowers or facilitates spiritual senses that people are unable to generate without divine grace.

"John Smith," with whom Wesley carried on theological correspondence during the early years of the Methodist revival, described Wesley as having a doctrine of "perceptible inspiration."[83] Smith claimed that such a doctrine consisted of "a divine and supernatural illapse from heaven," which implied that God's call upon the soul is "supernatural, miraculous, or uncommon" and thus eliminates rational assent to truth.[84] Wesley did not seem to mind the label "perceptible inspiration," but he disagreed with Smith's criticism that his writings were unreasonable and self–contradictory. Wesley considered any contradiction "only a *seeming* one."[85] For example, he saw no contradiction in speaking of the reasonableness of salvation, and of the divine assurance one may experience through the inspiration of the Holy Spirit. He believed he had established the reality of some kind of perceptible inspiration that helps Christians to gain a *conscious* sense of assurance of their salvation. Such a concept is found in Scripture, is sufficiently reasonable, and is confirmed by the experience of thousands of witnesses.[86]

The reasonableness of Wesley's view did not need to follow a precise logical form because its truth did not depend on the form of argument itself. Rather, the reasonable truthfulness of Wesley's view was based on other considerations than formal logic — namely, Scripture and experience. For Wesley, the appeal to experience for confirmation of biblical truths was the supreme apologetic for Christian beliefs, for in this way the philosophical demand for empiricism appeared firmly met.[87]

## The Extent of Knowledge

The question may be asked as to what extent God's inspiration truly enlightens the believer about the spiritual, or "invisible," world. One could argue for the presence of Platonic–like intuitionism in Wesley's understanding of the assurance of salvation. But Wesley appears less Platonic and more like Locke in the larger Aristotelian tradition passed down through Christian history.

Both Aristotle and Locke retained a place for intuitive knowledge about metaphysical reality; they were not total skeptics like Hume. Locke, for example, argued that we have intuitive knowledge of our own existence and subsequently of the existence of God.[88] In an argument much like Descartes's, Locke affirmed that the mind in self–reflection perceives its own acts, establishing its certain existence. Having affirmed his self–existence, Locke thought he possessed an Archimedean point on which to establish the existence of God. In a variation of the cosmological argument, Locke argued that a being (God) must necessarily exist who is adequate to produce all the effects manifest in experience. Browne later applied similar reasoning to the idea of God, arguing for the existence of God as the First Cause (using Aristotelian terminology) and guaranteeing that conclusion by certain observable phenomena, namely, miracles.[89]

Locke carefully distinguished the relationship between faith and reason, yet found them complementary. Earlier we noted that Locke defined faith as "the assent to any proposition not thus made out by the deductions of reason, but upon the credit of the proposer, as coming from God, in some extraordinary way of communication."[90] Let us look closer at how Locke defined reason.

> 1. *According to reason,* are such propositions whose truth we can discover, by examining and tracing those *ideas* we have from *sensation* and *reflection;* and by natural deduction find to be true or probable. 2. *Above reason,* are such propositions whose truth or probability we cannot by reason derive from those principles. 3. *Contrary to reason,* are such propositions as are inconsistent with, or irreconcilable to, our clear and distinct *ideas.* Thus the existence of one God is according to reason; the existence of more than one God contrary to reason; the resurrection of the dead, above reason.[91]

Locke counted on reason to accomplish a great deal within its proper sphere of influence. (although we may not agree with how he categorized the proper functions of reason). And Wesley aligned much of his own thinking with Locke's epistemological worldview.

*The Knowledge of God*

With regard to natural theology or natural knowledge of God, Wesley said we have no innate ideas. Yet he contended that we do have experientially related knowledge that God exists.

> If indeed God had stamped (as some have maintained) an idea of himself on every human soul, we must certainly have understood something of these, as well as his other attributes; for we cannot suppose he would have impressed upon us either a false or imperfect idea of himself. But the truth is, no man ever did, or does now find any such idea stamped upon his soul. The little which we do know of God (except what we receive by the inspiration of the Holy One) we do not gather from an inward impression, but gradually acquire from without. "The invisible things of God," if they are known at all, "are known from the things that are made"; not from what God hath written in our hearts but from what he hath written in all his works.[92]

Wesley believed that we infer or deduce from creation a knowledge of God's existence. Using variations of the cosmological and teleological arguments similar to those of Locke, Browne, and the greater Roman Catholic tradition, Wesley argued that "the whole creation speaks that there is a God"[93] and "together with his existence, all his attributes or perfections; His eternity…His omnipresence; His omnipotence…; His wisdom, [are] clearly deduced from the things that are seen, from the goodly order of the universe."[94] He maintained that we have knowledge that God exists as surely as we know that we ourselves exist.

> But to all that is or can be said of the omnipresence of God, the world has one grand objection: they cannot see him. And this is really at the root of all their other objections. This our blessed Lord observed long ago: "Whom the world cannot receive, because they see him not." But is it not easy to reply, "Can you see the wind?" You cannot. But do you therefore deny its existence, or its presence? You say, "No; for I can perceive it by my other senses." But by which of your senses do you perceive your soul? Surely you do not deny either the exis-

tence or the presence of this! And yet it is not the object of your sight, or of any of your other senses. Suffice it then to consider that God is a Spirit, as is your soul also. Consequently, "him no man hath seen, or can see," with eyes of flesh and blood.[95]

Like Locke, Wesley posited the existence of God in a way analogous to arguing for one's self–existence, though Wesley used less formal logic. One may interpret Wesley as arguing more from the standpoint of common sense — an interpretation that coincides with his intent to speak "plain truth for plain people" by abstaining "from all nice and philosophical speculations."[96] The best example of Wesley's argumentation from common sense comes in his remarks about Locke's *Essay Concerning Human Understanding*. First he quoted from Locke as to the substance or real essence of humanity, then in reply appealed to common sense as putting the conclusion beyond dispute.

> "Though the word 'man' signifies nothing but a complete idea of properties united in a substance; yet we commonly suppose it to stand for a thing having a real essence on which those properties depend." I do suppose it, and so does every one that has common sense.[97]

This quote demonstrates the more formal logic Locke used to confirm metaphysical knowledge of the essence of humanity and Wesley's informal use of logic on the subject.[98] Though Wesley's use of logic was closer to what philosophers would today call *informal* rather than *formal*, his arguments still prove equally compelling to those who possess "common sense" and "common honesty."[99]

Wesley believed that besides recognizing God's existence, people may infer knowledge from creation regarding human immorality, a future world, a future state, and judgment.[100] Wesley saw no threat to orthodoxy in this view, as critics of classical natural theology might protest; he did not allow classical natural theology to absorb or tame the riches of divine revelation as found in Scripture.[101]

Both Aristotle and Locke thought humankind can attain a degree of metaphysical knowledge, though Locke was more cautious as to the extent of that knowledge. By seeking the general or metaphysical causes of things, Aristotle expected to find intuitively certain general principles. Unlike contemporary empirical sciences, Aristotle sought *certain* rather than *probable* knowledge. And while Locke opted for probable knowledge from the senses, he still believed we could have *certain* knowledge about our own existence and the existence of God. Locke recognized an inconsistency here, but believed that common sense required it.[102] In so arguing, Locke went beyond his first definition of knowledge and consequently appeared inconsistent in his philosophy.[103] Yet, according to Locke, there comes a point when God immediately communicates a "new set of discoveries…which reason vouches the truth of, by the testimony and proofs it gives that they come from God.[104]

One finds a similar, though more common–sense–oriented, approach in Wesley. He did not consider his writings inconsistent, uncritical, or intellectually inadequate if they generally followed the popular philosophy of British empirical thinking as represented by Locke. On the contrary, many of Wesley's seeming inconsistencies stem more from his loyalty to British empirical and Anglican thinking than to defects in his logic.

For example, take his analogy between the physical and spiritual senses, which reflects both the Anglican and empirical sources of his thought. In his analogy Wesley spoke of the intuitions or insights made available to the experience of Christian believers through the grace of God. Outler describes this process as *transempirical intuitionism,* emphasizing the Platonic influences in Wesley's thought. Cell, with a slightly different emphasis, describes this process as *transcendental empiricism,* pointing to Wesley's intention to speak of Christian beliefs in the context of an empirical worldview — only Wesley had an expanded worldview that included all dimensions of human experience, including religious experience.

Simply because Wesley made references to divinely inspired intuitions or insights does not mean that he was uncritically mixing (or confusing) intuitionist and empiricist philosophies. Locke used similar terminology in the development of his ideas, yet it was in the context of an empirical worldview. His philosophical ideas were well received in Britain and continued to gain widespread intellectual acceptance throughout Wesley's lifetime. If Wesley seemed uncritical or inconsistent, this may reflect more of a disagreement with the philosophy of Locke and of the Enlightenment era than a defect in Wesley's theological method.

We should be careful not to project modern ideas onto the past merely because they enjoy current acceptance among a majority of people. Both Locke and Wesley produced germinal ideas in philosophy and theology. But germinal thinkers do not always have the luxury of investigating every conceivable implication of or objection to their ideas. Locke and Wesley did not have the benefit of our modern perspective, which draws on nearly three centuries of critical reflection on their philosophy and theology. We need to approach our study of Locke and Wesley with a sense of intellectual prudence and modern humility if we expect to glean the seeds of their genius.

According to Wesley, we possess ideas of God, though not the innate ideas of intuitionism. Wesley scholars who see him predominantly as an intuitionist miss the continuity of his thought with the early empirical tradition of Locke, which allowed for a degree of intuitive knowledge. When Wesley appealed to intuitive knowledge, it does not mean that he had veered toward the Cambridge Platonists or even the mystics, though he occasionally quoted from the former and acknowledged the influence of the latter in the early formation of his thought. But what may have begun as an eclectic use of ideas drawn from a variety of. sources developed for Wesley into a more intentionally biblical approach that sought intellectual and methodological presuppositions from Lockean philosophy and the greater Aristotelian tradition of logic.[105]

When Wesley appears unsystematic or inconsistent in providing a logical statement of his intellectual convictions, it often reflects some of Locke's limita-tions in holding a truly mediational position between the established rationalist tradition of philosophy and the burgeoning empiricism of the scientific revolu-tion.[106] While Wesley will never appear the most systematic theologian in histo-ry, his ideas and methodology become more coherent when seen in his histor-ical and intellectual context. That context includes the Aristotelian logical tradi-tion as traced through Locke's philosophy, especially as transmitted through the writings of Browne, whose Lockean adaptations were considered to fit more readily into the New Testament emphasis on faith.

### The Source of Knowledge

Wesley's use of the analogy of senses indicates that he generally wanted to stay in the British empirical camp, at least the kind of Lockean empiricism that allowed a prominent place for Christian belief. Wesley knew of some of Hume's skeptical writings, but neither he nor most of England gave much attention to what Hume had to say.[107] Like Locke, Wesley rejected the ideas of contempo-rary thinkers such as David Hartley, who argued that mental operations of the soul may be explained in mathematical or mechanical terms.[108] Physiological components are important to our empirical knowledge, but just as later empiri-cists such as Hume criticized Locke for forsaking direct mechanistic conceptions of reflective intellectual analysis, so Wesley rejected them as well. Instead, Wesley stressed the psychological features of perception, for example, when he said, "By 'feeling' I mean being inwardly conscious of."[109]

Wesley never satisfactorily resolved whether such a feeling or sense was something supernaturally bestowed by God or whether it was naturally or innately present in all people but inoperable due to human sinfulness. He spoke of faith as a spiritual sense given only by God, yet he also described "natural man" as being in "a state of...deep sleep; His spiritual senses are not awake: They discern neither spiritual good nor evil."[110] Wesley probably did not con-ceive of this question in either–or categories. For him, such issues resolved into a both–and worldview that entails a synergistic understanding of how God ini-tiates encounters with people and how people must respond to his initiative. As such, our feelings of being inwardly conscious of God have transcendent as well as psychological characteristics.

Certainly Wesley would have emphasized the transcendent, objective dimension of our encounter with God. But he would not have denied that such encounters have psychological, subjective effects on a believer's life.

Wesley conceived of "natural man" as always possessing some kind of pre-venting, or prevenient, grace. For example, he referred to humanity's conscience — which all people possess, whether Christian or non–Christian — as prevent-ing grace. But how can "natural man" truly be called "natural" if such a person is always in possession of divine grace? In one sense, we may say that for Wesley there existed theoretically the concept of a "natural man," but empirically no purely "natural" person existed. This is because all people experience the presence of God's divine grace — for example, a conscience whether or not they have become Christians. Wesley still made a distinction between: a "natural man" and a "spiritual man," but the "natural" person was not considered to have completely lost the work of God's grace in his or her life.

An important consequence of all this for Wesley was that no one remains without excuse in regard to their sin. All people experience the conviction of sin due to the preventing or prevenient work of God's grace in their conscience. Wesley wrote,

> Yet this is no excuse for those who continue in sin, and lay the blame upon their Maker by saying: "It is God only that must quicken us; for we cannot quicken our own souls." For allowing that all the souls of men are dead in sin by *nature*, this excuses none, seeing there is no man that is in a state of mere nature; there is no man, unless he has quenched the Spirit, that is wholly void of the grace of God. No man living is entirely destitute of what is vulgarly called "natural conscience." But this is not natural; it is more properly termed "preventing grace." [111]

Thus Wesley argued that all people know "Some great truths, as the being of God, and the difference between moral good and evil," because God "has in some measure 'enlightened everyone that cometh into the world,'" and knowledge of them is confirmed by "the traces of them [great truths]…found in all nations." [112]

For Wesley, proper reasoning about spiritual things entails .a prerequisite "apprehension of divine things." [113] Faith becomes that spiritual sense by which people have actual perception of divine things. In this regard faith serves as both the faculty (potential) and the act (process) of perceiving God and the things of God.

> Faith implies both the perceptive faculty itself and the act of perceiving God and the things of God. And the expression "seeing God" may include both, the act and the faculty of seeing him. [114]

So Christian believers may perceive or experience a distinct, divine "impression" (and subsequent assurance) of "being in favour with God." [115] Wesley did not insist on using the term *impression,* and he expressed his hope that someone might "find a better [term]; be it 'discovery,' 'manifestation,' 'deep sense,' or whatever it may be." [116] Note also how Wesley emphasized the "substance" of a doctrine and not the "philosophical illustrations of it." [117] He was not concerned about philosophically or theologically resolving all the aspects involved in articulating how God impresses truth upon people. It was enough to know that God, the ultimate source of all knowledge, did in fact reveal knowledge to people in discernibly different though complementary ways.

Brantley comments, "Thus, far from making a false and arbitrary, i.e., merely metaphorical, identification between the way one perceives the natural world and the way one feels the influxes of grace, Wesley implies that these two ways of 'knowing' are analogous to each other, i.e., founded in the same creation, derived from the same Source and therefore really related." [118] In general, Wesley was content to recognize and preach the *facts* of God's self–revelation and salvation to people and spent little time discussing the *manner* of how people discovered or sensed religious knowledge (even though we may wish he had done otherwise).

## The Role of Logic

Divine revelation discloses to people what reason alone cannot reveal, for example, the mysteries of the Incarnation, the Trinity, and the Atonement. But once disclosed, these mysteries of Christianity do not violate canons of logic. That is, they do not violate logic considered true or false, depending on considerations (such as experimental evidence) other than the form of their argument. This reasoning reflects the informal rather than formal nature of Wesley's logic, and it confirms his expectation to write theology that is logically reasonable.

Wesley put the rich tradition of Aristotelian logic that he inherited at Oxford to good use in his thought and ministry. Though recognizing that Christianity cannot be justified by formal logical equations, he staunchly affirmed the reasonableness of the Christian faith on the basis of tradition, reason, experience, and most of all Scripture. He defined logic as a proper use of inductive and deductive reasoning and accurate evidence. In his "Address to the Clergy" he suggested that knowledge of logic is second in importance only to knowledge of Scripture.

> Some knowledge of the sciences also, is, to say the least, equally expedient [as history]. Nay, may we not say, that the knowledge of one, (whether art or science,) although now quite unfashionable, is even necessary next, and in order to, the knowledge of the Scripture itself? I mean logic. For what is this, if rightly understood, but the art of good sense? of apprehending things clearly, judging truly, and reasoning conclusively?[119]

Reason, which is ultimately a gift from God (since humans are created in God's rational as well as moral image), serves as a guide, especially in understanding Scripture:

> Now, of what excellent use is reason, if we would either understand ourselves, or explain to others, those living oracles! And how is it possible without it to understand the essential truths contained therein?[120]

With the proper use of reasoning capabilities, which primarily involve logic, we may rationally assess the claims of religious belief. Laurence W. Wood points out that "Whereas the great metaphysical systems of the seventeenth century — Descartes, Malebranche, Spinoza, Leibniz — saw reason to be the realm of eternal truths held in common by the human and the divine mind, the eighteenth–century thinkers looked upon reason as an intellectual activity."[121]

Wesley's confidence in the powers of reason was strongest in his early years. He tempered that confidence later on in writing about the powers of reason in contrast to the powers of God's grace; but he still maintained that religious belief is capable of rational assessment and rational justification. Brantley observes "that at least for Wesley, if not for those who came within his sphere of influence, it was not a question of either empiricism or grace. His was a both/and logic."[122]

Wesley considered himself an expert logician and debater, and at Oxford he taught logic and moderated debates between students. He approved of Aristotle's simple approach to logic and disapproved of unnecessary additions, as found, for example, in the Roman Catholic "School–men" and in Locke's philosophy.[123] Wesley often responded to his critics by pointing out logical inconsistencies in their theological positions and their arguments against him. As the Methodist movement grew, he sought to develop preachers for every aspect of the ministry and exhorted them to study logic. He provided a "Compendium of Logic" that they could study in developing sermons and possible disputations with critics.

Other examples of Wesley's use of logic may be found throughout his writings. Perhaps the best example in his theological method is found in his sermon "The Means of Grace." Here he employed a manner of logic, borrowed from Bishop Robert Sanderson, in treating a specific problem, namely, "whether there are any means of grace."[124] Wesley enumerated the steps he used in writing the sermon: "The introduction, concerning the importance of the question, and the occasion of its being first disputed; and the conclusion, containing a recapitulation of the whole, with the corollaries arising therefrom."[125] These steps follow the logical order prescribed by Sanderson, as described in section 1, "Of Treating on a Simple Theme," in the appendix to Wesley's "Compendium of Logic."[126] For an illustration of Sanderson's section 2, "Of Treating on a Problem," see Wesley's sermon "The Nature of Enthusiasm."[127]

While not all of Wesley's sermons follow the explicit logical format of the "Compendium," they all reflect logical structure in the organization of religious themes and in substantiating ideas drawn from Scripture as well as extrabiblical sources. Certainly Wesley sought to present his writings in a logical format so that they would be easier to read and also more compelling in stating his case for the reasonable truthfulness of scriptural, experimental religion.

## The Limitations of Reason

Wesley appealed to reason as much as possible, but he realized that it had its limitations. These limitations were acknowledged more explicitly in Wesley's later works than earlier in his life and ministry. No doubt the abuses of ratiocination among his rationalistic contemporaries and among the Methodists themselves prompted Wesley to articulate some boundaries to reason. We already noted that during his pre–Aldersgate years, Wesley argued that "Faith is a species of belief, and belief is defined 'an assent to a proposition upon rational grounds.' Without rational grounds there is therefore no belief, and consequently no faith."[128] After the revival began, Wesley still confidently claimed reason as a source of religious authority in the "Appeals." Although reason never produces faith, Wesley always considered it capable of regulating the life of faith.[129] And he progressively criticized those whom he thought held improper views of reason.

Wesley first criticized those who were inclined toward mysticism and "enthusiasm," which was ironic since the Methodist revival had been accused of enthusiasm. He also cited problems with deistic rationalism, which he considered an aberration of true reason. In the 1750s, Wesley recognized and addressed still other viewpoints that he felt overstated reason. For example, in 1759 he took issue with John Downes's rationalistic definition of faith.[130] In 1765 he cautioned the editor of the *London Magazine* not to be "so positive" in what he reasoned;[131] he confessed that he no longer "was sure of everything" except "what God has revealed to man."[132] As we have seen, he never gave up his confidence in the powers of reason, but did moderate his views on the reliability of reason as a source of religious authority.

By the 1780s when Wesley wrote the sermons entitled "The Imperfection of Human Knowledge" and "The Case of Reason Impartially Considered," he still affirmed reason's continued role in theology, yet clearly cautioned against its abuses.

> Let reason do all that reason can; Employ it as far as it will go. But, at the same time, acknowledge it is utterly incapable of giving either faith, or hope, or love; and, consequently, of producing either real virtue, or substantial happiness. Expect these from a higher source, even from the Father of the spirits of all flesh.[133]

Reason remained essential to the whole theological task, but no one could consider it sufficient to know divine truths.[134] Even with regard to the existence of God, which Wesley believed that all people infer from creation, we cannot finally *demonstrate* God's existence beyond all doubt, nor can we search out God to perfection.[135] To understand the unity and infinity of God we must ultimately rely on knowledge of God as revealed in Scripture.[136]

True reason knows its limits. By recognizing the limitations of reason we learn humility, resignation, and faith (or trust) in God. Ultimately we need faith to provide sufficient knowledge of that which has eternal significance, that is, knowledge that leads us to God and to salvation.[137] To Wesley, faith still represented the "grand *desideratum*" — the grand *fact* of knowledge concerning God and all things pertaining to our salvation.[138] Yet faith also represented the *manner* or means of the knowing process.

In a sense, Wesley conceived of faith as a process of knowing that in itself constituted knowledge. Faith may then be understood and communicated rationally in much the same way that we understand and communicate other knowledge, though we may not fully understand all of the mannerisms or dynamics of faith. But then, Wesley considered *no* philosophy to contain complete and final knowledge of epistemology.

In conclusion, Wesley was not unreasonable or illogical in his attempt to articulate the nature of faith in the intellectual milieu of the predominant British empirical tradition. And like most intellects of the past, Wesley failed to tell us all that we now want to know about his views on particular topics such as reason. But we can still see the vital role reason played, even with its limitations, in Wesley's approach to theology and Christian faith.

# 7

# The Authority of Experience

Many consider Wesley's insights into experience as a source of religious authority one of his greatest contributions to the development of Christian theology.
He did not set out to be theologically innovative, but he was the first to incorporate explicitly into his theological worldview the experiential dimension of
the Christian faith along with the conceptual.[1] From his earliest theological writings in the "Sermons on Several Occasions," Wesley sought "to guard those who
are just setting their faces toward heaven (and who, having little acquaintance
with the things of God, are the more liable to be turned out of the way), from
formality, from mere outside religion, which has almost driven heart–religion
out of the world."[2]

Wesley feared that some of his Methodist followers as well as other
Christians might succumb to a kind of spiritually dead orthodoxy that demonstrated none of the living power and vitality of a personal relationship with God
through Jesus Christ. For example, Wesley began his short tract entitled
"Thoughts upon Methodism" with the following paragraph:

> I am not afraid that the people called Methodists should ever cease to exist,
> either in Europe or America. But I am afraid, lest they should only exist as a dead
> sect, having the form of religion without the power. And this undoubtedly will
> be the case, unless they hold fast both the doctrine, spirit and discipline with
> which they first set out.[3]

Fearful of the threat of reverting to this recurring kind of conceptualist orthodoxy (and potentially rigid scholasticism), Wesley sought to maintain a healthi-
er, more holistic view of the experiential dimension of Christian faith. He did
not consider it a theological innovation. The confirmatory power of experience,
he argued, was essential to the true believer's life. But by acknowledging such a
crucial role for experience, particularly the religious kind, Wesley serendipitously added experience as an essential religious authority to the existing Anglican
affirmation of Scripture, tradition, and reason.

Since the time of Wesley, theologians have been more willing to recognize
experience as an undeniable and valuable source of religious authority.

## Experimental Religion

In calling his religious methodology "experimental," Wesley generally meant that religion was related to or based on experience — experience that includes more than just our cognitive understanding of Scripture and tradition. Of course, theology does not then become based primarily on experience; Scripture remains the primary source of religious authority. But theology should be founded on or derived from experimentation that tests every potential source of religious authority, including religious experience.

Each of us evaluates, consciously or subconsciously, the cumulative evidence for and against religious belief. We then affirm or reject, believe or disbelieve that which best coincides with the evidence. Although we may believe that such a decision is facilitated and even initiated by divine grace, there remains an element of genuine human involvement in the act of faith.

Wesley believed that the truths of Scripture are (or will be eschatologically) confirmed in experience. Consequently we must respond to that which God has revealed historically through Scripture and at present through the work of the Holy Spirit. Although the confirmatory role of experience pertains especially to the assurance of salvation,[4] it also pertains to other truths of Scripture and to doctrines of orthodox Christianity.[5]

In Wesley we find that the development of theology resulted from efforts carried out under controlled conditions with the intent of discovering the truths of religion. The controlled conditions, or experimental methods, may not have been systematically conceived or rigorously employed, but they were present. Wesley self–consciously sought to articulate a conception of Christianity that was reasonable, given all the evidence, yet not formalistic. In so doing he tried very hard not to deprive Christianity of its spiritual vitality.

After stating his intent in the "Sermons on Several Occasions" to present "the true, the scriptural, experimental religion," Wesley warned against two threats to heart–religion.[6] We have already seen how both threats lay in the tendency to overemphasize the cognitive, formal dimension of religious belief at the expense of the affective, vital dimension of Christian experience, which involves a personal, interacting, and loving relationship with God.

### Empirical and Experiential Knowledge

The experimental study of religion deals with knowledge that is both *empirical* and *experiential*. Although these categories are not used by Wesley, they help to illustrate the subtlety of his theology of experience.[7]

*Empirical* knowledge is that founded on experience, observation, facts, sensation, practice, concrete situations, and real events. It is *a posteriori* knowledge derived from sense experience and is generally capable of public assessment. An example of empirical knowledge is the arguments from classical natural theology for the existence of God. It also includes testimonies and accounts of miracles from Christian believers past and present. These examples have to do with experiences where no direct sense or impression of the presence of God occurs, or at least where the intensity of the awareness of God tends to be less marked. Nevertheless, they serve as potential evidence for cumulative case arguments on behalf of the reasonableness of Christian belief.

*Experiential* knowledge relies on understanding, insights, or information that derive from personal or interpersonal sense experiences. It contrasts with empirical experience, which is confined to sensation, perception, or observation of the types of experiences that people share. Experiential knowledge derives from introspection, self–analysis, private conscious states, and other means. It is not the same thing as *a priori* knowledge, which is derived from reason without reference to sense experience;[8] rather. it is based on sense experience, but not on the kinds of empirical experiences that provide knowledge easily capable of public assessment.

Personal experiences are difficult to assess publicly because they are so individualistic as to prevent others from fully comprehending their significance. They tend to be meaningful only to the person or persons experiencing them. For example, it is not always possible to articulate why you love someone and hate another, or why you act one way rather than another. These difficulties are especially true with regard to religious experiences in which there occurs a direct awareness or impression of God — that personal being whose very existence transcends our ability to verify from empirical experience alone.

Although this kind of knowledge involves the personal participation of the knower, it is not purely psychological or *subjective,* because we genuinely come into contact with an *objective,* albeit empirically hidden, reality. Richard Brantley argues that Wesley's "analogy of proportionality [between physical and spiritual senses] helped Wesley to think that what is felt is a theologically satisfying substitute for what is seen philosophically — that as the intellect remains convinced of what the senses have to tell, so the intellect trusts emotion to be not illusory but spiritually veridical, i.e., to correspond to religious fact."[9] Thus Wesley believed that Christians may in fact experience certain experiential knowledge of God and of God's salvation for one's life.

Wesley saw the difficulty in articulating how Christians may claim to have experiential knowledge of God and of spiritual truths pertaining to God's salvation. Although he did not generally feel compelled to get involved in philosophical speculations, Wesley did attempt to provide an explanation of his appeal to experiential knowledge. This explanation appeared during the early years of the Methodist revival, primarily in "An Earnest Appeal," "A Farther Appeal," and subsequent writings rebutting criticisms of his use of experience as a source of religious authority. We have already seen how Wesley developed his ideas along the lines of Aristotelian logic and Lockean philosophy, including the way in which Peter Browne broadened the method of experimentation to include dimensions of religious experience transcendent of empirical sense data.[10]

In "An Earnest Appeal" we discover how Wesley developed Browne's ideas in his analogy between the natural and spiritual senses. These senses were thought to give people sufficient data or ideas with which to properly reason to true conclusions about "the things of God."[11] Natural senses perceive empirical data that provide ideas about the physical world. In this regard, Wesley's conception of the natural senses functioned in the same way by which Locke established his philosophy of empirical knowledge.

Likewise, the spiritual senses perceive experiential data of a religious nature that provide ideas about the spiritual world. On this score, Wesley believed he did justice not only to Scripture passages dealing with spiritual seeing and hearing, but also to contemporary scientific and philosophical advances in the theory of knowledge. Wesley, in fact, thought himself more thoroughly inductive because he had taken into consideration commonly recognized, nonempirical experiences that contribute to religious understanding. Unfortunately, the spiritual senses God created in people became distorted due to the presence of sin. And without "the *evidence* of things not seen,"[12] thought Wesley, no one could hope to reason properly about things pertaining to God.

Summarizing his views on the subject of natural and spiritual senses, Wesley said,

> You know, likewise that before it is possible for you to form a true judgment of them it is absolutely necessary that you have a *clear apprehension* of the things of God, and that your ideas thereof be all *fixed,* distinct, and *determinate.* And seeing our ideas are not innate, but must all originally come from our sense, it is certainly necessary that you have senses capable of discerning objects of this — not those only which are called "natural senses," which in this respect profit nothing, as being altogether incapable of discerning objects of a spiritual kind, but *spiritual* senses, exercised to discern spiritual good and evil. It is necessary that you have the *hearing* ear and the *seeing* eye, emphatically so called; that you have a new class of senses opened in your soul, not depending on organs of flesh and blood, to be "the *evidence* of things not seen" as your bodily senses are of visible things, to be the avenues to the invisible world, to discern spiritual objects, and to furnish you with ideas of what the outward "eye hath not seen, neither the ear heard."[13]

Wesley believed that God preveniently provides grace to all people so that they might have the kind of faith that activates and facilitates our spiritual senses of hearing, seeing, and feeling God. Thus, from Wesley's perspective, faith not only cleanses people from the guilt of sin, but also helps them to reason correctly concerning the things of God.

## Christian Experience of Faith

Although his concept of faith was rationally oriented, Wesley believed faith relies on the evidence of religious experience and is not a matter of reason alone. Even the devils, "Mohametans," and Roman Catholics possess rational kinds of faith, but their faith remains minimal and inadequate for salvation.[14] In affirming the experiential dimension of religious faith, Wesley thought he would avoid recurring rationalistic tendencies of formal, dogmatic religion.

Wesley also sought to avoid the concept of faith at the other end as a kind of mysticism, or "enthusiasm," of which he was sometimes accused. He did not like exotic religious experiences. He feared people who overvalued feelings, which is why he devoted an entire sermon to the subject "The Nature of Enthusiasm." But he saw that, despite some excesses in reports people gave about their experiences of God, there remained an inevitable variableness in the operations of the Holy Spirit on the souls of men. Thus the test for whether a witness is true or false should not be feelings alone. The appropriate way to "test the spirits" (1 John 4:1) should include criteria taken from Scripture, tradition, and reason as well as from experience.

Wesley's concept of faith reflects several elements from other traditions: the historic Roman Catholic emphasis on intellectual affirmation *(assensus)* of the content of classical orthodox beliefs, which includes Scripture; the Reformation concept of personal trust *(fiducia)*; and a dynamic, synergistic element that includes a place for God's initiative in bestowing faith and for people's responsibility in "reasoning justly" and acting faithfully in religious experience. This understanding of faith appears in a letter Wesley wrote to "John Smith."

> I believe, (1.) That a rational assent to the truth of the bible is one ingredient of Christian faith. (2.) That Christian faith is a moral virtue in that sense wherein hope and charity are. (3.) That men ought to yield the utmost attention and industry for the attainment of it. And yet, (4.) That this, as every Christian grace, is properly supernatural, is an immediate gift of God, which he commonly gives in the use of such means as he hath ordained.[15]

Thus every Christian believer may experience a sense of certainty about his or her personal faith in God and in God's salvation for one's life.[16]

What of the reliability of the testimonies to faith made by others? May we have the same sense of certainty with regard to their accounts of faith? Mitsuo Shimizu notes that Wesley did not suggest infallible certainty in judging the witness of others, but did commonly argue for the truth of Christianity and of Christian beliefs based on faith experiences described by believers.[17] Although we cannot determine the veracity of their witness with absolute certainty, we can have reasonable certainty of what they say after having examined the consistency of their witness and the quality of life that has resulted as expressed in their attitudes and actions. If a person's testimony is experimentally investigated and sufficiently verified in accordance with Scripture, tradition, and reason, it is reasonable to judge such witness as true and worthy of consideration as evidence of the truth of Christianity.[18]

## Relationship to Other Views of Experience

To a certain extent Wesley reacted against the rationalistic tendencies developing in Anglican and Reformed theologies, especially deism. By contrast, he sought to deal with the many vital dimensions of human life and religious experience. Perhaps for him, a person's experience of God represented an aspect of life that had remained relatively untouched by the critical minds of the eighteenth century because of their rationalistic phobias against anything that resembled enthusiasm. However, since he believed that true religious experiences would not contradict but only confirm and illumine Scripture, Wesley investigated the concrete religious experiences of people, expecting to uncover new truths about God and about people's relationship with God.

Although Wesley introduced experience into his theological method somewhat serendipitously, he believed he had precedent for doing so from the history of true, spiritual Christianity as found throughout church tradition. He considered his use of experience an explicit statement of what had always been tacitly assumed by genuine Christian believers. Especially concerning the witness of the Holy Spirit in our lives, Wesley appealed not only to Scripture but to Anglican and ancient church tradition. After having examined several scriptural passages in "A Farther Appeal," he gave the following summary statement on the actual *felt* presence of the Spirit of Christ in the believer:

> From these passages it may sufficiently appear for what purpose every Christian, according to the doctrine of the Church of England, does not "receive the Holy Ghost." But this will be still more clear from those that follow; wherein the reader may likewise observe a plain, rational sense of God's revealing himself to us, of the inspiration of the Holy Ghost, and of a believer's feeling in himself the mighty working of the Spirit of Christ.[19]

Perceiving — literally feeling — God's presence is a powerful epistemological guarantee for the truth of Christian belief.[20] It confirms the already existing words of Scripture, which itself provides the *terminus a quo* of religious truths.

In addition to the influence of the Anglican tradition, Wesley drew on the writings of Roman Catholic mystics who counterbalanced the formalistic tendencies of Reformed theology in the Church of England. The early influence of these Roman Catholics in Wesley's devotional readings cultivated his appreciation for certain ascetic virtues and for an almost mystical contemplation of God. Wesley eventually moved away from the mystical influence of such people as the Marquis de Renty, but he continued to hold up their exemplary lives for convincing people of sin and for challenging Christians to go on in perfection.[21]

In particular Wesley mentioned in "On God's Vineyard" the long–term influence of Francis of Sales and Juan de Castañiza.[22] These men modeled lives of holy living, both inwardly and outwardly, and thus verified that actual, experienced perfection is the privilege of believing Christians. Their examples, like many others, proved crucial in confirming and vitalizing for Wesley the full extent of religious truth and holiness described in Scripture.

## Diversity of Religious Experience

We have discovered that religious experience includes a wide spectrum of experiences. On the one hand, we have *empirical* knowledge that may serve religious purposes similar to that of classical natural theology. Such knowledge is founded on sense experience, observation, facts, sensation, practice, concrete situations, and real events. On the other hand, we have *experiential* knowledge that may also serve religious purposes, reflecting a personal relationship with God. This knowledge is founded on introspection or self–analysis, personal sensations or perceptions, and generally, inwardly oriented observations that are not easily communicated outwardly. Both kinds of knowledge play a role in Wesley's theology, though experiential knowledge defies easy categorization and application beyond the meaningfulness of a particular religious experience to a person.

As I mentioned earlier, the first kind, empirical knowledge, is derived from sense experience and is capable of public assessment. No direct sense or impression of the presence of God occurs, or at least the intensity of the awareness of God tends to be less marked. Yet this knowledge may provide clues to discerning a limited degree of spiritual truths. Such experiences alone offer insufficient knowledge about God, especially the divine provision for salvation through Jesus Christ. But cumulatively, Scripture, tradition, reason, and experience make a compelling case for Christian beliefs.[23] Faith is still required, but that faith is neither irrational nor nonrational and it does not lack a full investigation of relevant evidence.

The second kind, experiential knowledge, relies on instances of understanding, insight, or information derived from private sense experience. These personal instances may include experiences originating in the spiritual senses. Experiential knowledge, particularly of a religious nature, is not so conducive to public assessment as empirical knowledge. The former tends to be more meaningful in relation to the particular person or persons who have had or shared the experience. Examples include the experience of conversion and the internal "witness of the Spirit," both of which played important roles in the evangelistic and apologetic aspects of Wesley's life and ministry.[24] Wesley gave little credence to visions, dreams, and mystical experiences, but he saw these phenomena as similar to the other examples in that religious experience generally claims to have a direct awareness or impression of God.

These experiential data, which from Wesley's perspective were valid experimental evidence, were reasonably obtained through such means as introspection or self-analysis. They were also subject to error. But Wesley believed that — given *all* the evidence available from experience, Scripture, tradition, and reason — religious belief is capable of rational assessment *and* rational justification (at least to the degree that any human knowledge can be rationally justified).

We will now examine the variety of religious experiences Wesley used in formulating theology. First we will look at outward, empirical experiences as a source of evidence for religious belief. Then we will investigate examples of inward, religious experiences, especially as related to the so-called spiritual senses and to the Christian assurance of salvation. The latter form of evidence clearly proved to be the most compelling to Wesley, both personally and theologically. But both reveal the completeness with which Wesley considered the experimental, or inductive, study of religious experience.

## Outward Experiences

Earlier we noted that Wesley affirmed arguments of classical natural theology with regard to proofs of the existence of God. In fact, he appealed to variations of the cosmological and teleological arguments in his writings. In "A Farther Appeal," he suggested a form of cosmological argument by affirming that the existence of God is demonstrated by the existence of creation and its creatures.

> What a miserable drudgery is the service of God unless I love the God whom I serve! But I cannot love one whom I know not. How then can I love God till I know him? And how is it possible I should know God, unless he make himself known unto me? By *analogy* or proportion? Very good. But where is that proportion to be found? What proportion does a creature bear to its creator? What is the proportion between finite and infinite?
>
> I grant, the *existence* of the creatures demonstratively shows the *existence* of their Creator. The whole creation speaks that there is a God.[25]

Wesley did not claim to have discovered the divine nature of God, but he was convinced of God's existence based on cosmological arguments that use analogies of proportion. Thomas Aquinas also doubted an innate ability to know the divine nature, but he developed the analogy of proportion to show how the likeness between God and creatures is based on their proportionate participation in the reality signified by the concept.[26] Wesley apparently followed this Thomistic line of argumentation.

Elsewhere Wesley spoke more boldly with regard to the general revelation we have of God through knowledge derived from the natural senses. He appealed to a variation on the teleological argument when he said that "together with his [God's] attributes or perfections; His eternity... — His omnipresence; His omnipotence...; — His wisdom, [are] clearly deduced from the things that are seen, from the goodly order of the universe."[27]

The Deists, who were still popular during Wesley's lifetime, were the strongest proponents of the teleological argument, pushing natural theology to the point of usurping the primary religious authority of Scripture. But Wesley, like Anselm and Aquinas, remained fully orthodox in his theology and did not allow natural theology to tame or absorb the riches of divine revelation as found in Scripture.[28] From Wesley's perspective, arguments for the existence of God served more to confirm and elaborate on one's concept of God than to prove the existence of God without appealing to Christian faith and teaching.

His concern for accumulating facts related to religion reflects Wesley's conscious obedience to the inductive study and correlation of the experiences of others in the service of theology. In chapter 3 we looked at Wesley's work "Doctrine of Original Sin" as the classic example of how he used inductive method in the investigation of a historic, biblical doctrine. Wesley sought to show that our universal experience of sin, pervading our past and present, manifestly confirms the reality of sin. Though some critics disagreed with Wesley's interpretation of the evidence and chose not to use the biblical term "sin," he considered the demonstrative evidence for the Christian understanding of sin overwhelming. In other writings Wesley offered additional evidence for the doctrine by pointing out the conviction of sin that people experience.[29] The only reason why the conviction of sin at times seems ineffectual is because people have deceived themselves into thinking there is nothing wrong with their actions and therefore they need not be responsible for them.

Wesley also believed in extraordinary or miraculous events as evidence for the truth of Christian beliefs. These arguments are almost without exception variations on the teleological argument (the argument from design), because they point to events and experiences that seem to require an intelligent source for their existence. For example, the miracles of Jesus are demonstrative signs of his divine messiahship.[30]

The divine inspiration of Scripture was also thought by Wesley to be substantiated by "four grand and powerful arguments which strongly induce us to believe that the Bible must be from God; viz., miracles, prophecies, the goodness of the doctrine, and the moral character of the penmen."[31] Each of these arguments may be used as evidence for the existence of God and for the revelation of God in Scripture.

While accepting miracles as a source of religious authority in certain matters, Wesley did not haphazardly accept them for every aspect of Christian faith and practice. He required that appeals to miracles be carefully considered and accounts of miracles be thoroughly investigated — just as every other source of religious authority needs to be rationally and experimentally analyzed. Such extraordinary events need to be evaluated and correlated in relation to Scripture, tradition, and reason as a series of epistemological checks and balances. For example, when asked to present miraculous credentials on behalf of his ministry, Wesley responded,

> What is it you would have us prove by miracles? that the doctrines we preach are true? This is not the way to prove that. (As our first Reformers replied to those of the Church of Rome, who, you may probably remember, were continually urging them with this very demand.) We prove the doctrines we preach by Scripture and reason, and, if need be, by antiquity.[32]

Wesley made it quite clear that some aspects of religious belief should not be decided on the basis of miracles, just as Jesus refused to perform miraculous signs for the unbelieving crowds (Matt. 12:38–41). Wesley said, "It is therefore utterly unreasonable and absurd to require or expect the proof of *miracles* in questions or such a kind as are always decided by proofs of quite another nature."[33]

Wesley surely saw a place for extraordinary or miraculous events in understanding religious beliefs, but they functioned more in confirmation of truths reasonably established primarily by Scripture.[34] Nevertheless, the confirmation of such extraordinary experiences was a relevant part of a thoroughly experimental methodology and should not be quickly passed aside as only part of an ancient, superstitious worldview. A truly experimental methodology will not automatically pass off accounts of miracles simply because they offend modern, scientific presuppositions. Rather, one must remain as objective as possible by being methodologically open to investigations sufficiently comprehensive to evaluate the trustworthiness of purported miracles both past and present.

The confirmatory function of experience played a key role in Wesley's

understanding of theological method. He believed that empirical knowledge —
accumulated accounts of people's experiences (religious and nonreligious) that
are open to public assessment — contributes to the confirmation and
understanding of biblical truths. Observing how people become Christians
proves profitable in a number of ways. To begin with, it brings encouragement
to individual believers. Wesley wrote that "it is certain no part of Christian history is so profitable as that which relates to great changes wrought in our souls:
these, therefore, should be carefully noticed and treasured up for the
encouragement of our brethren."[35] Moreover, examining the religious experiences of people serves to confirm the truthfulness of classical orthodox doctrines. For example, from experience Wesley distinguished two kinds of
Christians: those who chose to live the "more excellent way" of holy living, and
those who received God's justifying grace but rejected his sanctifying grace.

> For long experience and observation I am inclined to think, that whoever finds
> redemption in the blood of Jesus, whoever is justified, has then the choice of
> walking in the higher or the lower path. I believe the Holy Spirit at that time sets
> before him the "more excellent way," and incites him to walk therein; to choose
> the narrowest path in the narrow way; to aspire after the heights and depths of
> holiness, after the entire image of God. But if he does not accept this offer, he
> insensibly declines into the lower order of Christians. He still goes on in what
> may be called a good way, serving God in his degree, and finds mercy in the
> close of life, through the blood of the covenant.[36]

In defense of his doctrine of entire sanctification, Wesley cited frequent
instances of people being perfected in love.[37] Later in life he discovered by
experience that he needed to amend his understanding of the doctrine. Harald
Lindström helpfully documents how Wesley's experiences in the Methodist
revival altered some of the extreme emphases he placed on the entirely sanctified in 1740 in the preface to *Hymns and Sacred Poems.*[38]

Another example of how Wesley used religious experiences in his theological writings relates to his defense of Arminianism. Although there did not seem
to be a direct Arminian influence in the early formation of his theology, Wesley
later defended Arminian doctrine in the *Arminian Magazine.* Issues of the magazine had four parts — a defense of Arminianism, a life of some outstanding
Christian, a number of letters, and various poems and hymns. People's personal stories in the magazine served as a practical means of communicating
Arminian theology and also as an empirically oriented means for bolstering the
case for its truthfulness.

By holding up experience as a source of religious authority, Wesley was able
to pass beyond proofs of truth advanced by contemporary, subjectivistic
thinkers such as George Berkeley and Samuel Clarke. Accordingly, George
Eayrs considers Wesley to have made a significant contribution to thought in his
century and for all time because he argued from religious experience.[39] On the
doctrine of sanctification, Eayrs says, "As a philosopher, he [Wesley] analyzed
and synthesized the contents of his consciousness and that of Christian persons,
together with its results in character and conduct."[40] Wesley regarded experi-

ence so highly that it sometimes made him wonder whether he had interpreted Scripture properly; for him the additives of tradition and reason served as safeguards for the correct interpretation of Scripture.[41]

Despite Wesley's regard for experience, it never became a source of doctrine per se. On the contrary, experience primarily served to confirm scriptural truth and to enhance biblical interpretation, since he saw the truth of human and religious experiences as coinciding with the truth of Scripture. Wesley always rejected criticism of enthusiasm. He defended himself by declaring that his consistent affirmation of Scripture was more important than any private or secret impulse. Thus he refuted the notion of his being an enthusiast on the grounds that he was not "One who vainly images a private revelation [or] One who has a vain confidence of his intercourse with God" — a definition devised by Locke and taken as typical of eighteenth–century usage for enthusiasm.[42] Moreover, he affirmed the rationality of his theology of religious experience, in response to John Downes's accusations of enthusiasm, by saying, "I am no enthusiast; for I resolve none of my notions into immediate inspiration. I have something to do with reason."[43]

## Inward Experiences

We turn now from empirical knowledge to experiential knowledge, which plays the most important role in Wesley's experimental understanding of religion. Experiential knowledge comprises experiences that provide a direct awareness or impression of God. This kind of experience gives a person a sense of understanding or insight that is generally obtained through introspection, self–analysis, or private conscious states.

Although such experiences require the personal participation of the knower in acts of understanding, they do not make that understanding *subjective*. All acts of understanding require some degree of personal involvement in the knowing process. Thus it is neither an arbitrary nor a passive experience, but a responsible act on a person's part. Knowledge derived from a personal, experiential encounter with God is *objective* in the sense of establishing contact with a real, albeit hidden, reality. According to Wesley, the fullness of the reality of God and of God's salvation is hidden from our natural senses, though not from our spiritual senses. Such senses were created in us by God and may now be reactivated by his grace to counteract the distortion of those spiritual senses by sin. With the experiential knowledge gained through our contact with God, the potential for discovering future religious insights — perhaps inconceivable to us now — becomes unlimited.

Experiential knowledge functioned decisively for Wesley in the entire range of religious understanding. At an early age he argued with his father in a letter over matters of holiness and stated that "experience is worth [a] thousand reasons."[44] Even before his Aldersgate experience Wesley demanded more than scriptural proof for doctrines, especially those relating to the instantaneous nature of justification by faith. In his journal he describes how he came to believe in instantaneous conversion. He had doubted that conversions occurred instantaneously, even though a literal interpretation of Scripture seemed to indicate it was true.

At first Wesley clung to experience as a defense against Scripture, but he could not long resist the "living witnesses to it."[45] He met person after person who had instantaneously experienced forgiveness and the assurance of salvation. He became so convinced and convicted of his unbelief that he totally committed his life to God and subsequently experienced the heart–warming assurance of God's gracious presence. He could finally say that such salvation "is confirmed by *your* experience and *mine*."[46]

These references to religious experience in Wesley's early life illustrate its long–term methodological importance as a source of religious authority in helping him to respond to the immediate theological needs of his personal life and ministry.

Wesley had a particular fascination with the experimental investigation of personal conversion experience. Conversion was, for him, one of the two primary ways in which believers experience a direct awareness of God, the other being assurance of salvation. Wesley spent a lifetime analyzing and delineating the order of salvation (*ordo salutis*).[47] More than one hundred specific conversion experiences are described in his sermons, journals, and letters.

In his investigations Wesley perceived that there is "irreconcilable variability in the operations of the Holy Spirit on the souls of men."[48] One cannot become dogmatic in interpreting every last detail of a religious conversion. Nevertheless, the actual experiences provide a tremendous sense of assurance both to the person who experiences conversion and to those who witness the fruit of it in the person's life.

This assurance of salvation Wesley often referred to as "the witness of the Spirit." Sometimes this witness occurs simultaneously with the religious experience of conversion; sometimes it comes later. Wesley discussed the subject specifically in two sermons, "The Witness of the Spirit, I–II." He described the witness of God's Holy Spirit as follows:

> But what is that testimony of God's Spirit, which is superadded to, and conjoined with, this [testimony of our own spirit]? How does he "bear witness with our spirit that we are the children of God"? It is hard to find words in the language of men to explain "the deep things of God." Indeed, there are none that will adequately express what the children of God experience. But perhaps one might say, (desiring any who are taught of God to correct, to soften, or strengthen the expression,) The testimony of the Spirit is an inward impression on the soul, whereby the Spirit of God directly witnesses to my spirit, that I am a child of God; that Jesus Christ hath loved me, and given himself for me; and that all my sins are blotted out, and I, even I, am reconciled to God.[49]

Parallel to this witness of the Spirit, according to Wesley, is the Christians' own spirits witnessing to them through the conscience that they have been reconciled to God through the salvation offered by Jesus Christ.[50] They then receive a spiritual consciousness, which Wesley described this way:

Now this is properly the testimony of our own spirit; even the testimony of our own conscience, that God hath given us to be holy of heart, and holy in outward conversation. It is a consciousness of our having received, in and by the Spirit of adoption, the tempers mentioned in the word of God, as belonging to his adopted children; even a loving heart toward God, and toward all humankind; hanging with childlike confidence on God our Father, desiring nothing but him, casting all our care upon him, and embracing every child of man with earnest, tender affection: − A consciousness that we are inwardly conformed, by the Spirit of God, to the image of his Son, and that we walk before him in justice, mercy, and truth, doing the things which are pleasing in his sight.[51]

Wesley strongly affirmed the witness of the Spirit because he had experienced it in his own life. His familiar journal entry about having a "heart strangely warmed" bears repeating to emphasize the experimental importance of experiential knowledge in Wesley's theological understanding:

In the evening I went very unwillingly to a society in Aldersgate Street, where one was reading Luther's preface to the Epistle to the Romans. About a quarter before nine, while he was describing the change which God works in the heart through faith in Christ, I felt my heart strangely warmed. I felt I did trust in Christ, Christ alone for salvation: And an assurance was given me, that he had taken away *my* sins, even *mine,* and saved *me* from the law of sin and death.[52]

Later on, Wesley said that Christians "cannot be satisfied with any thing less than a direct testimony from his Spirit, that he is 'merciful to their unrighteousness, and remembers their sins and iniquities no more.'"[53] Such experience is the privilege of all believers. [54] It occurs before "the witness of our own spirit," but is attendant with "the fruit of the Spirit."[55] The witness of our own spirit or consciousness plus the actual change that occurs in our lives − the manifestation of the fruit of the Spirit − provides added evidence of the reality of God, of his salvation, and of all his truth as revealed to us through Scripture.[56]

Thus Wesley concluded that Christians indeed experience directly the witness of the Holy Spirit − a witness of which we may have an assured sense of consciousness. In a letter to Dr. Conyers Middleton, Wesley confidently referred to the felt sense of confirmation one experiences inwardly of the truths of Christianity.

I now am assured that these things are so: I experience them in my own breast. What Christianity (considered as a doctrine) promised is accomplished in my own soul. And Christianity, considered as an inward principle, is the completion of those promises. It is holiness and happiness, the image of God impressed on a created spirit, a fountain of peace and love springing up into everlasting life. [57]

In this instance Wesley referred to religious experience in the experiential sense of the term. This is a distinction from mysticism − which Wesley was critical of − in that in this witness of the Spirit one does not participate in an object per se, namely, in oneness with the divine being. But neither did Wesley have a purely empirical concept of experience in which data are limited to knowledge obtained or confirmed through the natural senses. Wesley saw a relation between spiritual and physical experiences, and he was interested in examining both. But when it came to Christianity, Wesley was primarily concerned with the inner, spiritual knowledge that comes through a personal relationship with God.

Besides these two religious experiences of conversion and the witness of the Holy Spirit, Wesley made mention of visions and dreams and mystical experiences. But he remained very cautious, almost skeptical, of the claims people made, because of the lack of care given to interpreting such experiences and the possibility of human or demonic cause rather than divine.[58] Wesley said more than once that Christians should not rely on visions.[59] He held a similar distrust for dreams, yet showed a recurring fascination for them.[60] In his early years, Wesley had also been fascinated by mystical writers. But despite certain "excellences" he perceived in their writings, he recognized many defects so that he eventually broke with their company as in the case of William Law — and became progressively critical of their mysticism. [61]

## Limitations of Experience

Wesley knew that religious excesses often occurred in understanding visions, dreams, and mystical experiences as well as experiences of conversion and the witness of the Holy Spirit. Because one could easily misinterpret or miscommunicate religious experiences, Wesley insisted that each experience be tested for reliability.

The primary test for Wesley was Scripture; that criterion remained manifestly clear. Wesley often criticized people like the mystic Madame Guyon, who placed greater reliance on "inspirations" than the "written Word."[62] He also criticized Baron Emmanuel Swedenborg's dreams and reveries, saying that "his tales are often exceeding lively, and as entertaining as the tales of the fairies; But I dare not give up my Bible for them; and I must give up one or the other."[63]

Despite Wesley's firm belief that miracles occurred in the past and still occurred in his time, he emphasized that even miracles cannot supersede the authority of Scripture.[64] A failure to evaluate religious experience according to Scripture results in both unhealthy theology and unhealthy Christian practice. (For example, in his sermon "The Mean of Grace," Wesley criticized the quietistic tendency toward "stillness" in Quakerism because of its antinomian tendencies.)[65]

Along with Scripture, tradition and reason provide safeguards to unchecked interpretations of religious experience, according to Wesley. Of course, the history of the church over two thousand years offers countless examples of theological extremism and heresy. These instances help us to prevent repeating the errors, from the extremes of mysticism or enthusiasm on the one hand and from formal, rationalistic religion on the other. Wesley always tried to steer a middle path between the two, keeping a healthy balance between knowledge and vital piety.

In Wesley's view, reason especially serves to help us discern a proper interpretation of individual and corporate religious experiences. He could use reason as a criterion because he considered such experiences reasonably justified and thus capable of rational assessment. Religious experience is not something so privatistic and subjective that it cannot be understood or communicated to others. If we regard religion as fundamentally reasonable, then our experience must appear equally reasonable. Thus experimental investigation of experience helps to illumine and existentially bring to life the cognitive truths we affirm in Christianity.

In summary, experience justifiably stands alongside Scripture, tradition, and reason as authoritative criteria for the Christian faith. All need to be taken into consideration when we reflect on basic Christian beliefs. In the words of Robert Monk, "These authoritative elements in fact become a believer's own, through experience, since it keeps them from being only irrelevant externals."[66] Confirming interpretation of Scripture by religious experiences of both a private, experiential nature and a public, empirically observable nature is the most comprehensive method of discovering genuine knowledge of a religious nature.

Colin Williams says that for Wesley, experience "is the appropriation of authority"[67] — it confirms the truthfulness of Scripture, tradition, and reason. This confirming function of religious experience uplifts the primary authority of Scripture rather than usurping it. Although Wesley said that he would revise his understanding of the Bible if experience contradicted it, he assumed that people's experiences would not ultimately contradict Scripture. William M. Arnett rightly observes that for Wesley the relationship between Scripture and experience did not represent a question of either–or but of both–and.[68]

## A Summary of Religious Authority

As we have seen, Wesley did not consider himself an innovator of theological method. He saw himself as a theological conservative, preserving the classical orthodox tradition of Christianity. This was so much the case that in one sermon he said, "But whatever doctrine is *new* must be *wrong*; for the *old* religion is the only *true* one; and no doctrine can be right unless it is the very same 'which was from the beginning.'"[69]

More specifically, Wesley saw himself fitting comfortably within the context of the greater Reformed and, particularly, Anglican tradition. Although he sought spiritually and morally to renew Anglicanism along with the whole of Britain, he preserved his theological conservatism due to his unwillingness to go to extremes on religious experience.[70] In so doing, he strongly affirmed Scripture as the primary source of religious authority for all aspects of his personal life, ministry, and theological writings. Scripture naturally flowed from Wesley's pen as though a second language, and he always brought followers and critics alike back to the biblical starting point of true Christianity.

Conforming to Anglican tradition, Wesley considered his theology and ministry to reflect the best of church tradition, especially the church of Christian antiquity. Tradition contains the lived experience of countless generations of Christians and thus transmits both the doctrines and accounts of the vital lives of Christians and Christian communities. These along with Scripture provide the measure by which to pattern current Christian beliefs and practices. Tradition further helps us to interpret problematic portions of the biblical text and to protect us from extreme or unhealthy applications of the faith.

Reason played a vital role in Anglican tradition as the mediator between competing theological methods that appealed primarily either to church tradition or to Scripture. As mediator, reason served to integrate Scripture and tradition into a more holistic, relevant understanding of the Christian faith. Wesley totally agreed with this orientation in Christianity as reasonable and credible in the progressively secular age of the Enlightenment. Within this Anglican tradition he felt the ministerial call to work toward the preservation or renewal of that vital, spiritual core of piety that characterized the essence of *true* Christianity throughout the ages.

The appeal to experience, broadly conceived, fit logically into Wesley's theological and philosophical worldview. On the one hand, it seemed the obvious thing to do, namely, to appeal explicitly to the historical Christian experience of salvation: "new birth" through repentance and justification, the indwelling of the Holy Spirit, and the observable fact of sanctified living. On the other hand, Wesley intentionally included experience in his theological method so as to prevent Christians — Methodists in particular — from succumbing to the recurring rationalistic and formalistic kind of religion that quenched the vitality of the Holy Spirit in a believer's life. Above all else, Wesley sought to provide a mediating view of Christianity that avoids the extremes of mystic enthusiasm or antinomianism on the one side and dead orthodoxy that suppresses the true "heart–religion" on the other.

In seeking this holistic dimension of religious faith, Wesley's emphasis on experience ushered in a new era in theological method. Although he may not have understood the full implications of his methodology, he altered and enriched the categories for approaching the task of theology. Like Pietism on the Continent, Wesley recognized that no theology should be categorized or systematized in a way that leaves out the authenticating and animating dimension that religious experience contributes to our understanding of doctrine and the Christian life. The importance of believers' religious experiences could no longer be tacitly assumed for the individual or for theological method. Because Wesley's own theological consciousness had changed at Aldersgate, he irrevocably introduced experience into the realm of theological method in the consciousness of eighteenth–century England and of future theologians.[71]

In so doing, Wesley anticipated the nineteenth–century turn toward experience as the foundation and eventually the primary source of religious authority for Christian theology. Of course, he did not have a direct influence on the development of liberal Protestant thinking, for he was too conservative — too biblical — to affect such a shift.[72] But historians and theologians alike, in the words of Umphrey Lee, "have long recognized that Wesley and Methodism, taken in its broadest sense, contributed to the breaking up of the old orthodoxy and of eighteenth–century rationalism."[73] Others such as George Cell claim that no one more than Wesley brought the subjective factor to bear on one's interpretation of Scripture and formulation of Christian thought.[74]

Yet Wesley, had he foreseen the theological direction of nineteenth–century liberal Protestantism, would have repudiated its willingness to go to extremes on religious experience. In seeking to bring balance to the "knowledge and vital piety" of Christianity, Wesley would have called for a return to biblical religion and, with it, a more catholic understanding effected by the integration of the complementary religious authorities of tradition, reason, and experience. Scripture must always remain the primary religious authority, which is a fact modern Wesleyan scholars sometimes forget as they reduce all aspects of the Wesleyan quadrilateral to sources of equal authority. Nevertheless, Wesley bequeathed a general framework of theological method and religious authority that continues to provide insight for contemporary approaches to the subject.

Wesley's work remains relevant because, on the one hand, he sought to retain a historically conceived and spiritually vital core of biblical beliefs, and on the other hand, he did not fear to introduce extrabiblical sources of religious authority in the attempt to discern "the true, the scriptural, experimental religion."

# 8

# Conclusion:
# Wesley and Evangelicalism

The eighteenth century was a watershed in Western intellectual history. During the burgeoning Enlightenment era, John Wesley responded to the need for Christians to affirm Scripture and classical orthodoxy. He had the privilege and burden of living at a transitional time when Christians needed to present anew their beliefs and life experiences in Jesus Christ. Rather than return to Scripture alone or to the creeds and confessions of the Reformation, Wesley reconceived historic Christianity in light of Enlightenment thinking. The result of his theological work involved more of an approach to Christianity than a completed system. But his approach succeeded in the eighteenth century in terms of both theological method and spiritual renewal.

Because Wesley refused to allow particular philosophies or theological systems to dictate his thinking, his writings continue to offer insights to those who wish to approach Scripture and classical orthodoxy in the most relevant and compelling way possible.

Throughout his writings Wesley was aware of the immanent work of the Holy Spirit in the people's lives and in the task of theology. Questions of authority were living and dynamic because of the presence and ultimate authority of the Holy Spirit in the believer's life and theology. For this reason Albert Outler emphasizes the theme of *participation* in Wesley's theology.

> Thus, we can see in Wesley a distinctive theological *method*, with Scripture as its pre-eminent norm but interfaced with tradition, reason and Christian experience as dynamic and interactive aids in the interpretation of the Word of God in Scripture. Such method takes it for granted that faith is human re-action to an antecedent action of the Holy Spirit's prevenience, aimed at convicting our consciences and opening our eyes and ears to God's address to us in Scripture.[1]

Given the need for divine guidance in the task of theology, Wesley approached Scripture, tradition, reason, and experience as interdependent sources of religious authority. Although they would not fit into a neat theological system, they did hold together in a correlative structure that served to meet the ministerial and. theological needs of his day.

Amid a rising, tide of biblical criticism by deists, Wesley affirmed the inspiration and primary religious authority of Scripture as authenticated by the inner testimony of the Holy Spirit. He affirmed Scripture without reacting wholesale to contemporary criticisms of it. Instead he sought to have dialogue with critics. He tried to understand, appreciate, and use the best of their works without doing injustice to the gospel message of salvation. The authority and trustworthiness of Scripture remained intact, though Wesley recognized an increasing need for the critical study of the Word. His appeals to tradition, reason, and experience serve to complete a circle of hermeneutics that begins and ends with Scripture.

Wesley demonstrated a broad knowledge of historic Christianity, both East and West, which few of his contemporaries shared. He looked to classical orthodoxy as a source of religious authority that genuinely complements our knowledge of biblical truths. *Sola Scriptura* remains sufficient for salvation. But Christian tradition serves as a supplemental resource for the theological and ministerial needs of contemporary Christians.

Wesley did not confine his theology and ministry to the Reformation tradition alone. On the contrary, he freely appropriated knowledge from Roman Catholic; Eastern Orthodox, and other Christian traditions. Such traditions offered valuable insights for distilling the content and vitality of the one true tradition of scriptural religion. His catholic spirit toward diverse traditions made him suspect among many of his contemporaries and among some evangelicals today. But his inclusive, universal approach continues to make his theology relevant to our time.

The appeal to reason as a genuine source of religious authority was well established in Anglican thinking before the time of Wesley. Wesley saw no cause to fear the use of reason and the discipline of logic. He affirmed the popular belief in the reasonableness of Christianity. He did not expect reason to confute anything found in Scripture, so he did not hesitate to regard reason as a safeguard to Christian faith.

However, Wesley did not employ reason uncritically, nor did he sympathize with theological systems that were heavily influenced by rationalistic methodologies.[2] He considered reason to have limitations, particularly in its epistemological power. But reason serves as a tool or means for reflecting on theology and the Christian life, so our faith should be compatible with good reason or logic. The content of our faith does not begin with reason; it confirms and complements the thoughts and experiences of Christians. Thus Wesley affirmed reason an essential part of his methodological approach to theology.

Wesley's appeals to experience represent his best known and most controversial contribution to theological investigation. The experiential, or experimental, dimension of his theology primarily pertained to the experience of God's Holy Spirit in the life of believers. Christians have the privilege of experiencing the forgiveness, love, and presence of the divine. Subsequent experiences of a changed life and attitudes represent assurances of salvation.

But Wesley's confidence in experience extended beyond the experience of the divine. He did not disparage a difference between experiences of the objective reality of God and concomitant experiences of subjective feelings, emotions, and thoughts. So he took the liberty of appealing to empirically observable experiences in order to confirm, illustrate, and sometimes redefine Christian beliefs. Although, for him, experience never provided the source of doctrine, it played an inescapable role in the discipline of theology.

In introducing experience as a source of religious authority, Wesley did not see himself doing something innovative in the history of Christian thought. He considered experience a self–evident and essential aspect of true, scriptural religion. But he included experience explicitly, whereas before it had been only a tacit part of theological endeavors. In making experience a source of religious authority, he anticipated a germinal shift in the development of theological method. Unlike Wesley, many theologians coming after him were unable to hold experience in tension with Scripture and classical orthodoxy. But as an enduring example of evangelical theology with an emphasis on a personal relationship with God, Wesley maintained a healthy and orthodox relationship between experience and the primacy of scriptural authority.

The interplay between these various sources of religious authority have come to be known as "the Wesleyan quadrilateral." The term is more of a shorthand reference to their interdependent relationship than to a well–developed or defined statement of Wesley's concept of theological method and religious authority. But the quadrilateral serves as a helpful model or tool for investigating the complexity and dynamic of Wesley's approach to theology.

Unfortunately, there has been more understanding and appreciation of Wesley's theological method outside evangelical traditions than within them. The catholicity of his thought has especially appealed to contemporary Christians who wish to approach their hermeneutics and theology in a way that transcends denominational history. Scripture alone, tradition alone, reason alone, or experience alone does not satisfy contemporary demands for understanding the comprehensiveness and relevance of the Christian faith. Even holding two or three of these components in combination does not satisfy the need for a more catholic or universal treatment of both the content and the vitality of Christianity. The model of the Wesleyan quadrilateral seeks to satisfy the need for greater evangelical catholicity in theology.

The Wesleyan quadrilateral is not a perfect model or paradigm. Few models or paradigms are. But it begins to answer some of the challenging questions of theological method and religious authority faced by contemporary Christians. This is particularly true among evangelicals, with whom Wesley is akin both spiritually and intellectually.

Contemporary evangelicalism faces a number of challenges to its existence, not the least of which is its self–identity. Certainly evangelicalism is becoming progressively diverse socially and culturally as well as theologically. In its identity as well as its theology, evangelicalism must adapt to encompass the diversity of individuals, churches, and theologies that call themselves evangelical. There are those within evangelicalism who wish to restrict the number of others who may refer to themselves as such, on theological, historical, or experiential grounds. But for the most part, evangelicals are recognizing the growing need to become united amid a healthy diversity.

Wesley provides a number of ways in which to hold in tension the perennial dilemma of maintaining a recognizable sense of evangelical unity in the midst of theological diversity. His catholic spirit offers a practical basis for becoming more inclusive of beliefs not essential to historic Christianity. Theologically his quadrilateral understanding of Scripture, tradition, reason, and experience provides a conceptual basis for incorporating all historic authority claimants according to priorities and functions assigned to them by a distinctly evangelical perspective. As a model of evangelical theology, the Wesleyan quadrilateral offers an enduring method by which to represent Scripture and classical orthodoxy in the most relevant and compelling way possible. It seeks to be contemporary methodologically, comprehensive in its approach (though not as a system), and inclusive of evangelical concerns that extend beyond mere doctrine.

In this final chapter we will discuss how the Wesleyan quadrilateral may serve as a contemporary model of evangelical theology.

## The Wesleyan Quadrilateral

No one uses a single religious authority, and evangelicals are no exception. One of the basic beliefs of evangelicalism is the primacy of scriptural authority, but primacy does not mean exclusivity. *Sola Scriptura* has long been held up as a faithful model of evangelical theology. Yet it does not deny the usefulness of other sources of religious authority.

For example, Richard Muller notes that *"sola Scriptura* was never meant as a denial of the usefulness of the Christian tradition as a subordinate norm in theology."[3] He states that the Reformers and the Protestant orthodox held Scripture as the absolute and therefore prior norm, but allowed tradition a derivative and important secondary role in doctrinal statements.

Muller's observation serves to free evangelicals from any biblicism that rejects insight from resources other than Scripture. But it does not go far enough. It does not satisfy the growing concerns of many evangelicals for greater catholicity in such matters as biblical hermeneutics, theological formulations, and cooperation in ministry. Evangelical theology needs to have a dynamic sense of the interdependent sources of religious authority. It is naive and critically suspect to think otherwise.

Evangelical theology needs to begin by becoming more explicit in recognizing the variety of resources from which it draws in its biblical and theological studies. Several evangelical authors already recognize this need for theological catholicity; it appears in their calls for greater induction, integration, contextualization, contemporization, and so on. The question does not involve which sources of religious authority one uses. It involves the interplay one allows them to have and the degree of recognition permitted in the task of theology. Analysts of evangelicalism such as Gabriel Fackre readily recognize this fact, for example, in hermeneutics. Fackre says,

> Every evangelical hermeneutic, functionally if not formally, finds some place in its authority structure for church and world. . . . These hidden operations argue for a more self–conscious, and therefore more critical, appreciation of ecclesial and secular factors in hermeneutical theory and practice.[4]

We do not need to read far in evangelical literature to discover a growing concern for catholicity. Evangelical catholicity is a major theme in the various writings of Donald G. Bloesch, wherein he seeks to present a "catholic evangelicalism" or "evangelical catholicism."[5] Millard Erickson spends the first 150 pages in *Christian Theology* emphasizing the need for greater evangelical consensus on theological method, the relationship between theology and philosophy, the critical study of Scripture, contemporizing the Christian message, and the use of theological language.[6]

Evangelicals need to conceptualize their theological method in a way that explicitly recognizes the interplay between the various sources of religious authority that it uses. The Wesleyan quadrilateral provides one attempt to produce greater self–consciousness and thus greater criticalness and appreciation for the complexity of doing theology.

Wesley does not have the final word for refining theological method, but he represents one historic model firmly grounded in the evangelical tradition. The historicity of the Wesleyan quadrilateral gives it credibility. Some contemporary attempts at theological catholicity among evangelicals have appeared out of a concern for defending the faith. (Even in his commendable attempt to facilitate "evangelical–catholic unity," Bloesch admits that his theology "will necessarily have a polemical ring.")[7] Rather than positively stating the beliefs and life experiences of evangelicalism, these theologians have often been preoccupied with responding to actual or perceived threats to the existence of evangelical theology. This has tended to limit the appeal of their thought to relatively modern concerns — for example, biblical inerrancy, "the second blessing," or the millennial reign of Jesus Christ on earth.

Such concerns are important, but their newness precludes them from the kind of historic respect afforded more established approaches to Scripture and classical orthodoxy. The Wesleyan quadrilateral possesses that historical precedent. Although Wesley had to defend his faith (often among fellow Christians), it was not his theological method that he had to defend.

The quadrilateral also has a contemporary relevance due to its emergence in the Enlightenment era, which continues to exert its intellectual force today. The Enlightenment has often misdirected evangelicals toward concerns more relevant to modern science and philosophy than biblical theology; yet evangelicalism requires a method of theology readily capable of dialogue with Enlightenment and modern issues.

Let us summarize the benefits that our historic understanding of the Wesleyan quadrilateral offers to contemporary evangelicals. We will do so by reviewing the distinctive characteristics of the quadrilateral.

## Catholicity

The earliest understanding of *catholicity* in church history was universality. Wesley had this meaning in mind in his sermon "Catholic Spirit" when he emphasized the need for universal love among Christians.[8] The sermon has several levels of meaning for catholicity: love as the highest Christian virtue, tolerance of theological opinions among Christians, and so on. But Wesley implies in the sermon and makes explicit in other writings a more pervasive catholicity or universality. Three aspects of catholicity are relevant to theological method and religious authority.

### Theological Catholicity

Wesley sought to incorporate all historic claimants to authority into his approach to theology and therefore identified tradition, reason, and experience as sources of religious authority complementary to Scripture, which has primacy. Wesley did not consider himself an innovator in theological method. In coining the term "quadrilateral," Outler states,

> The "quadrilateral" requires of a theologian no more than what he or she might reasonably be held accountable for: which is to say, a familiarity with Scripture that is both critical and faithful; plus, an acquaintance with the wisdom of the Christian past; plus, a taste for logical analysis as something more than a debater's weapon; plus, a vital, inward faith that is upheld by the assurance of grace and its prospective triumphs, *in this life.*[9]

Outler points out what he considers germinal in Wesley's theology. Christians need to broaden their understanding of the valid sources of religious authority and to learn how to integrate rather than isolate them. They at least need to make explicit — as Wesley did — what they already do implicitly. To do otherwise is to make theology incompatible with learned inquiry. Wesley strongly believed that Christians need to have intellectual integrity about what they believe, and that integrity includes a more self–conscious and therefore critical integration of all historic claims to authority.

Of course, Wesley was convinced of the ultimate reasonableness of Christianity. He saw that in this life, Christians are unable to substantiate their worldview intellectually more than any other. He understood that every worldview is dependent on certain faith assumptions, beliefs, and presuppositions. But he felt we can make an excellent case for Christianity being as reasonable as any other worldview. In fact, with the confirming witness of the Holy Spirit, Wesley considered the truths of Scripture and classical orthodoxy eminently convincing.

### Practical Catholicity

Another aspect of Wesley's catholic spirit is the practical dimension of his thought. Wesley desired that both his theology and his ministry should be relevant to the needs of people both inside and outside the church. He was willing to test his theological ideas in the crucible of daily life. Experience is not the substance of true religion, but it lends itself to analysis and development. On this basis Wesley could be as inductively studious of experience as of Scripture. He opposed any biblicism or traditionalism that was irrelevant to the greater needs of individuals *and* of the society in which we live. His characteristic attentiveness to insights from Scripture, tradition, reason, and experience repeatedly brought into focus the need for practical participation in social concerns.

Today this participation requires an expanded sensitivity and involvement in matters of ethics, justice, and peace that are social as well as personal. He was concerned as much for the spiritual and moral well being of society as for the spiritual and moral well being of individuals. These concerns touched a wide range of human needs. Experience alone as a source of religious authority did not arouse such sensitivities in Wesley. But experience as a necessary corollary to Scripture, tradition, and reason served to complete the holistic perspective and applicability of his theology.

*Ecumenical Catholicity*

Wesley's openness to a variety of sources of religious authority reflects an ecumenical extension of his catholic spirit. He often distinguished between the essentials of Christian belief and mere theological opinions. From his perspective, the essentials should be held to a minimum, primarily reflecting doctrinal summaries of Scripture found in Christian antiquity.

His willingness to bring Scripture into relationship with tradition, reason, and experience relieved Wesley of the dangers of an absolutism resistant to a healthy pluralism. A genuinely catholic theology demanded liberty in organizing one's beliefs and in applying those beliefs in ministry. Wesley saw a number of ways for Christians to become more united, not the least of was common religious experience. But the clue to understanding Wesley's ecumenicity is his regard for Christian antiquity as a source of Christian truth second only to Scripture.

To Wesley, creeds and confessions from the divided church represent divided beliefs. Such beliefs are helpful to particular groups, but they should not be made essential for Christian unity; they serve to divide rather than unite those seeking to proclaim the gospel of Jesus Christ. With this conviction Wesley could associate and minister with those from the Reformed tradition such as George Whitefield, whose views of double predestination Wesley strongly rejected. Wesley also approached Roman Catholics in an ecumenical interest to base cooperation in ministry on essential areas of agreement rather than areas of disagreement, which would inhibit.

Christian antiquity offers a minimum of beliefs, particularly as stated in the ecumenical creeds, on which to begin cooperation — cooperation that should unify efforts in mission and could unify more as we learn to work with rather than against one another.

## Emphasis on Approach to Theology

The Wesleyan quadrilateral represents a model or approach for reflecting on and formulating theology rather than a completed system of theology. Wesley

would have considered it a benefit rather than a liability not to have constructed a systematic theology. Doing theology is an ongoing process. Theological
conclusions should be developed, but held tentatively. They must be left open
to the leading of the Holy Spirit, to reformulation in light of new insights or
experiences, and to reevaluation in the face of ever new and complex questions
asked by a progressively secular society.

This attitude puts great emphasis on the responsibility of individual believers and groups of believers in hermeneutical and theological discourse. But contemporary Christians cannot become dependent on external sources of religious authority that do not personally involve them in the knowing process.
Formal theological systems tend to diminish our ability to understand the complexity of our world and make our life experiences relevant to our beliefs. By
contrast, the Wesleyan quadrilateral offers a model capable of dealing with new
and complex problems that confront Christians. The cumulation of theological
insights provides a pool of knowledge from which we may profitably draw at
any time, a resource that continually requires faithful scrutiny and reaffirmation.

The ongoing need for Christians to respond theologically to questions and
life experiences should deter us from becoming prematurely set in our doctrinal beliefs.

## Paradigmatic Character

Wesley did not fully define his approach to theology, but the force of his
fourfold guidelines made their presence apparent throughout his writings. He
functioned in a gestalt–like understanding of the dynamic interplay between
Scripture, tradition, reason, and experience. That gestalt does not readily lend
itself to exhaustive analysis, which would delineate each particular presupposition and rule of his theological method. Nor would Wesley want to limit the
vital interplay between the four sources of religious authority. Consequently the
quadrilateral serves best as a model or paradigm for theology. A full set of rules
need not exist for such a paradigm to succeed. Consensus in understanding a
paradigm is not absolutely necessary; the paradigm may represent a contested
concept among those who use it.

The quadrilateral as a paradigm sets the parameters of religious authority in
theological studies, namely, the primary authority of Scripture with the complementary sources of tradition, reason, and experience. Thus the quadrilateral can
embrace several overlapping traditions of theology without being coextensive.

## Simplicity

A great benefit of *sola Scriptura* is the sheer simplicity of its formulation as a
model of theology. "Scripture alone!" became the heart cry of Reformers seeking to extricate themselves from the magisterium of the Roman Catholic
Church and return to a more pristine and reliable source of religious authority.
Today evangelicalism remains firmly ensconced in the tradition of *sola Scriptura,*
but with the increasing need to become more self–conscious — and therefore

more critical — in its appreciation of ecclesial and other factors in hermeneutical and theological endeavors.

The quadrilateral communicates simply and clearly that more than one source of religious authority is at work in the task of theology. It further expresses the need for a more comprehensive and integrative approach. The ease of referring to the quadrilateral enhances its desirability as a model of evangelical theology. But the simplicity of reference does not negate the quadrilateral's complexity and relevance for contemporary evangelicals. Outler suggests, "This complex method, with its fourfold reference, is a good deal more sophisticated than it appears, and could be more fruitful for contemporary theologizing than has yet been realized."[10] He supports this idea by showing how Wesley preserved the primacy of scriptural authority, profited from the wisdom of tradition, interacted with the disciplines of critical reason, and stressed the Christian experience of grace with all its existential force.

## Experimental Emphasis

Wesley's concern for heart–religion should be considered as critical to Christians as his method of approaching theology. The two are inseparable. Wesley was always concerned about allowing the witness of the Holy Spirit to have free reign in the hearts and minds of believers. This divine presence represents chiefly the experiential dimension of his thought.

The presence of the Holy Spirit encouraged Wesley not to fret over the lack of a well–defined system of beliefs. He believed that the Holy Spirit leads us to all truth, beginning but not ending with the truth of salvation. Thus Wesley's intention was always to hold in tension the content of classical orthodoxy and the vitality of a personal relationship with Jesus Christ.

Wesley was continually running into misunderstandings, and it puzzled him greatly that people could not grasp the paradox inherent in the Holy Spirit's work in believers' lives. That is, although we may not be able to explain every aspect of Christian faith, we know enough to provide a reasonable account of what we believe. Opponents rejected experience as a genuine source of religious authority without realizing the paradoxical understanding Wesley had in view. Wesley would perhaps have benefited from later developments in the concept of paradox, which hold that theological statements appearing on the surface to be absurd or even self–contradictory are nevertheless true or may be true in experience.

The existential aspect of faith was as important to Wesley as the intellectual substratum of faith. He considered both planes of investigation essential to doctrinal considerations. The doctrinal content and spiritual vitality of Christianity must always be held in tension.

## Classical Orthodoxy

Wesley stressed that his theology faithfully represented both Scripture and classical orthodoxy. The two are complementary resources for Christian faith and practice. Wesley considered Scripture sufficient for salvation, but perceived that Scripture does not touch explicitly on every theological and ministerial need of the church. For that reason he turned to classical Christian orthodoxy, particularly the early ecumenical creeds and the patristic writings of the Western and Eastern churches. For him, these provided substance for Christian faith and practice second only to Scripture.

Wesley understood classical orthodoxy as affirming the primacy of scriptural authority, so he expected all true Christian tradition to align with Scripture. In addition, he was open to learning from a variety of Christian traditions, believing that they all help to confirm, illuminate, and apply classical orthodoxy. But in his mind there remained only one authentic, living tradition of Christian belief and practice, and it was this concept Wesley primarily intended in his references to tradition. Sometimes he referred to it as "the primitive church" or "Christian antiquity." Whatever he called it, he believed that classical orthodoxy was the second most important source of Christian truth. Were Wesley living and writing today, would he not very likely pass over more recent statements of faith in favor of the ancient creeds affirmed by the undivided church?

## Historical Precedence

We have already suggested that the historical precedence of Wesley's model of theology gives it an enduring quality and a sense of long–term value that makes it more appealing than contemporary evangelical attempts to achieve a more catholic approach to theology — as impressive as some of those attempts are. The quadrilateral's positive approach to restating Christianity in the context of the Enlightenment gives it a universal air free of a defensive or apologetical agenda. To be sure, Wesley had to defend his beliefs before both Christian and secular critics. But he was not criticized for the catholicity of his approach to theology.

The theological and revivalistic success of the Wesleyan quadrilateral in the eighteenth century, coupled with its proven relevance to evangelicals in the subsequent Wesleyan, Holiness, Keswick, and Pentecostal movements, demonstrates its durability in the evangelical tradition. Rather than seeking to devise something innovative or new, evangelicals should appropriate the rich theological tradition that extends back through the Protestant Reformation. In the past, evangelicals have tended to remain within their respective movements, rarely acknowledging or appreciating insights offered by other professed evangelicals. This is as true among the Wesleyan, Holiness, Keswick, and Pentecostal movements as among the Lutherans, Reformed, Anabaptists, and Baptists.

The Wesleyan quadrilateral is part of this greater evangelical tradition. Wesley avoided anything he considered unreasonable or precritical for his theology. Instead his theology was constantly reforming — a Reformation ideal — to meet the new and complex questions of a progressively secular society. Even today we cannot take wholesale Wesley's historic understanding of Scripture, tradition, reason, and experience. It anticipates continual rethinking and reapplication so that it will function with as much relevance and success tomorrow as if did in the eighteenth century.

## Religious Authority

To complete this discussion of the Wesleyan quadrilateral, we need to see some of its implications for an evangelical understanding of the different sources of religious authority. The four components have already been examined at some length, so here we will only suggest additional ways by which the quadrilateral can enhance our understanding. The implications and relative importance of each component depend on a person's own religious history. But the quadrilateral has much to offer as a model for those who seek evangelical catholicity.

In the quadrilateral, all the historical claimants to authority — Scripture, tradition, reason, and experience — function interdependently according to priorities and roles assigned to them by an evangelical doctrine of revelation. No single source of religious authority alone is sufficient, but each one may have distinctive implications and relevance within the framework of the quadrilateral.

### Scripture

Neither Wesley nor the quadrilateral controverts the primacy of scriptural authority. Those who use the Wesleyan quadrilateral to diminish the primary authority of Scripture misinterpret Wesley's belief and Outler's intention in coining the term "quadrilateral." But while Scripture is viewed as primary, it should not be considered exclusive. Such an understanding would be inappropriate for Wesley as well as for Christian antiquity and the Protestant Reformation.

Through the centuries Christians have progressively come to an awareness of the variety of religious authorities at play in their hermeneutical and theological work. Some traditions have been willing to recognize those sources of religious authority as genuine and necessary to their theology. Wesley merely made explicit what had developed implicitly in Christian theological method, defining tradition, reason, and experience as correlatives to the primary religious authority of Scripture. In this he achieved a more genuinely integrative approach to theology.

Wesley's theology developed in the context of the evangelical principles of *sola gratia*, *sola fide*, and *sola Scriptura*. He affirmed the intent of these principles, but felt their authoritativeness had been overstated as a response to the late medieval abuses of Roman Catholic authority. Wesley regarded them as primary, but not exclusive, as Outler readily attests:

> The great Protestant watchwords of *sola fide* and *sola Scriptura* were also fundamentals in Wesley's doctrine of authority. But early and late, he interpreted *solus* to mean "primarily" rather than "solely" or "exclusively."[11]

Without denying the evangelical principles of the Protestant Reformation, Wesley modified them in a way that could account for a broader perspective on religious authority.

Wesley affirmed the inspiration and authority of Scripture, but he did not address questions of inerrancy that have received so much attention in our day. It is still a matter of debate where Wesley would have hung his hat on these issues, just as it is regarding Luther and Calvin. Because these men lived in an earlier age, a degree of reserve is required as to how we should interpret them. But it is at least true that the epistemological concerns of Wesley were not those of modern fundamentalism. Larry Shelton comments,

> That Wesley does not function as a Fundamentalist is evidenced by his empha-
> sis on the saving purpose of Scripture, its sacramental function, the *testimonium*
> and reliability as canons for authority, and his attitude of catholicity. Therefore,
> his use of Scripture should not be analyzed by the means of Fundamentalist
> canons, but by the canons of Classical Christian orthodoxy.[12]

The Wesleyan quadrilateral should not be understood as advocating biblical inerrancy. Instead Wesley probably would have found himself agreeing with Donald Bloesch, who said, "We do not deny the element of biblical truth in all these doctrines [including biblical inerrancy], but in and of themselves they can-not be considered evangelical essentials."[13] In keeping with his catholic spirit, Wesley undoubtedly would have considered inerrancy a theological opinion, not an essential. It would not constitute something worthy of preventing evan-gelical brothers and sisters from fellowship with one another and from joining in cooperative ventures in ministry. In this same catholic spirit, Wesley undoubt-edly would have sought to incorporate the best insights from inerrantists and infallibilists. His inclusive approach would have sought to understand, appreci-ate, and employ contributions available from all who wish to uphold Scripture and historic orthodoxy.

Wesley did not contribute anything particularly innovative in the way of bib-lical hermeneutics. His approach was generally inductive, historical–literal, and soteriologically motivated, like the Protestant tradition that preceded him. Thus Wesley was not a slavish literalist. He was open to textual criticism and occa-sionally resorted to allegory in order to interpret problematical texts. Most important, Wesley interpreted Scripture in the setting of tradition, reason, and experience. Scripture remained the source of religious authority based on its unique inspiration. But tradition was an authoritative resource of interpreting Scripture; reason was the means by which to reach logical conclusions; and experience represented Wesley's belief in the illumination of the Holy Spirit in both the authors and the readers of Scripture.

The interplay between Scripture, tradition; reason, and experience deterred Wesley from a static and mechanical literalism, while the affirmation of the pri-macy of scriptural authority prevented unfaithful and capricious renditions of classical orthodox theology. Despite his theological tolerance, Wesley recog-nized the limitations of theological pluralism. From his perspective, Scripture remained the epistemological safeguard against placing virtue in pluralism for its own sake.[14]

## Tradition

Even with the uniqueness of his integration of experience into theological method, Wesley's emphasis on classical Christian orthodoxy may represent his most important contribution to contemporary evangelicalism. Since the Reformation, Protestants have been unable to develop a consistent theory of tradition that includes the diversity of historic attempts to be faithful to the most ancient tradition of Scripture and Christian antiquity. Too often "tradition" goes back no further than Luther, with the exception of a few church fathers who are included as much for their popularity among the Reformers as for their popularity today.

The lack of a theory of tradition becomes especially poignant among contemporary evangelical Christians. Evangelicals begin with Luther or Calvin and then retreat to their own nineteenth–century backgrounds, where most of their sense of tradition is still located. All too often the primary focus of church tradition reflects the concerns of the Enlightenment and modern eras rather than classical orthodoxy. For many, the fundamentalist–modernist controversy continues to set the basic criteria for what it means to be "truly evangelical." And so the historic criteria of Christian antiquity and the ecumenical councils of the undivided church are forgotten. In addition, contemporary Christians unwilling to use criteria of tradition from the past two centuries are sometimes ignored or ostracized by so–called evangelicals despite the commitment of the former to the more historically orthodox beliefs!

Certainly the theological issues of the past two centuries are immensely important. But they cannot form the criteria for historic evangelicalism. Those criteria require a more historic, catholic understanding of Scripture and classical orthodoxy.

Wesley deemed the content of Christian antiquity particularly important. This is because Christian antiquity contributed real substance to the verification of revelation in the canonical New Testament. As to the content of classical orthodoxy, Wesley allowed the ecumenical creeds to summarize Christian beliefs rather than the confessions and creeds of the Reformation. He often appealed to the Anglican articles of religion, but only to the extent that he believed they reflected Scripture and classical orthodoxy. Wesley could be as critical of Anglicanism as he was complimentary. But his hope was to preserve the integrity of the teachings of Christian antiquity. He believed that the Holy Spirit inspired (though not in the same way as Scripture) the early ecumenical decisions of the Christian church. He also trusted that the Holy Spirit continues to abide in the church and preveniently leads and preserves true believers into truth.

Rather than systematic theologies that often contribute little more than commentary on classical orthodoxy, perhaps what evangelicals need most is ancient church doctrine as the core of their beliefs. Most evangelicals affirm the historic creeds in theory, but in practice allow other doctrinal summaries to take precedence. Generally evangelicals see church tradition as an imperfect commentary on Scripture that is helpful only when it properly interprets Scripture – that is, in the way they themselves interpret it. Instead they should be wrestling with Christian antiquity as an indispensable resource for evangelical self–identity.

Some contemporary evangelicals are trying to correct the impoverishment of having ignored the work of the Holy Spirit in the ancient church. For example, Thomas Oden in his *Systematic Theology* proposes "to set forth an ordered view of the faith of the Christian community upon which there has generally been substantial agreement between the traditions of East and West, including Catholic, Protestant, and Orthodox."[15] Oden refers to Irenæus, Origen, Chrysostom, and Aquinas as often as he does to Luther, Calvin, Wesley, and Barth. Likewise, John J. Davis in *Foundations of Evangelical Theology* defines evangelical theology as "systematic reflection on Scripture and tradition and the mission of the church in mutual relation, with Scripture as the norm."[16]

Wesley embraced those who affirmed the essentials of Scripture and classical orthodoxy. He did not quibble over what for the most part he considered to be mere differences of theological opinion. This attitude reflects the "catholic spirit" of which he wrote. He did not condone doctrinal compromise. He did not condone unchecked latitudinarianism, or what we would today call pluralism. But he considered an inclusive spirit of toleration a more constructive alternative to the kind of sectarianism that prevented unity of Christian mission and fellowship. Wesley sought to include rather than exclude those who wished to be a part of the Evangelical Revival of eighteenth–century England. Consequently he was open to a broader–based conception of evangelicalism that transcended the theological opinions of his day.

Today evangelicals need to incorporate a greater sense of catholicity in their relationship with one another as well as in their theology. Bloesch rightly points out that "the Reformers themselves sought a theology that would be at the same time Evangelical and Catholic."[17] Only in recent years has American evangelicalism come to recognize, happily or unhappily, its own diversity. People from the Wesleyan, Holiness, Keswick, and Pentecostal movements have played a greater role in American evangelicalism than has often been recognized or acknowledged.[18] These branches of evangelicalism need to become incorporated in a way that enriches and strengthens evangelicalism as a whole. Wesley's catholic spirit contributes to this associative process, as does his method of theology as found in the Wesleyan quadrilateral.

In Outler's words, "Wesley's complex way of theologizing has the ecumenical advantage of making fruitful linkages with other doctrinal traditions without threatening to supplant any of them and without fear of forfeiting its own identity."[19]

## Reason

From Wesley's theological perspective, reason is instrumental by nature. It does not contribute substance to any theological discussion, but it rightly orders revelation. Wesley actually made no distinctive contribution in his use of reason and logic. What he did was to incorporate into theology some intellectual developments of the Enlightenment era, attempting to maintain a healthy tension between concerns of the various theologies and philosophies. He was unconcerned with intellectual worldviews that only reflected the traditions of Platonic or Aristotelian approaches to theology; he did not seek Platonic ideals divorced from experience, nor trace all things back through an Aristotelian system of causes and effects. He did, however, tend to be more empirically oriented, concentrating on what works as much as on what is true.

In particular, Wesley's emphasis on experience — including the experience of a personal relationship with God — communicates a strong relational dimension to his epistemological thought. He considered this relational aspect present in Scripture and the early church, though it had eroded over centuries of rationalistic theologies more concerned with the form than the vitality of true religion. Along with cultivating relationships with God and others, Wesley was concerned for personal growth that includes the rational, affective, and moral aspects of a person as well as the spiritual.

Wesley was acutely aware of various polarities in the world of reason and in everyday life. He sought to hold these in tension rather than dismiss them on the one hand or synthesize them into a philosophical or theological system on the other. For example, he believed that while our primary knowledge of God comes through the intuited presence of the Holy Spirit, there is an experiential or experimental knowledge that includes Scripture and felt religious experiences. Wesley saw the need to preserve the primary religious authority of Scripture, yet with it the need to incorporate other sources of religious authority, specifically tradition, reason, and experience.

The number of polarities that Wesley wrestled with was extensive. He often thought of himself as a *via media,* or mediating position, between them. These polarities are well summarized by William F. Abraham.

> Wesley's significance as a theologian rests fundamentally on his ability to hold together elements in the Christian tradition that generally are pulled apart and expressed in isolation. Thus he integrates contrasting emphases that are vital to a healthy and comprehensive vision of the Christian faith.
>
> Consider the following disjunctive pairs: faith, works; personal devotions, sacramental practice; personal piety, social concern; justification, sanctification; evangelism, Christian nurture; Bible, tradition; revelation, reason; commitment, civility; creation, redemption; cell group, institutional church; local scene, world parish. Very few in the history of the church have been able to live so well with the tensions such partners generate; Wesley was certainly one of these few. For this reason alone, he deserves to be read and pondered.[20]

Wesley did not try to resolve these polarities or resort to compromise. He was willing to hold them in tension, believing that the appropriate balance shifted depending on the times and the particular needs of people. The Wesleyan quadrilateral serves to hold together the paradoxical aspects of Christian living in the healthiest and most productive way. In a spirit reflective of Wesley's theology, Outler writes, "The ruling premise throughout is my conviction that every thoughtful Christian must accept responsibility for the overcoming of polarities without compromise, for affirming pluralism without drifting into indifferentism, for learning to live in the Scripture, the Christian past, and modern world all at once."[21]

Evangelicals need to become less concerned with rational system–building or system–maintaining, and more concerned with a theological approach that allows an inevitable diversity of opinions. System–building is not found in Scripture or Christian antiquity. It did not occur in Eastern Orthodoxy either, but rather developed in the West with its fascination with the powers of reason:

The Reformers reordered the ecumenical creeds, but did not substantially advance their theology. This has led some scholars to believe that systematic theologies are merely lengthy catechisms, or exhaustive exercises in questions and answers. Many evangelicals still consider systematic theology both possible and necessary. Millard Erickson contends that "Each theologian must decide upon a particular theme...in approaching theology."[22] Gordon R. Lewis and Bruce A. Demarest advocate the development of "a comprehensive, noncontradictory set of convictions on topics significant for Christian life and service."[23] John Davis argues at great length for both the possibility and legitimacy of systematic theology.[24]

Other evangelicals are moving more toward the conception of theology as an ongoing process, pilgrimage, or art. Donald Bloesch states, "Evangelical theology is a *theologia viatorum* (a theology of wayfarers), not a *theologia comprehensorum* (a theology of those who have arrived conceptually)."[25]

The Wesleyan quadrilateral does not emphasize the quality of the end product so much as the quality of approach or the means to achieve the end product. From Wesley's perspective, theology involved more of a means of addressing religious issues than a part of the end — an intricate, systematic whole. Wholeness came through process rather than completion. The quadrilateral may have dogmatic (positive) and apologetic (negative) functions, but the emphasis tends to land less on the doctrinal aspects than on living faith.

## Experience

Wesley considered the analysis and integration of experience in relationship to true religion a necessary theological enterprise. He also regarded the inward witness of the Holy Spirit as the strongest proof of Christianity. As a result, he explicitly included experience with tradition and reason as sources of religious authority complementing the primacy of scriptural authority. He saw a personal, experiential dimension in all knowing processes. In particular he felt that theology and even our interpretations of Scripture rely on a certain element of subjectivity that cannot be completely rationalized.

. Wesley also sought to hold in tension the polarities between direct apprehension of the transcendent and the rational inference in the task of theology. Too many in his day had forsaken one for the other in facile solutions to the new and complex questions of a progressively secular society. Although he never achieved complete balance between these polarities, Wesley brought the disparate epistemological concerns together in a theological method capable of being more inclusive and eclectic.

Much of contemporary Christianity has a deficient understanding of the role of experience in theology. This is as true among nonevangelical as among evangelical Christians. Evangelicals persist in becoming either phobic or fanatic in integrating experience into their theology, worship, and so on. They seem to lack a theology of experience that adequately accounts for the vitality of the Holy Spirit in the life of believers, the experiential participation of believers in the divine, the internalization of Christian truth in a believer, and the spiritual transformation of a believer.

Since the time of the Reformation, emphasis on the Holy Spirit and on the experience of the Holy Spirit in a believer's life has been neglected in many Protestant churches and left to so–called sects. Shirley Guthrie poignantly notes that in the original version of the Westminster Confession there was no chapter on "God the Spirit."[26] In a post–Pentecostal and charismatic era, it seems incredible that evangelicals such as Bloesch can write a two–volume work, *Essentials of Evangelical Theology,* without a single chapter explicitly dedicated to the doctrine of the Holy Spirit. Others admit to certain positive values of experience, but spend more time emphasizing its negative values. For example, Davis caricatures the recent evangelical resurgence in the experiential vein as dangerous for the most part when contrasted with his preeminent concern for scriptural authority.[27] Yet Christians are called beyond Scripture and classical orthodoxy to authentic experience with God, and evangelicals need to reflect more seriously upon how to integrate experience into their theology and into their lives.

The historic study of experience in theology has most often occurred in the form of natural theology. This rationalistic approach to experience has ebbed and flowed in popularity among Christians and among evangelicals in particular. But even more rationally oriented evangelicals such as Carl F. H. Henry recognize a place for religious experience. He states, "The objectivity and validity of religious experience concerns not merely the formal rational structures of consciousness, not merely man's immanent epistemological constituents, but also the sphere of metaphysical reality over and above this."[28] Colin Brown criticized natural theology, yet concluded that "it seems legitimate on the basis of both common experience and the witness of the biblical writers to speak of a revelation in nature and a natural awareness of God."[29]

Wesley's references to experience involved something distinctly different from classical natural theology. He considered experience an indispensable vivification of revelation and of insights of Scripture and tradition when judged by right reason and coherence. The kind of experience to which Wesley referred was not "religious affection," but the witness of the Holy Spirit. For Wesley, this kind of evangelical experience is utterly crucial. Abraham comments, "Without a deep encounter with the living God wherein we become aware of the things of the Spirit through the witness of the divine Spirit, we are in darkness and death."[30]

Contemporary theologians have all too often given a psychological interpretation to experience. They relate this to the Romantic tradition, which does not quite explain how Wesley understood experience. Wesley was not talking about subjective experience; he was talking about the inner witness of the Holy Spirit to heirship with Jesus Christ. That view of experience would become the distinctive thing in Wesley as over against anything in his hermeneutics or his use of reason and logic. It would also give a link with tradition, something that evangelicals seem almost unable to understand about Wesley. Experience is not ahistorical, but is inextricably linked with tradition. From Wesley's perspective, the Holy Spirit's continued life and direction in the church — which represents his meaning of tradition — is an essential extension of the witness of Scripture.

## Final Remarks

The concerns of the Wesleyan quadrilateral need to be integrated into any future conception of evangelical theology. Such concerns involve a more self–conscious and critical approach to theology that integrates all historic authority claimants, including Scripture, tradition, reason, and experience. It involves an affirmation of scriptural authority as primary, but not exclusive. It involves an affirmation of tradition that extends beyond the nineteenth century to classical orthodoxy in Christian antiquity. It involves an affirmation of rational methods of inquiry, viewing theology more as an ongoing process than a completed system. And it involves an affirmation of experience as a genuine source of religious authority.

My conclusion is that the Wesleyan quadrilateral provides a critical model of theological method that can meet the new and complex questions of the modern world. It affirms the explicit integration of all four historical components as interdependently related in the task of doing theology. The need for greater catholicity in how one approaches biblical hermeneutics and theology and in relations with other Christians is growing among evangelicals. Those who wish to pursue these goals will find in the quadrilateral invaluable insights for developing a more thoroughly catholic model of evangelical theology.

# NOTES

## Introduction
## Wesley and the Quadrilateral

1. Albert C. Outler, introduction, *Works* (Bicentennial ed.), 1:67. Cf. Albert C. Outler, "John Wesley: Folk "Theologian," *Theology Today* 34, no. 2 (1977): 150–60.

2. See Colin W. Williams, *John Wesley's Theology* (Nashville: Abingdon, 1960).

3. Randy L. Maddox, "Responsible Grace: The Systematic Nature of Wesley's Theology Reconsidered," *Wesleyan Theological Journal* 19, no. 2 (1984): 7–22. Cf. H. Ray Dunning, "Systematic Theology in a Wesleyan Mode," *Wesleyan Theological Journal* 17, no. 1 (1982): 15–22; and the Wesleyan systematic theologies developed by Richard Watson, *Theological Institutes*, 2 vols. (New York: Lane & Scott, 1851); William B. Pope, *Compendium of Christian Theology*, 3 vols., 2nd ed. (N.p.: Phillips & Hunt, 1880); and H. Orton Wiley, *Christian Theology*, 3 vols. (Kansas City: Beacon Hill, 1940).

4. See John Deschner, *Wesley's Christology* (1960; reprint, Grand Rapids: Zondervan, 1988); Kenneth J. Collins, Wesley on Salvation: A Study in the Standard Sermons (Grand Rapids: Zondervan, 1989); and Harald Lindström, *Wesley and Sanctification* (1980; reprint, Grand Rapids: Zondervan, 1983).

5. Mildred Bangs Wynkoop, *A Theology of Love* (Kansas City: Beacon Hill, 1972), 11, 15–16.

6. Ibid., 11.

7. Donald W. Dayton, "Yet Another Layer of the Onion; or, Opening the Ecumenical Door to Let the Riffraff In" (Paper delivered to the American Theological Society at Lutheran School of Theology, Chicago, 30 October 1987), 27–28.

8. Preface to the third edition, §6, *Works* (Jackson ed.), 1:iv.

9. "Principles of a Methodist," §13, *Works* (Jackson ed.), 8:365. For further examples of the quadrilateral in Wesley's writings, see chapter 2.

10. Outler, *Works* (Bicentennial ed.), 1:183n4.

11. For a discussion of these terms, see Richard A. Muller, *Dictionary of Latin and Greek Theological Terms* (Grand Rapids: Baker, 1985), 33.

12. Dayton, "Yet Another Layer," 28.

13. Use of the quadrilateral reflects an analogue model rather than a replica model. An analogue model should not be understood as a precise representation of real features being modeled. Cf. the discussion of models and religious language in Norman L. Geisler and Winfried Corduan, Philosophy of Religion, 2nd ed. (Grand Rapids: Baker, 1988), 272–91.

14. Albert C. Outler, "The Wesleyan Quadrilateral in John Wesley," *Wesleyan Theological Journal* 20, no. 1 (1985): 11.

15. Ibid., 16.

16. Because Wesley did not explicitly articulate his theological method, the attempt to investigate the particulars of Wesley's procedures proves difficult. This difficulty, however, involves more than the lack of an explicit statement. The great theorist of intellectual history Thomas B. Kuhn suggests that the historical search for rules — in individuals as well as in particular communities — is more difficult and satisfying than the search for paradigms; it is frustrating to find coherence in rules alone (see Kuhn, *The Structure of Scientific Revolutions*, 2nd ed. [Chicago: University of Chicago Press, 1970], 43–4).

A paradigm, Kuhn argues, may be identified without necessarily agreeing on or even attempting to produce a full interpretation or rationalization of it. The lack of a standard interpretation or an agreed–on set of rules will not prevent a paradigm from guiding research. In support of his thesis, Kuhn refers to the scientific philosophy of Michael Polanyi. Polanyi infers that the existence of a paradigm need not even imply that any full set of rules exists, since much of a person's success in a particular discipline depends on "tacit knowledge," that is, knowledge acquired through practice and not explicitly articulated (Kuhn, 44n1.: referring to Michael Polanyi, *Personal Knowledge* [Chicago: University of Chicago Press, 1958] esp. chaps. 5–6, pp. 69–202).

17. Muller, *Dictionary of Latin and Greek Theological Terms*, 107.

18. George Marsden, ed., *Evangelicalism and Modern America*, (Grand Rapids: Eerdmans, 1984), ix.

19. William J. Abraham, *The Coming Great Revival: Recovering the Full Evangelical Tradition* (San Francisco: Harper & Row, 1984), 72–73, using the term "essentially contested concept" introduced by W. B. Gallie, *Philosophy and the Historical Understanding* (London: Chatto and Windus, 1964), chap. 8.

20. Abraham, *The Coming Great Revival*, 73.

21. Donald G. Bloesch, *The Future of Evangelical Christianity: A Call for Unity amid Diversity* (Garden City, N.Y.: Doubleday, 1983), 5, 48–52. Cf. Donald G. Bloesch, *Essentials of Evangelical Theology*, 2 vols. (San Francisco: Harper & Row, 1978), 2:1.

22. Outler, "The Wesleyan Quadrilateral in Wesley," 9. Cf. problems related to the quadrilateral as a sufficient model of Wesley's theological method in R. Larry Shelton, "The Trajectory of Wesleyan Theology," *Wesleyan Theological Journal* 21, no. 2 (1986): 159–75.

23. Gabriel Fackre, "Evangelical Hermeneutics: Commonality and Diversity," *Interpretation* 43, no. 2 (1989): 127n29–30. Fackre draws a connection with Mercersburg Theology because of its rejection of sectarianism and concern with Christian union. Mercersburg Theology reflects the nineteenth–century thought of John W. Nevin and Philip Schaff, who taught at the seminary for the German Reformed Church in Mercersburg, Pennsylvania. Although Nevin and Schaff rejected sectarianism, the extent of their catholic spirit is questionable due to their criticism of revivalism and individual salvation.

24. Ibid., 127.

25. Ibid., 127–28.

26. Ibid., 128.

27. Ibid., 129.

28. Bernard Ramm, *After Fundamentalism: The Future of Evangelical Theology* (San Francisco: Harper & Row, 1983), 27.

29. Bruce Demarest and Gordon Lewis, *Integrative Theology*, 3 vols. (Grand Rapids: Zondervan, 1987– ), 1:9.

# Chapter 1
## The Background of Theological Method

1. Peter A. Angeles, *A Dictionary of Philosophy* (London: Harper & Row, 1981), 171.

2. R. McKeon, "Methodology (Philosophy)," *New Catholic Encyclopedia*, 16 vols. (New York: McGraw–Hill, 1967), 9:744.

3. "Method, Theological," *A New Dictionary of Christian Theology*, ed. Alan Richardson and John Bowden (London: SCM Press; 1983), 363.

4. J. J. Mueller" *What Are They Saying About Theological Method?* (New York: Paulist Press, 1984), 1. Mueller provides a helpful introduction to the whole topic of theological method.

5. The name "Methodist" was originally given in mockery of Wesley and his colleagues during their college years at Oxford. See "A Short History of Methodism," §5, *Works* (Jackson ed), 8:348.

6. For example, see *The Science of Theology*, ed. Paul Avis, History of Christian Theology (Grand Rapids: Eerdmans, 1986), vol. 1, esp. pt. 1: "Patristic and Medieval Theology" by Gillian R. Evans, and pt. 2: "Reformation to Enlightenment" by Alister E. McGrath. Cf. Gerald R. Cragg, *The Church and the Age of Reason* (New York: Atheneum, 1961); *From Puritanism to the Age of Reason: A Study of Change' in Religious Thought Within the Church of England: 1660–1700* (Cambridge: Cambridge University Press, 1950); and *Reason and Authority in the Eighteenth Century* (Cambridge: Cambridge University Press, 1964).

7. See Henry R. McAdoo, *The Structure of Caroline Moral Theology* (London: Longman's, Green, 1949) and *The Spirit of Anglicanism: A Survey of Anglican Theological Method in the Seventeenth Century* (New York: Scribner's, 1965).

8. J. A. Fichtner, "Tradition (in Theology)," *New Catholic Encyclopedia* 14:228. Fichtner quotes J. Beumer.

9. Cf. Evans in *Science of Theology*, ed. Avis, 6.

10. See "The Definition of Faith of the Council of Chalcedon," *A Select Library of Nicene and Post–Nicene Fathers of the Christian Church*, trans. and ed. Philip Schaff and Henry Wace, 14 vols. (Reprint, Grand Rapids: Eerdmans, 1979), 14:262.

11. Anselm, "Proslogion," trans. M. J. Charlesworth, *Philosophy in the Middle Ages*, ed. Arthur Human and James J. Walsh (Indianapolis: Hackett, 1974), 150. Here Anselm echoes the dictum attributed to Augustine concerning the relationship of belief and authority to reason: *Crede, ut intelligas,* "Believe in order that you may understand." See Augustine, *Sermon* 43.7, 9, quoted by Richard A. Muller, *Dictionary of Latin and Greek Theological Terms,* 85.

12. Thomas Aquinas, *Summa Theologica*, pt. 1, Q.1, art. 8, *Philosophy in the Middle Ages,* 483.

13. McAdoo, *Spirit of Anglicanism,* 2.

14. Martin Luther, "Preface to the Wittenberg Edition of Luther's German Writings, Dr. Martin Luther's Preface," trans. Robert R. Heitner, *Selected Writings of Martin Luther, 1517–1520*, ed. Theodore G. Tappert, 4 vols. (Philadelphia: Fortress, 1967), 1:9.

15. Martin Luther, "That These Words of Christ, 'This Is My Body,' etc., Still Stand Firm Against the Fanatics," *Luther's Works*, ed. Robert S. Fischer, Amer. ed., gen. ed. Helmut T. Lehmann, 55 vols. (Philadelphia: Muhlenberg, 1961), 37:14.

16. John Calvin, "Prefatory Address to King Francis," *Institutes of the Christian Religion,* trans. Ford Lewis Battles, ed. John T. McNeill, 2 vols. (Philadelphia: Westminster, 1960), 1:18.

17. See Calvin, "The Knowledge of God the Creator," 1.6.1, 1.7.1, 1.8.1, *Institutes of the Christian Religion*, 1:69–71, 74–75, 81–82.

18. McAdoo, *Spirit of Anglicanism*, 3.

19. The Council of Trent, §95, *The Church Teaches: Documents of the Church in English Translation*, trans. and ed. John F. Clarkson et al. (St. Louis: B. Herder, 1955), 45.

20. Fichtner, "Tradition (in Theology)," *New Catholic Encyclopedia*, 14:227.

21. Thomas Cranmer (1489–1556) served as the chief instrument of Henry VIII for overthrowing the papal supremacy in England. John Jewel (1522–1571) became a stronger supporter of the Anglican settlement, writing persuasive defenses for the Church of England. Richard Hooker (c. 1554–1600) was perhaps the greatest apologist of the Elizabethan Settlement of 1559 and perhaps the most accomplished advocate that Anglicanism has ever had. In terms of their relationship to Wesley, Frank Baker observes that Wesley "firmly accepted the *via media* of the Church of England, as incorporated in Cranmer's *Book of Common Prayer*, and expounded in turn by Jewel as the fulfillment of the Scripture and the Fathers and by Hooker as the crown of human reasoning" (Baker, *John Wesley and the Church of England* [Nashville: Abingdon, 1970], 1).

22. See Raymond Aaron Houk, introduction, *Hooker's Ecclesiastical Polity*, bk. 8 (New York: Columbia University Press, 1931), 68.

23. Paul E. More, "Spirit of Anglicanism," in *Anglicanism*, ed. Paul E. More and Frank L. Cross (Milwaukee: Morehouse–Gorham, 1935), xix.

24. Robert Sanderson, preface, §xxi, *XXXV, Sermons*, 7th ed. (London: T. Basset, 1681), D.

25. See Outler, *Works* (Bicentennial ed.), 1:593n9: quoting from Peter Heylyn, *Historia Quinquarticularia, or a Historical Declaration of the Five Controversial Points Reproached in the Name of Arminianism* (London, 1660), 508, and Thomas Fuller, *Good Thoughts in Bad Times; Mixt Contemplations in Better Times* (1645); cf. *Thoughts and Contemplations*, ed. James O. Wood (London: SPCK, 1964), 124.

26. Latitudinarians represented a group of seventeenth–century Anglican divines who remained in the Church of England, but attached relatively little importance to matters of dogmatic truth, ecclesiastical organization, and liturgical practice.

27. Edward Stillingfleet, preface, *The Irenicum, or Pacificator: Being a Reconciler as to Church Differences* (London, 1662; reprint, Philadelphia: M. Sorin, 1842), xiv–xv. Stillingfleet's reference to the *Via media* comes from either Horace's *aurea mediocrites*, "the golden mean," or Ovid's *in medio tutissimus ibis*, "thou shalt pass not safely midway between both extremes."

28. John Tillotson, preface, *The Works of the Most Reverend Mr. John Tillotson*, 10 vols. (Edinburgh: Wal. Ruddiman & Company, and A. Murray & J. Cochran, 1772), 1:xi.

29. Richard Hooker, preface, *Of the Laws of Ecclesiastical Polity*, 4 vols., Folger Library Edition of the Works of Richard Hooker, gen. ed. W. Speed Hill (Cambridge, Mass.: Belknap Press of Harvard University Press, 1977), 1:17.

30. Ibid., 1:34–36.

31. McAdoo, *Spirit of Anglicanism*, 143; cf. 1–23.

32. Ibid., 320, selecting passages from Hooker, bk. 5, chaps. 6–8, *Laws of Ecclesiastical Polity*, 32–40.

33. Francis Paget, *An Introduction to the Fifth Book of Hooker's Treatise of the Laws of Ecclesiastical Polity* (Oxford: Clarendon, 1907), 284.

34. Alister E. McGrath in *The Science of Theology*, ed. Paul Avis, *History of Christian Theology* (Grand Rapids: Eerdmans, 1986), 1:179. Paget agrees with this assessment in *Introduction to the Fifth Book of Hooker's Ecclesiastical Polity*, 284.

35. Robert Sanderson, collected ed., *Library of Anglo–Catholic Theology,* 99 vols. (Oxford: Oxford University Press, 1841–1863), 2:114.

36. John Pearson, to the reader, *An Exposition of the Creed* (Oxford: Oxford University Press, 1833), xix–xx. Note that even Pearson, the seventeenth–century champion of orthodox Christian beliefs, placed reason in his order of discussion ahead of antiquity and the primitive fathers. Although Pearson tried to preserve the importance of fidelity to orthodox Christian beliefs, he recognized that right reason must first be assumed in order to undertake the investigation of any theological issue.

37. Jeremy Taylor, epistle dedicatory, "A Discourse of the Liberty of Prophesying, with its Just Limits and Temper: Showing the Unreasonableness of Prescribing to other Men's Faith, and the Iniquity of Persecuting Differing Opinions," *The Whole Works of the Right Rev. Jeremy Taylor,* 15 vols. (London: C. and J. Rivington; T. Cadell; Longman, Rees, Orme, Brown, and Green; J. Booker; J. Richardson; Hatchard and Son; R. H. Evans; J. Duncan; J. Cochran; Oxford: J. Parker; Cambridge: J. J. Deighton, 1828), 7:cccxxxiv. Elsewhere Taylor mentions his dependence on the work "done by the incomparable Mr. Hooker" in the epistle dedicatory, "Ductor Dubitantium, or the Rule of Conscience," *Works,* 11:cccxlii.

38. A. Keith Walker, *William Law: His Life and Thought* (London: SPCK, 1973), 164.

39. McAdoo, *Spirit of Anglicanism,* 348. Anglicans mentioned by McAdoo do not exhaust the list of theologians who appealed to Scripture, tradition, and reason in theological methodology. Lancelot Andrewes, George Bull, Francis Atterbury, and others reflect similar approaches to theological method.

40. Ibid., v.

41. Ibid., 357 (emphasis mine).

42. Ibid., 413.

43. Preface, *Christian Library,* 1:v.

44. Jeremy Taylor, epistle dedicatory, *The Rule and Exercise of Holy Dying* (Boston: Little, Brown, 1864), xxi–xxii.

45. McAdoo, *Spirit of Anglicanism,* 310.

46. Ibid., 311.

47. See McAdoo's discussion on Cambridge Platonist and Latitudinarian approaches to theological method in *Spirit of Anglicanism,* 70, 91, 134–37, 161–67, 175.

48. See Taylor, "The Liberty of Prophesying," 3.3, *Works,* 7:497–98. Cf. the epistle dedicatory to the same treatise in *Works,* 7:cccxxviii–xxix.

49. William Law, "Some Animadversions upon Dr. Trapp's Late Reply," *The Works of the Reverend William Law, M.A.,* 9 vols. (1762; reprint, London: G. Moreton, 1893), 6:204.

50. More, introductory essay, *Anglicanism,* ed. More and Cross, xx.

51. No name is given for the initials R. M. in the author's preface to *A Summary of Divine Truths Agreeable to the Faith Profess'd by the Church of England, confirm'd by Scripture and Reason* (London, 1711).

52. McAdoo, *Structure of Moral Caroline Theology,* 9.

53. Pearson, epistle dedicatory, *Exposition of the Creed,* xiii.

54. McAdoo, *Spirit of Anglicanism,* v.

55. See the posthumous works by Isaac Newton (1642–1727), including *The Chronology of the Ancient Kingdoms* (1728) and *Observations upon the Prophecies of Daniel and the Apocalypse of St. John* (1733). Cf. other theological works by Robert Boyle, including *The Excellency of Theology Compared with Natural Philosophy* (1673) and *The Christian Virtuoso* (1690). Boyle's will bequeathed money for the establishment of a series of eight lectures (the "Boyle Lectures"), to be given to some church in London against unbeliev-

ers.

56. McAdoo, *Spirit of Anglicanism,* 262.

57. McGrath in *Science of Theology,* ed. Avis, 190.

58. Hooker, preface, *Laws of Ecclesiastical Polity,* 1:29.

59. Taylor, epistle dedicatory, *Holy Dying,* xxi.

60. Ibid.

61. See the chapter "Of Enthusiasm" in Locke, *An Essay Concerning Human Understanding,* 2 vols. (1690; reprint, New York: Dover, 1959), 2:428–41, esp. 432. Cf. Samuel Johnson's definition of "Enthusiasm," which he credited to Locke, in *A Dictionary of the English Language* (1755; reprint, New York: Arno, 1979).

62. Peter Browne, *The Procedure, Extent and Limits of Human Understanding* (1728; reprint, New York: Garland, 1976), 33.

63. Ibid., 34, 462. Cf. the development of Browne's ideas and analogy in *Things Divine and Supernatural, Conceived by Analogy with Things Natural and Human* (1733; reprint, New York: Garland, 1976).

64. See Richard E. Brantley, *Locke, Wesley, and the Method of English Romanticism* (Gainesville, Fla.: University of Florida Press, 1984), 34.

65. McAdoo, *Spirit of Anglicanism,* 312.

66. See Maximin Piette, *John Wesley in the Evolution of Protestantism,* trans. J. B. Howard (New York: Sheed and Ward, 1937), 121, cf. 110.

67. See McAdoo, *Spirit of Anglicanism,* 405.

68. William R. Cannon, *Theology of John Wesley* (New York: Abingdon, 1946), 19.

69 See Piette, *Evolution of Protestantism,* 181–82.

70. For a more complete discussion of Anglican theological method, particularly concerning Scripture, tradition, and reason, see my work *Theological Method in John Wesley* (Ann Arbor, Mich.: University Microfilms, 1988), 40–57.

71. For example, see James McEldowney, "John Wesley's Theology in Its Historical Setting" (Diss., University of Chicago, 1943); Vivian H. H. Green, *The Young Mr. Wesley* (London: Epworth, 1961); Robert Monk, *John Wesley: His Puritan Heritage* (Nashville: Abingdon, 1966); Onva K. Boshears, Jr., "John Wesley, the Bookman: A Study of His Reading Interests in the Eighteenth Century" (Diss., University of Michigan, 1972); and R. D. Matthews, "'Religion and Reason Joined': A Study in the Theology of John Wesley" (Diss., Harvard University, 1986).

72. Other religious figures whose personal lives have received similar scrutiny from religious scholars include Augustine, Luther, and Søren Kierkegaard. In some ways it seems an injustice to study the theology of these men without becoming aware of the effect of their personal lives upon their theology. It is the case with Wesley that we cannot fully understand or appreciate his theology without studying it in the context of his personal and spiritual development and the development of his revival ministry.

73. See Wesley's preface to Tillotson's "Sermon 1: Of the Ordinary Influence of the Holy Ghost on the Minds of Christians," *Christian Library,* 27:3.

74. Samuel Wesley, *Advice to a Young Clergyman,* reprinted as an appendix in Thomas Jackson's *The Life of the Rev. Charles Wesley,* 2 vols. (London: John Manson, 1841), 2:500–534. In his book Samuel Wesley also recommended the works of Tillotson, Stillingfleet, Aldrich, Sanderson, Pearson, More, Cudworth, Norris, Clarke, and William Chillingworth."

75. Piette, *Evolution of Protestantism,* 474.

76. Albert C. Outler, "The Place of Wesley in the Christian Tradition," in *The Place of Wesley in the Christian Tradition,* ed. Kenneth E. Rowe (Metuchen, N.J.: Scarecrow, 1976),

19. Susanna Wesley owned a copy of the English translation of *Pugna Spiritualis,* translated into English by Richard Lucas in 1698, usually attributed to the Spanish Benedictine Juan de Castañiza (c. 1536–1599), though later it has more often been attributed to Lorenzo Scupoli (c. 1530–1610), a Spanish Theatine. Henry Scougal (1650–1678), a Scottish theologian and mystic, remained an important devotional source to Wesley, for example, as evidenced by Wesley's recommendation of Scougal to his Methodist assistants in the "Minutes of the Third Annual Conference," 14 May 1746, Q.15, *John Wesley* 162.

77. For example, see Susanna Wesley's letters in volume 25 of the *Works* (Oxford ed.): 164–67, 8 June 1725; 172–73, 21 July 1725; 178–80, 18 August 1725; 183–85, 19 October 1725; 326–27, 21 February 1732; 344–46, 25 October 1732; 377–78, 14 February 1734; and so on. Susanna Wesley even quoted from classical writers such as Seneca in *Works* (Oxford ed.), 25:215, 22 April 1727.

78. Cf. Outler's discussion of these deans in his introduction to *John Wesley* (New York: Oxford University Press, 1980), 6.

79. See Francis Atterbury, preface, *Sermons and Discourses on Several Subjects and Occasions,* 5th ed. (London: T. Woodward, 1740), 8. While at Oxford, Wesley mentioned reading Atterbury's sermons along with those of Samuel Clarke in his letter "To the Revd. Samuel Wesley, Jun.," 6 December 1726, *Works* (Oxford ed.), 25:202.

80. See Outler, "The Place of Wesley in the Christian Tradition," 20. Wesley acknowledged the influence of Guyse and Doddridge on his interpretation of Scripture in the *Notes upon the New Testament,* 8.

81. Outler, introduction, *Works* (Bicentennial ed.), 1:77.

82. Cf. Piette, *Evolution of Protestantism,* 290.

83. In this work Law also contended with Benjamin Hoadly and Bernard Mandeville. See Law's prefatory advertisement to the "Case of Reason," *Works,* 2:v.

84. See Law, introduction, "Case of Reason," *Works,* 2:57–58.

85. Outler comments that Wesley "had always considered the piety and devotion of Roman Catholics like De Renty, Lopez, Fenelon, *et al.,* authentic; thus, he always insisted that truly 'catholic spirit' must also include the Romans." See Outler, *Works* (Bicentennial ed.), 2:71n32; cf. 1:35–36.

86. Outler, "The Place of Wesley in the Christian Tradition," 31.

87. See McAdoo's discussion of and quotes from F. Holland in *Spirit of Anglicanism,* 404–5. McAdoo comments that "Holland's introductory essay is a valuable indication of the way in which a scholarly country clergyman of 1725 thought about theological method."

88. See "A Short History of the People Called Methodists," §3, *Works* (Jackson ed.), 13:304.

89. See "Minutes of the Third Annual Conference," 14 May 1746, Q.15, *John Wesley,* 163.

90. Outler, introduction, *John Wesley,* 12.

91. Outler, introduction, *Works* (Bicentennial ed.), 1:77, 79–80.

92. See George C. Cell, *The Rediscovery of John Wesley* (New York: Henry Holt, 1935); Cannon, *Theology of John Wesley;* and Monk, *John Wesley: His Puritan Heritage.* Cf. John Deschner, *Wesley's Christology, an Interpretation* (Dallas: Southern Methodist University Press, 1985; reprint, Grand Rapids: Zondervan, 1988); Colin Williams, *John Wesley's Theology Today* (New York: Abingdon, 1960); and Martin Schmidt, *John Wesley: A Theological Biography,* trans. Norman Goldhawk, 2 vols. in 3 (New York: Abingdon, 1962).

93. The suggestion that Aldersgate served as a *terminus a quo* (a point of origin), for

Wesley does not imply that it was the only or most important point of transition in either his personal life or his public ministry. The suggestion merely serves to identify certain significant changes that occurred soon after Aldersgate and that seem, at least indirectly, related to his experience there. No attempt is made to determine a *terminus ad quem* (a final limiting point in time), because in both his personal life and his public ministry Wesley underwent continued growth and development.

94. Interestingly, Clifford Hindley argues that the influence of experimental philosophy predisposed Wesley to the sense of personal assurance preached by the Moravians. Hindley says, "The way of thinking presupposed [by Wesley] in all the passages so far considered, and the readiness with which Wesley accepted the Moravian teaching about and assurance and waited for it to be confirmed in his own experience, derive unmistakably from a common source — the belief that the only source of knowledge available to us is some experience of sense" ("The Philosophy of Enthusiasm: A Study in the Origins of 'Experimental Theology,'" *London Quarterly and Holborn Review* 182 [1957]: 101).

95. Outler, introduction, *John Wesley*, 14.

96. Ibid., 15–16.

97. See Wesley's preface to "An Extract of Mr. Richard Baxter's Aphorisms of Justification," *Works* (Jackson ed.), 14:216.

98. *Journal* (Curnock ed.), 2:101, 12 November 1738. This extract refers to "The Doctrine of Salvation, Faith, and Good Works, Extracted from the Homilies of the Church of England." See the bibliographic description of the work by Richard Green in *The Works of John and Charles Wesley: A Bibliography* (London: C. H. Kelly, 1896). The extract was included in the earliest collected *Works* of Wesley, but was omitted from subsequent editions.

99. Outler, introduction, *John Wesley*, 16.

100. Ibid., 121–23.

101. See Outler, introduction to "Church and Sacraments," *John Wesley*, 306.

102. Sanderson, preface, XXI, XXXV, *Sermons*, D.

103. See Pearson, epistle dedicatory and preface, *Exposition of the Creed*, xiv, xviii–xix.

104. "To Cradock Glascott," 11 May 1764, *Letters* (Telford ed.), 4:243.

105. "To Dr. Warburton, Bishop of Gloucester,'! 26 November–1762, *Letters* (Telford ed.), 4:376; cf. 376–78.

106. "A Farther Appeal:" vol. 23, *Works* (Bicentennial ed.), 11:163–66, esp. 166.

107. Wesley said that it was in pursuit of an advice given by Bishop Taylor in "Rules of Holy Living and Dying" that he began to keep his personal journal. See Wesley's preface to the *Journal* (Curnock ed.), 1:83.

108. Taylor, epistle dedicatory, *Holy Dying*, xxi.

109. Taylor, "The Worthy Communicant," quoted in *The Golden Grove: Selected Passages from the Sermons and Writings of Jeremy Taylor,* ed. Logan P. Smith (Oxford: Clarendon, 1930), 143.

110. See Outler, introduction, *John Wesley*, 306.

111. For example, see the extract from Norris's "Reflections upon the conduct of Human life, with reference to learning and knowledge" in *Christian Library* 30:35–68. Cf. Outler on the role of John Norris in the development of Wesley's thought in *Works* (Bicentennial ed.), 1:59; 276n46; and 433n7.

112. See Wesley's various remarks on electricity in the *Journal* (Curnock ed.), 3:320, 16 October 1747; 4:53–54,17 February 1753; 4:190–91, 9 November 1756; 4:357, 30

October 1759; and 5:247, 4 January 1768.

113. See preface, "The Desideratum: Or, Electricity made plain and useful. By a Lover of Mankind, and of Common Sense," *Works* (Jackson ed.), 14:24144.

114. Ibid.

115. See "Remarks upon Mr. Locke's 'Essay on the Human Understanding:" *Works* (Jackson ed.), 13:455–64. The complete series of Wesley's remarks may be found in volumes 5–7 of the *Arminian Magazine*. Wesley made references to having read Browne's philosophical commentaries on Locke as early as 1729. See references to Browne's writings in the series of letters between Wesley and Mary Pendarves in "To Mrs. Mary Pendarves," 3 October 1730, 28 December 1730, 4 February 1731, in *Works* (Oxford ed.), 25:250, 261, 269; and "From Mrs. Mary Pendarves," 13 February 1731, in *Works* (Oxford ed.), 25:271.

116. Cf. Hindley, "The Philosophy of Enthusiasm," 99–109, esp. 108; and Brantley, *Locke, Wesley,* 27–102, esp. 30, 34.

117. Preface, §6, "Sermons on Several Occasions," *Works* (Bicentennial ed.), 1:106.

118. See Robert E. Cushman's excellent study in *John Wesley's Experimental Divinity* (Nashville: Abingdon, 1989), esp. chap. 2: "A Little Body of Experimental and Practical Divinity," 34–48.

119. Hindley convincingly argues that it is only in this empiricist atmosphere that we can rightly understand the epistemological thought of Wesley and his method of investigating the truths of Christian belief ("The Philosophy of Enthusiasm," 99).

120. Paget, *Introduction to the Fifth Book of Hooker's Ecclesiastical Polity,* 284. Cf. Charles Gore, *Roman Catholic Claims,* 4th ed. (London: Longman's, Green, 1892), 6.

121. McAdoo, *Spirit of Anglicanism,* vi.

122. Ibid., 312.

123. Ibid., 313.

124. Piette, *Evolution of Protestantism,* 436.

# Chapter 2
## An Overview of Wesley's Theology

1. Randy L. Maddox critiques my work *Theological Method in John Wesley* by claiming that it makes condescending or negative assessments of Wesley's' theological abilities or that it apologizes for the fact that his theology is popular; eclectic, occasional, and relatively nonspeculative ("John Wesley–Practical Theologian?" Wesleyan Studies Group, American Academy of Religion Annual Meeting, Chicago, 20 November 1988, 16n54). But neither *Theological Method* nor this book has anything but respect for the theological abilities of Wesley. If anything, these. works were written to encourage respect for Wesley as a theologian. That respect will come only when people first recognize the motivation behind his writings, his method of approach, and the ends he sought to achieve. This book proposes that Wesley has not received sufficient scholarly recognition because critics have used historically and theologically inappropriate criteria with which to understand and appreciate his theology.

2. *Journal* (Curnock ed.), 5:116, 14 May 1765.

3. Charles Wesley, "A Collection of Hymns for the use of the People called Methodists, 1780," Hymn 461, 1.5, *Works* (Oxford ed.), 7:644.

4. Henry R. McAdoo, *The Spirit of Anglicanism: A Survey of Anglican Theological Method in the Seventeenth Century* (New York: Scribner's, 1965), v.

5. Ibid.

6. Preface, §§3, 5, "Sermons on Several Occasions," *Works* (Bicentennial ed.), 1:104–5.

7. John Dillenberger and Claude Welch, *Protestant Christianity: Interpreted Through Its Development* (New York: Scribner's, 1954), 123–40.

8. "The Scripture Way of Salvation" (1765, sermon 43), §1, *Works* (Bicentennial ed.), 2:156.

9. Ibid., §2.

10. "A Farther Appeal," I.3, *Works* (Bicentennial ed.), 11:106: "Now if by salvation we mean a present salvation from sin, we cannot say holiness is the condition for it: for it is the thing itself. Salvation, in this sense, and holiness, are synonymous terms."

11. Ibid., 1.1, 11:105.

12. Mitsuru Samuel Fujimoto, "John Wesley's Doctrine of Good Works" (Diss., Drew University, 1986).

13. "Salvation by Faith" (1738, sermon 1), *Works* (Bicentennial ed.), 1:109130. Even Albert C. Outler, who edited the four volumes of sermons in the new scholarly edition of Wesley's works, suggests that Wesley stresses "soteriology as the focus of his entire theology." See Outler, an introductory comment, *Works* (Bicentennial ed.), 1:103.

14. See "The Almost Christian" (1741, sermon 2); "Awake, Thou That Sleepest" (1742, sermon 3); "Scriptural Christianity" (1744, sermon 4); and "Justification by Faith" (1746, sermon 5) in *Works* (Bicentennial ed.), 1:131–99.

15. See Luke Tyerman, *The Life and Times of the Rev. John Wesley, M.S., Founder of the Methodists*, 3 vols. (London: Hodder and Stoughton, 1870–71), 1:234.

16. Preface, §3, "Sermons on Several Occasions," *Works* (Bicentennial ed.), 1:104, and "On God's Vineyard" (1787, sermon 107), 1.1, *Works* (Bicentennial ed.), 3:504.

17. Preface, §5, "Sermons on Several Occasions," *Works* (Bicentennial ed.), 1:105. Cf. "On God's Vineyard" (1787, sermon 107), 1.1, *Works* (Bicentennial ed.), 3:504, and "A Plain Account of Christian Perfection," §S, *Works* (Jackson ed.), 11:367.

18. "The Nature of Enthusiasm" (1750, sermon 37), §22, *Works* (Bicentennial ed.), 2:54.

19. See "A Plain Account of Christian Perfection," §10, *Works* (Jackson ed.), 11:373.

20. Oden notes, "From 1763 onward (and from 1773 on in America) it has been generally assumed by preachers through the connection that to preach contrary to 'our doctrines' would be to preach counter to and against Wesley's teaching as defined textually in the Sermons and Notes (and after 1784, the Articles of Religion)" (Thomas C. Oden, *Doctrinal Standards in the Wesleyan Tradition* [Grand Rapids: Zondervan, Francis Asbury Press, 1988], 27).

21. Albert C. Outler, "The Wesleyan Quadrilateral in John Wesley," *Wesleyan Theological Journal* 20, no. 1 (1985): 8.

22. "Minutes of Some Late Conversations," 25 June 1744, *Works* (Jackson ed.), 8:275.

23. See Albert C. Outler, ed., "The Theological Study Commission on Doctrine and Doctrinal Standards: Interim Report to the General Conference" (1970): quoted by Oden, *Doctrinal Standards*, 25. Oden further notes that "Chronologically, the sequence of doctrinal definition moved from *Minutes* (beginning 1744) to *Sermons* (beginning 1746) to *Notes* (1754) to *Articles* (1784)" (*Doctrinal Standards*, 26). Cf. Thomas B. Neely, *Doctrinal Standards of Methodism* (New York: Revell, 1918), 104.

24. Outler, "The Wesleyan Quadrilateral," 8. Other works edited by Wesley include the fifty–volume *Christian Library* and numerous extracts from other authors published in pamphlet form.

25. Richard E. Brantley, *Locke, Wesley, and the Method of English Romanticism* (Gainesville, Fla.: University of Florida Press, 1984), 65. Elsewhere Brantley argues that, by studying the connections between the thought of Locke and Wesley, we discover a *consistency* of method throughout Wesley's writings. Brantley states, "1 argue, in other words, that John Wesley's method, if not always self–conscious, is assuredly present throughout his writings; his defenses of faith are enhanced by Locke's experiential idiom, which, though hardly so pervasive in Wesley's works as, say, his scriptural reference, is nonetheless so clearly a major feature of them as to demonstrate that beside being syncretic and steeped in tradition his theology articulates his understanding of empiricism" (*Locke, Wesley,* 23).

26. Ibid., 66.

27. Ibid., 103–128 (the chapter entitled "Wesley's Intellectual Influence).

28. Cf. Robert Tuttle, *John Wesley: His Life and Theology* (Grand Rapids: Zondervan, 1978), 336.

29. For example, Randy L. Maddox argues that there is "an orienting concept in Wesley's theology; namely, the concept of responsible grace" ("Responsible Grace: The Systematic Nature of Wesley's Theology Reconsidered," *Wesleyan Theological Journal* 19, nor 2 [1984]: 24–34, esp. 27). In a related discussion, Mitsuru Fujimoto argues, "The axial theme of Wesley's theology is) '1 grace (prevenient, convincing, justifying, sanctifying, perfecting, and finally glorifying). . . . But such a principle must be definitely followed by another *primary* principle: wherever grace and faith are, there are good works" ("John Wesley's Doctrine of Good Works," 3). Cf. the articles by M. Douglas Meeks, "John Wesley's Heritage and the Future of Systematic Theology," 38–46, and by H. Ray Dunning, "Perspective for a Wesleyan Systematic Theology," 51–55, in *Wesleyan Theology Today: A Bicentennial Theological Consultation,* ed. Theodore Runyon (Nashville: Abingdon, Kingswood, 1985).

30. Umphrey Lee, *John Wesley and Modern Religion* (Nashville: Cokesbury, 1936), 143.

31. Ibid.

32. See Outler's helpful discussion on the Wesleyan quadrilateral in "The Wesleyan Quadrilateral," 7–18. Cf. William Abraham, *The Coming Great Revival* (San Francisco: Harper & Row, 1984), 57–61; "The Wesleyan Quadrilateral in the American Episcopal Tradition," *Wesleyan Theological Journal* 20 no. 1 (1985): 34–44; and "The Wesleyan Quadrilateral," in Runyon, *Wesleyan Theology Today,* 119–26. Also, Leon Hynson, "The Wesleyan Quadrilateral in the American Holiness Tradition," *Wesleyan Theological Journal* 20, no. 1 (1985): 19–33, and comments made by Thomas C. Oden in *The Living God,* vol. 1 of *Systematic Theology* (San Francisco: Harper & Row, 1987), 330–39.

33. Oden, *The Living God,* 1:332. Oden continues: "For a functional view of this method, one sees it best operating in the central Anglican formularies, the *Homilies,* the *Book of Common Prayer,* the Thirty–nine Articles of Religion, the works of Cranmer, Jewel, Hooker, Gibson, Thorndike, Jackson, Taylor, and Wesley, as well as in Scholastic Lutherans like Gerhard, and in some measure in Calvinists like A. J. Niemeyer, as well as in many post–Tridentine Catholics" (1:332). Generally Oden considers the main strand of quadrilateral–like thinking developing through the Anglican tradition and leading up to the theology of Wesley.

34. The presence of the so–called quadrilateral in Wesley should not be confused with "the Four Pillars of Methodism," which alludes to Wesley's belief that "Christianity is built upon four grand pillars; viz., the power, understanding, goodness, and the holiness of God." See "A Clear and Concise Demonstration of the Divine Inspiration of the Holy Scriptures,' *Works* (Jackson ed.), 11:484.

35. Richard Lovelace, "Recovering Our Balance:' *Charisma* (August 1987): 80.

36. At this point we may take the Liberty to digress and present an organic model for the Wesleyan quadrilateral. Such an endeavor should *not* be understood as a serious attempt to explain Wesley's theological method. Rather, consider it an exercise in free association in reflecting on Wesley's use of Scripture, tradition, reason, and experience.

In the sermon "What Is Man? Psalm 8:4," Wesley spoke of humanity in terms of (1) *body*, resembling a mechanism composed of various elements, (2) *soul*, capable of thinking and feeling, (3) *liberty*, which represents our distinctive ability to choose, and (4) *end* or goal of life — that which we are most "concerned to know, and deeply to consider." See "What Is Man? Psalm 8:4" (1788, sermon 116), *Works* (Bicentennial ed.), 4:20–27.

The *body* is analogous to *experience*, since it is composed of various sensible elements. The *soul* is analogous to *reason*, which cannot fully comprehend either the movements or end of the body. The *liberty* is analogous to *tradition*, because tradition reflects the history of the soul and body. The *end* or goal of life is analogous to *Scripture*, since only Scripture tells us of our sole end: to prepare for eternity. Of course, Wesley believed that the genuine task of theology — analogous to humanity — is moved by the "Almighty Spirit," the ultimate power source of all motion, thought, feelings, and choices in the universe.

Taken together, the body, soul, liberty, and end of humanity could serve as an organic model for how Scripture, tradition, reason, and experience interact. The analogy may not be exact, but it does come from ideas contained in the writings of Wesley rather than from others.

Remember that this attempt to describe the Wesleyan quadrilateral is *not* intended to be understood as anything other than an exercise in free association. More serious attempts at reconceptualizing the Wesleyan quadrilateral would profitably take less contrived approaches to the subject.

37. See Romans 12:4–5; 1 Corinthians 12:12–31; and Ephesians 4:14–16.

38. Preface to the third edition, §4, *Works* (Jackson ed.), 1:iv.

39. "Doctrine of Original Sin," *Works* (Jackson ed.), 9:432. Cf. another reference to "Scripture, reason, and experience" in "The Repentance of Believers" (1767, sermon 14), 1.2, *Works* (Bicentennial ed.), 1:336.

40. For example, see "To the Reader," *Arminian Magazine, Works* (Jackson ed.), 14:278–81.

41. "A Farther Appeal," *Works* (Oxford ed.), pt. 1, introduction, 11:105; pt. 1, V.27, 11:170; pt. 3, 1.9–10, 11:277; and pt. 3, III.29, 11:310–11.

42. "Principles of a Methodist," *Works* (Jackson ed.), §13, 8:365, and §28, 8:373.

43. "Principles of a Methodist Farther Explained," §§4–5, *Works* (Jackson ed.), 8:472–74.

44. "A Letter to the Right Reverend the Lord Bishop of Gloucester," III.1–10, *Works* (Oxford ed.), 11:534–38.

45. "To Dr. Conyers Middleton," 24 January 1749, III.1–12, *Letters* (Telford ed.), 2:383–88.

46. "Doctrine of Original Sin," *Works* (Jackson ed.), pt. 2, 1.1, 9:238–39; pt. 2, [II.]1, 9:261; pt. 2, [III.], 10, 9:273; and pt. 6, 9:432–33.

47. "On Sin in Believers" (1763, sermon 13), V.1, *Works* (Bicentennial ed.), 1:332–33.

48. "Means of Grace" (1746, sermon 16),I.1–6, *Works* (Bicentennial ed.), 1:378–80.

49. Preface, §5, "Sermons on Several Occasions," *Works* (Bicentennial ed.), 1:105–6.

50. Wesley frequently placed reason second in order after Scripture. We have already seen that Wesley claimed to present what is agreeable "to Scripture, reason, and

Christian antiquity." See preface to the third edition, §4, *Works* (Jackson ed.), 1:iv. In the title of "Doctrine of Original Sin," Wesley claimed to present the doctrine "according to Scripture, Reason, and Experience" (see *Works* [Jackson ed.], 9:191; cf. 191–353).

51. For additional discussion of the order of priority in the Wesleyan quadrilateral, see the introduction and chapter 4 of this book.

52. "Seek First the Kingdom" (1725, sermon 134), §10, *Works* (Bicentennial ed.), 4:220, and "The Circumcision of the Heart" (1733, sermon 17), §2, *Works* (Bicentennial ed.), 1:402.

53. See the contribution by John B. Cobb, Jr., to the series on the New Doctrinal Statements and the Primacy of Scripture in an article entitled "I say, 'Keep the Quadrilateral!,'" *Circuit Rider* 11, no. 5 (1987): 4–6. In an opposing viewpoint, Kenneth C. Kinghorn seems to maintain a more Wesleyan approach to the question of religious authority (Kinghorn, "I say, 'The Bible is the Decisive Source of Authority!,'" *Circuit Rider* 11, no. 5 [1987]: 6–7). Cf. the authors' responses to each other's article in the same issue of *Circuit Rider*: Cobb, "Response to 'Bible as Decisive Authority,'" 8–9, and Kinghorn, "Response to 'Keep the Quadrilateral,'" 8.

54. See "Causes of the Inefficacy of Christianity" (1789, sermon 122), §12, *Works* (Bicentennial ed.), 4:93.

55. See "On Laying the Foundation of the New Chapel" (1777, sermon 112), II.1–6, *Works* (Bicentennial ed.), 3:585–87.

56. See "An Earnest Appeal," §§2–4, *Works* (Oxford ed.), 11:45–46. Cf. Wesley's quotation of this passage in "On Laying the Foundation of the New Chapel" (1777, sermon 112), II.1, *Works* (Bicentennial ed.), 3:585.

57. See "On Laying the Foundation of the New Chapel" (1777, sermon 112), II.2–6, *Works* (Bicentennial ed.), 3:585–87.

58. In speaking against schism, Wesley said, "It is the nature of love to unite us together, and the greater the love the stricter the union. And while this continues in its strength nothing can divide those whom love has united. It is only when our love grows cold that we can think of separating from our brethren" ("On Schism" [1786, sermon 75], II.11, *Work;* [Bicentennial ed.], 3:64).

59. See "Catholic Spirit" (1750, sermon 39), *Work;,* (Bicentennial ed.), 2:79–95. Cf. "The Lord Our Righteousness" (1765, sermon 20), II.3, *Work;* (Bicentennial ed.), 1:454, and "On the Death of George Whitfield" (1770, sermon 53), III.7–10, *Work;* (Bicentennial ed.), 2:344–46.

60. "The Witness of Our Own Spirit" (1746, sermon 12), §6, *Work;* (Bicentennial ed.), 1:303.

61. See "The Lord Our Righteousness" (1765, sermon 20), II.3, *Work;* (Bicentennial ed.), 1:454.

62. Outler, introductory comment, *Work;* (Bicentennial ed.), 2:80.

63. Wesley frequently used this phrase. For example, see "The Lord Our Righteousness" (1765, sermon 20), II.20, *Work;* (Bicentennial ed.), 1:464; "The Nature of Enthusiasm" (1750, sermon 37), §36, *Work;* (Bicentennial ed.), 2:59; "On the Death of George Whitefield" (1770, sermon 53), III.1, *Work;* (Bicentennial ed.), 2:341; "On the Trinity" (1775, sermon 55), §2, *Work;* (Bicentennial ed.), 2:376; and "On the Wedding Garment" (1790, sermon 127), §14, *Work;* (Bicentennial ed.), 4:145.

64. "Catholic Spirit" (1750, sermon 39), III.5, *Work;* (Bicentennial ed.), 2:94.

65. Ibid., 2:95.

66. "Prophets and Priests" (1789, sermon 121), §21, *Work;* (Bicentennial   e d . ) , 4:83–84.

67. See "A Letter to a Roman Catholic," §16, *Work;* (Jackson ed.), 10:85.

68. See "The End of Christ's Coming" (1781, sermon 62), III.5, *Work;* (Bicentennial ed.), 2:483. Cf. Wesley's criticisms of Jean Jacques Rousseau, Voltaire, and David Hume in "The Unity of the Divine Being" (1789, sermon 120), §19, *Work;* (Bicentennial ed.), 4:68–69.

69. Although Wesley did not use the analogy of a tree, it seems to capture the organic nature of his understanding of the growth of theology. Wesley frequently quoted Scripture verses that draw an analogy between Christian believers and a tree (or vine) that must bear fruit, for example, Matthew 7:1718; 12:33; and Luke 6:43. Wesley was also aware of others' using the analogy of a tree for discussing various Christian truths, for example, as contained in the extract of John Arndt's "True Christianity" in the *Christian Library,* 1:409.

70. "On Laying the Foundation of the New Chapel" (1777, sermon 112), I.3, *Work;* (Bicentennial ed.), 3:582.

71. Brantley emphasizes the complexity and pervasive influence of Wesley's religious thinking beyond the Methodist movement itself. In his study of the influence of Lockean and Wesleyan thought on eighteenth–century English Romanticism, Brantley suggests that "Wesley's philosophical theology is satisfyingly complex, appropriately interdisciplinary, aptly inclusive, and almost the only available model for the broad concept of experience everywhere implicit in English Romantic epistemology" *(Locke, Wesley,* 26; cf.103–200, esp. 103–128 [chap. 3: "Wesley's Intellectual Influence"]).

72. See the heavy curriculum outlined for the Kingswood School, founded by Wesley, in "An Address to the Clergy," *Works* (Jackson ed.), 10:480–500.

73. Robert E. Cushman, *John Wesley's Experimental Divinity* (Nashville: Abingdon, Kingswood, 1989), 11. On pages 34–48 Cushman delineates nine principles of Wesley's experimental divinity: (1) present and immediate work of the Holy Spirit, (2) religious experience that is reproducible, (3) personal ownership of such Christian truths as original sin, (4) personal ownership to the point of "self–despair," (5)experienced gift of "saving faith," (6) experienced assurance, (7) awareness of the person and work of Jesus Christ, (8) verification of Scripture in experience, and (9) God's prevenient (or preventing) grace.

74. Roderick T. Leupp rightly observes that commentary on Wesley's thought has long recognized his empirical tendencies, though scholars have disagreed widely on the degree to which his thought was genuinely empirical. See Leupp, "'Art of God': Light and Darkness in the Thought of John Wesley" (Diss., Drew University, 1985), 223; cf. 192–206.

75. This may be seen in the works of Cambridge Platonists and Latitudinarians. Experimental method, of course, became very apparent in the scientifically oriented philosophy and theology of Locke, Robert Boyle, and Richard Bentley. But it also influenced a growing number of Anglicans such as Peter Browne and Vincent Perronet.

76. Samuel Johnson, *A Dictionary of the English Language* (n.p.; n.d.); see definition of "Experimental"

77. Preface, §6, "Sermons on Several Occasions." *Works* (Bicentennial ed.), 1:106.

78. To this understanding of *true* religion, Ted A. Campbell adds "that John Wesley conceived of Christian antiquity as a period in which an ideal of Christian individual and community life was realized. The 'ideal' Wesley believed to have been realized in Christian antiquity was that to which Wesley referred as 'true' or 'genuine Christianity', and whose paradigm Wesley found in Christ and in the Christianity of the New Testament" ("John Wesley's Conceptions and Uses of Christian Antiquity" [Diss.,

Southern Methodist University, 1984], 14).

79. "Upon our Lord's Sermon on the Mount, X" (1750, sermon 30), §2, *Works* (Bicentennial ed.), 1:651.

80. "On a Single Eye" (1789, sermon 125), §3, *Works* (Bicentennial ed.), 4:121–22.

81. George Eayrs, *John Wesley: Christian Philosopher and Church Founder* (London: Epworth, 1926), 58–59.

82. Brantley, *Locke, Wesley,* 43.

83. For a more complete discussion concerning definitions and distinctions between the terms *experimental, experiential,* and *empirical,* see chapter 7 of this book.

84. "An Earnest Appeal:" §9, *Works* (Oxford ed.), 11:47–48.

85. Cf. Wesley's distinction between the "faith of a servant" and "the faith of a son" in "On the Discoveries of Faith" (1788, sermon 117), esp. §13, *Works* (Bicentennial ed.), 4:35.

86. Eayrs comments, "It is admitted that he [Wesley] regulated and used his method upon a master principle or hypothesis; but every investigator is guided, more or less, by some principle or some assumption. . . . It seems to the present student that Wesley's working hypothesis may be found in a statement in the remarkable preface which he issued, in 1747, with the first volume of his *Standard Sermons (Works,* v., Preface). There Wesley utters this impressive confession: 'I am a spirit come from God, and returning to God'. This simple but profound statement includes his belief as to the origin, nature, consciousness, and conscience of man, and the purpose of his existence" *(John Wesley: Christian Philosopher and Church Founder,* 59–60).

87. Stanley B. Frost, *The Doctrine of Authority in the Works of John Wesley* (London: n.p., 1938), 104–5.

88. "Awake, Thou That Sleepest" (1742, sermon 3), III.6, *Works* (Bicentennial ed.), 1:154.

89. Wesley, *Wesleyan New Testament,* 433; quoted by George C. Cell, *The Rediscovery of John Wesley* (New York: Henry Holt, 1935), 65. Cell does not specify from which edition he quoted Wesley, but the quote probably comes from either the 1815 or 1818 editions; it does not appear in the original 1790 edition. In the introduction to his own edition of Wesley's translation, Cell confirms the experimental theme in Wesley by concluding his introduction in the following words: "Beyond controversy the primary resource of the Protestant faith has been the experimental and experiential knowledge of the Word of God" (Cell, introduction, *John Wesley's New Testament: Compared with the Authorized Version* [Philadelphia: John C. Winston, 1738], xiv). This statement implies both methodological study of Scripture as well as the experiential confirmation of its truths.

90. See Brantley, *Locke, Wesley,* 2. On page 23 Brantley states that "Wesley verbalized his experience. And *experience,* throughout this study, is conceived as a continuum from things, through ideas, to words."

91. Ibid., 3; quoting Frank Baker, *John Wesley and the Church of England* (New York: Abingdon, 1970), 3.

92. "On God's Vineyard" (1787, sermon 107), I.5, *Works* (Bicentennial ed.), 3:505–6.

93. See "The Way to the Kingdom" (1746, sermon 7), I.7, *Works* (Bicentennial ed.), 2:79.

94. Outler comments that Wesley agreed with William of St. Thierry that love is the surest way to truth and the highest goal of thought. See Outler's introductory comment to "Catholic Spirit" (1759, sermon 39), *Works* (Bicentennial ed.), 2:79.

95. "Popery Calmly Considered," IV.10, *Works* (Jackson ed.), 10:155–56.

96. See "Predestination Calmly Considered," §§42–44, *Works* (Jackson ed.), 10:227–29, and "Free Grace" (1739, sermon 110), §§11–12, *Works* (Bicentennial ed.), 3:548–49.

97. Mildred Bangs Wynkoop, *A Theology of Love* (Kansas City: Beacon Hill, 1972), 19.

98. For example, see John S. Simon, *John Wesley and the Religious Societies* (London: Epworth, 1921), esp. 157–58.

99. Colin Williams, *John Wesley's Theology Today* (New York: Abingdon, 1960), 149.

100. Preface, §2, "Sermons on Several Occasions," *Works* (Bicentennial ed.), 1:103–4.

101. Outler, introductory comment, "The Use of Money" (1760, sermon 50), *Works* (Bicentennial ed.), 2:263.

102. In 1747 Wesley first published *Primitive Physick, or an Easy and Natural Method of Curing Most Diseases* (1747; reprint, London: Epworth, 1960). This simple medical manual was reprinted twenty–one times by 1785.

103. See "A Plain Account of the People Called Methodists," XIII–XIV, *Works* (Jackson ed.), 8:265–6(.

104. "A Plain Account of the People Called Methodists," XIV.2, *Works* (Jackson ed.), 8:266.

105. See "A Plain Account of the Kingswood School," §1, *Works* (Jackson ed.), 13:289

106. See "A Plain Account of the People Called Methodists," XV, *Works* (Jackson ed.), 8:267–68.

107. See "The Use of Money" (1760, sermon 50), *Works* (Bicentennial ed.), 2:263–80.

108. See Outler, introductory comment, "The Danger of Riches" (1781, sermon 87), *Works* (Bicentennial ed.), 3:277.

109. Ibid., 3:228.

110. Vivian H. H. Green, *John Wesley* (London: Nelson, 1964), 158.

111. Williams, *John Wesley's Theology Today,* 197n13.

# Chapter 3
# Theological Method in Wesley

1. "On Faith, Heb. 11:6" (1788, sermon 106), I.1, *Works* (Bicentennial ed.), 3:493.

2. See "The Great Privilege of those that are Born of God" (1748, sermon 19), III.2, *Works* (Bicentennial ed.), 1:442. Larry Shelton argues that "the focus and function of the Holy Spirit as the context of his theological method [is not] usually recognized adequately." Consequently the role of the Holy Spirit in Wesley's theological method deserves greater recognition and development. See Shelton, "The Trajectory of Wesleyan Theology," *Wesleyan Theological Journal* 21, no. 2 (1986): 160.

3. "An Earnest Appeal," §6, *Works* (Oxford ed.), II:46. Gerald R. Cragg points out that Wesley "argues by analogy from our senses and knowledge based on their reports to faith and the assurance based on its testimony" — an idea that reflects Peter Browne's Lockean understanding of epistemology. See Cragg, *Works* (Oxford ed.), 57n1; d. Richard E. Brantley, *Locke, Wesley, and the Method of English Romanticism* (Gainesville, Fla.: University of Florida Press, 1984), 48–53.

4. Letter "To Mr. 'John Smith,'" 28 September 1745, §§11–12, *Works* (Oxford ed.), 26:156–57.

5. Colin Williams, *John Wesley's Theology Today* (New York: Abingdon, 1960), 34.

6. See Wesley's comments on the faith of deists ("On Faith" [1788, sermon 106], I.2,

*Works* [Bicentennial ed.], 3:494), and on their objection of the Bible ("On a Single Eye" [1789, sermon 125], §3, *Works* [Jackson ed.], 7:298).

7. See Wesley's discussion of faith as a disposition of the heart in "Salvation by Faith" (1738, sermon 1), I.4, *Works* (Bicentennial ed.), 1:120; cf. "The Almost Christian" (1741, sermon 2), (III).5, *Works* (Bicentennial ed.), 1:139.

8. "To Brian Bury Collins," 3 January 1781, *Letters* (Telford ed.), 7:47. 9. "On Eternity" (1786, sermon 54), §54, *Works* (Bicentennial ed.), 2:369.

10. See Williams, *John Wesley's Theology Today,* 27.

11. See Shelton's discussion on the agreement of Wesley with Luther and Calvin concerning the self–authentication of Scripture through the *testimonium Spiritus Sancti internum* ("The Trajectory of Wesleyan Theology," 160–61).

12. The term *experimental* does not mean the same as *empirical* in the sense that all truth must be empirically verifiable. Not all truths may be proved empirically, because not all truths are of an empirical nature. But all truths may be proved in our experiences of "life. For example, Wesley argued that experience proves that people are sinful, thus confirming the biblical doctrine of sin. See "On Sin in Believers" (1763, sermon 13), III.6–7, *Works* (Bicentennial ed.), 1:322–23; and "The Doctrine of Original Sin," pt. 1 ("The Past and Present State of Mankind"), *Works* (Jackson ed.), 9:196–237. Cf. chapter 7 in this book.

13. Umphrey Lee, *John Wesley and Modern Religion* (Nashville: Cokesbury, 1936), 300–322.

14. Schleiermacher, more than Coleridge, drew out the theological implications of formulating theology based on experience, particularly concerning our sense of absolute dependence on an infinite God.. See Friedrich Schleiermacher's works *On Religion: Speeches to its Cultured Despisers,* tr. John Oman (New York: Harper &: Row, 1958), 15–18, and *The Christian Faith,* ed. H. R. Mackintosh and J. S. Stewart (Edinburgh: T. &: T. Clark, 1928), 5–31, 94–128.

15. Scholars such as Brantley consider Wesley's adaptation of Lockean philosophy in theology a major advance in Western thought. Insofar as Wesley's works reflect the influence of Locke, Brantley says, "in particular [Browne's] *Procedure's* emphases on immediate revelation, they reveal what has not hitherto been widely acknowledged, namely, that his analogy between Methodist experience and Lockean method, i.e., between sense perception and the mind's response to the feeling of faith, constitutes an especially distinctive early modern blend of religion and philosophy" (*Locke, Wesley,* 101).

16. Frank Collier reports that Isaac Taylor, an otherwise sharp critic of Wesley and the Methodist movement, declared that the movement "presents itself as the starting–point of our modern religious history" due to Wesley's openness to what may be applied to theology from the work of physical scientists and empirical philosophers of his day. See Frank W. Collier, *John Wesley Among the Scientists* (New York: Abingdon, 1928), 11.

17 Collier suggests that Wesley was "an ardent disciple of the physical scientists of his day" (*John Wesley Among the Scientists,* 11).

18. Wesley drew his methodological ideas from a complex of sources currently popular at the time of his writing. He was impressed by the natural sciences and by the empirical philosophy of Locke. He also had high regard for the Oxford Aristotelian logical tradition so well described by Rex D. Matthews in "'Religion and Reason Joined': A Study in the Theology of John Wesley" (Diss., Harvard' University, 1986), 143–57. However, we must resist the temptation to align Wesley with only one source of theological method as Brantley and Clifford Hindley do with their excellent, though perhaps too narrowly conceived, research into the Locke–Wesley connection. See Brantley,

*Locke, Wesley,* 27–102, and Hindley, "The Philosophy of Enthusiasm: A Study in the Origins of 'Experimental Theology:' " *London Quarterly and Holborn Review* 182 (1957): 99–109.

Brantley argues "that Locke's rational empiricism (i.e., his epistemology of sense perception attended by induction and deduction), directly informs the religious 'epistemology' whereby Wesley claimed the saving faith he felt was his," but he also admits that Wesley's general trust in experience is only "a partly Lockean trust." Brantley recognizes other influences in Wesley's thought; he merely emphasizes the influence of Locke and Browne *(Locke, Wesley,* 13, 89–90).

19. "Of the Gradual Improvement of Natural Philosophy," introduction to the five–volume *Natural Philosophy,* found in the *Works* (Jackson ed.), 13:483.

20. See Preface, §6, "Sermons on Several Occasions," *Works* (Bicentennial ed.), 1:106.

21. "The Case of Reason Impartially Considered" (1781, sermon 70), II.3, *Works* (Bicentennial ed.), 2:594–95.

22. George Bayrs, *John Wesley: Christian Philosopher and Church Founder* (London: Epworth, 1926), 58–59.

23. Unfortunately Eayrs did not fully develop the inductive character of Wesley's theological method. Instead he interpreted Wesley as being "a mystic," albeit "a practical mystic," which detracts from interpreting Wesley in line with his heritage of theological method derived from British theology, philosophy, and *science.* See George Eayrs, *John Wesley: Christian Philosopher and Church Founder,* 17, cf.. 58–59.

24. John Taylor's book on original sin was first published in 1740, but Wesley read a later edition that included a supplement in answer to The *Vindication of the Scripture Doctrine of Original* Sin by D. Jennings and The Ruin *and Recovery of Mankind* by Isaac Watts. See John Taylor, The *Scripture–Doctrine of Original* Sin, *Proposed to Free and Candid Examination,* 3rd ed. (London: J. Waugh, 1750).

25. Preface, §4, "Doctrine of Original Sin," *Works* (Jackson ed.), 9:193–94. 26. Ibid., 9:194.

27. Introduction, "Doctrine of Original Sin," pt. 1, *Works* (Jackson ed.), 9:196.

28. "Doctrine of Original Sin," pt. 1, I, *Works* (Jackson ed.), 9:196.

29. "Doctrine of Original Sin," pt. 1, I.14, *Works* (Jackson ed.), 9:235.

30. See references to common sense in "Doctrine of Original Sin," pt. 1, II.4,10–11, *Works* (Jackson ed.), 9:213, 221, 230. Wesley's frequent references to *common* sense undoubtedly reflect his confidence, typical of his century, in people's commonsense ability to discern truth and goodness. It does not necessarily reflect Thomas Reid's eighteenth–century Scottish Common Sense Philosophy, with which Wesley was not all that familiar. On the contrary, both Robert Carrol and Mitsuo Shimizu argue that Wesley had already inherited a tradition of "common–sense Anglicanism" through William Chillingworth, John Tillotson, and Edward Stillingfleet. See Robert T. Carrol, The *Common Sense Philosophy of Religion of Bishop Edward Stillingfleet* (The Hague: Nijhoff, 1975), 4, and Mitsuo Shimizu, "Epistemology in the Thought of John Wesley" (Diss., Drew University, 1980), 37–46.

31. "Doctrine of Original Sin," pt. 1, II.13, *Works* (Jackson ed.), 9:234. 32. See Mark H. Horst, "Christian Understanding and the Life of Faith in John Wesley's Thought" (Diss., Yale University, 1985), 287–92.

33. Ibid., 285.

34. Randy Maddox, "John Wesley — Practical Theologian?" Wesleyan Studies Group, American Academy of Religion Annual Meeting, Chicago, 20 November 1988, 26n93, 27. Maddox adds, "The Enlightenment ideal of the dispassionate inductive observer has

proven to be not only impossible (even for the natural sciences), but subtley oppressive" (27).

35. "Doctrine of Original Sin," pt. 2, [II.]10, *Works* (Jackson ed.), 9:273 (emphasis mine).

36. "Doctrine of Original Sin," pt. 2, I.1, *Works* (Jackson ed.), 9:273.

37. Wesley spoke of Taylor's work as a hypothesis that failed to provide a consistent and comprehensive explanation of the facts of sin. See "Doctrine of Original Sin," pt. 2, I.1, *Works* (Jackson ed.), 9:239.

38. "Doctrine of Original Sin," pt. 2, [III], *Works* (Jackson ed.), 9:302.

39. "Doctrine of Original Sin," pt. 2, [II.]8, *Works* (Jackson ed.), 9:271, and pt. 2, I.12, *Works* (Jackson ed.), 9:251.

40. "Doctrine of Original Sin," pt. 2, I.13, *Works* (Jackson ed.), 9:252; pt. 2, [III], *Works* (Jackson ed.), 9:311; and pt. 2, [III], 18, *Works* (Jackson ed.), 9:284.

41. See "Doctrine of Original Sin," pt. 2, I.14, *Works* (Jackson ed.), 9:253, and pt. 3, VII, *Works* (Jackson ed.), 9:336.

42. "Doctrine of Original Sin," pt. 2, [II.]16, *Works* (Jackson ed.), 9:269.

43. For example, see "Doctrine of Original Sin," pt. 3, VII–VIII, *Works* (Jackson ed.), 9:336, 341.

44. Wesley appealed to other sources besides Jennings and Watts in evaluation of Taylor. For example, he often quoted from the *Dialogues* by James Hervey, especially chapter 11, "Theron and Aspasio."

45. See Wesley's extract from *The Ruin and Recovery of Mankind* by Watts in "Doctrine of Original Sin," pt. 4, *Works* (Jackson ed.), 9:353–97.

46. "Doctrine of Original Sin," pt. 3, I, *Works* (Jackson ed.), 9:317.

47. See "Doctrine of Original Sin," pt. 3, II, *Works* (Jackson ed.), 9:317–19.

48. See "Doctrine of Original Sin," pt. 3, III, *Works* (Jackson ed.), 9:325; cf. 320.

49. See Wesley's excerpts from Taylor in "Doctrine of Original Sin," pt. 3, IV, *Works* (Jackson ed.), 9:326–27.

50. See preface, §4, "Doctrine of Original Sin," *Works* (Jackson ed.), 193–94.

51. Taylor, quoted by Wesley in "Doctrine of Original Sin," pt. 3, VIII, *Works* (Jackson ed.), 9:339–40.

52. Wesley, quoting Ephesians 4:21, in "Doctrine of Original Sin," pt. 3, VIII, *Works* (Jackson ed.), 9:340; cf. 341.

53. "Doctrine of Original Sin," pt. 3, VIII, *Works* (Jackson ed.), 9:341.

54. Wesley did not use the term *correlation* in discussing his approach to theology, just as he did not explicitly formulate a statement of theological method. So we should not attempt to understand his correlational endeavors with the degree of specificity and intentionality with which, say, Paul Tillich undertook his "method of correlation" (Paul Tillich, *Systematic Theology,* 3 vols. [Chicago: University of Chicago. Press, 1951], 1:59–66). Instead we should understand Wesley's correlational endeavors from the more informal perspective of how he practically sought to integrate all sources of religious authority, including Scripture, tradition, reason, and experience.

55. Introduction, "Doctrine of Original Sin," pt. 4, *Works* (Jackson ed.), 9:353.

56. Wesley quoted extensively from the following sources: Isaac Watts, *The Ruin and Recovery of Mankind* (1741), and Thomas Boston, *Human Nature in its Fourfold State* (1720). See "Doctrine of Original Sin," pts. 4–7, *Works* (Jackson ed.), 9:353–464.

57. Preface, §3, "Doctrine of Original Sin," and pt. 6, *Works* (Jackson ed.), 9:193, 431.

58. "Doctrine of Original Sin," pt. 6, *Works* (Jackson ed.), 9:432.

59. Wesley implies this concern in "Doctrine of Original Sin," pt. 2, [III], *Works*

(Jackson ed.), 9:300.

60. "Doctrine of Original Sin," pt. 2, [II.]11, *Works* (Jackson ed.), 9:274.

61. "Doctrine of Original Sin," pt. 2, [III], *Works* (Jackson ed.), 9:291.

62. See "Doctrine of Original Sin," pt. 6, *Works* (Jackson ed.), 9:432.

63. Preface, §6, "Doctrine of Original Sin," *Works* (Jackson ed.), 9:195. By recognizing that he was not *indifferent* to this important doctrine, Wesley reveals some awareness concerning limitations in the Enlightenment ideal of complete objectivity.

64. "Doctrine of Original Sin," pt. 6, *Works* (Jackson ed.), 9:432.

65. Ibid.

66. "Doctrine of Original Sin," pt. 2, [III], *Works* (Jackson ed.), 9:314. Cf. preface, §6, "Doctrine of Original Sin," *Works* (Jackson ed.), 9:195.

67. Wesley often begins his sermons or writings by making observations (or by asking questions about things he has observed) and then proceeds to draw inferences from what he has observed both of life and of the Scriptures. For example, in his sermon "On Faith, Heb. 11:6," he begins by asking the question, "But what is faith?" He proceeds, first, by endeavoring "to point out the several sorts of faith" and, second, by drawing "a few inferences from the preceding observations." See "On Faith, Heb. 11:6" (1788, sermon 106), §1, I.1, II.1, *Works* (Bicentennial ed.), 3:492–93, 498. Cf. Brantley's excellent investigation into the connection between Lockean method and the approach Wesley took in formulating most of his writings *(Locke, Wesley,* 48–89).

68. The term *common sense* did not play a technical role in Wesley's theology or in that of Chillingworth, Tillotson, and Stillingfleet. Common sense only later became a crucial philosophical term for Reid's Scottish Common Sense Philosophy. Nevertheless, Wesley wrote in a context where people practically understood what he meant when referring to common sense. For the most part, common sense refers more to informal rather than formal canons of logic.

69. In correspondence with the critic who used the name "John Smith," Wesley affirmed that our spiritual senses possess what may be called "perceptible inspiration." Our spiritual senses are analogous to and are as reliable as our physical senses. Wesley says, "Therefore the *distinguishing doctrines* on which I do insist in all my writings and in all my preaching will lie in a very narrow compass. You sum them all up in perceptible *inspiration.* For this I earnestly contend; and so do all who are called mean that inspiration of God's Holy Spirit whereby he fills us with righteousness, peace, and joy, with love to him and to all humankind. And we believe it cannot be, in the nature of things, that a man should be filled with this peace and joy and love by the inspiration of the Holy Ghost without perceiving it, as clearly as he does the light of the sun." See "To 'John Smith,'" 30 December 1745, §13, *Works* (Oxford ed.), 26:181–82.

70. "The Witness of the Spirit, I' (1746, sermon 10), II.9 *Works* (Bicentennial ed.), 1:282.

71. Wesley uses these words from Locke's "Essay on Human Understanding" in order to communicate similar epistemological ideas. See "Remarks upon Mr. Locke's 'Essay on Human Understanding,'" *Works* (Jackson ed.), 13:455–56.

72. For example, see "On God's *Vineyard*" (1787, sermon 107), I.2–3, *Works* (Bicentennial ed.), 3:504–5.

73. Brantley, *Locke, Wesley,* 23.

74. These are the words of Locke, quoted by Hindley, "The Philosophy of Enthusiasm," 109n33.

75,. Brantley, *Locke, Wesley,* 33.

76. Ibid., 48.

77. "Remarks upon Mr. Locke's 'Essay on Human Understanding,'" *Works* (Jackson ed.), 13:456.

78. *Natural Philosophy,* 2:185.

79. Ibid., 2:210. Wesley's words reflect the ideas of Charles Bonnet in *Contemplation de la Nature,* 2nd ed., 2 vols. (Amsterdam: n.p., 1769), 1:67. Wesley actually included in his *Natural Philosophy* an English abridgment of Bonnet's *Contemplation of Nature.* Cf. other references to the gradual progression of the world in the letter "To Dr. John Robertson," 24 September 1753, *Works* (Oxford ed.), 26:518, and *Notes upon the Old Testament,* Genesis 1.2. For further discussion on this subject, see the chapter "Wesley and Evolution" in Collier, *John Wesley Among the Scientists* 148–204, esp. 187–95.

80. See Mildred Bangs Wynkoop, *A Theology of Love* (Kansas City: Beacon Hill, 1972), 347.

81. See Harald Lindström's revealing discussion of these later changes in Wesley's view of entire sanctification in *Wesley and Sanctification* (1980; reprint, Grand Rapids: Zondervan, 1983), 138–40.

82. Ibid., 139.

83. *Journal* (Curnock ed.), 5:492, 495, 17 December 1772.

84. See "An Earnest Appeal" and "A Farther Appeal," *Works* (Oxford ed.), 11:37–326.

85. Wesley should not be criticized for failing to consider every conceivable fact relevant to the study of religion. Although Wesley may appear selective with the facts of Scripture and experiences he chose to investigate, *he* believed that he had thoroughly dealt with all information relevant to studying    Christian doctrines.,

86. Wesley's use of a limited number of observed instances of sin may be best described as *ampliative induction,* which is defined as follows: "Reasoning from a limited number of observed instances to a general causal relationship" (Peter A. Angeles, *A Dictionary of Philosophy* [New York: Harper & Row, 1981], 132).

# Chapter 4
# The Authority of Scripture

1. Preface, §8, "Sermons on Several Occasions," *Works* (Bicentennial ed.), 1:107.

2. Wesley most often made explicit references to the authority of reason when speaking in conjunction with scriptural authority. And whenever he mentioned more than two sources of religious authority, he usually placed reason second in order after Scripture. So, especially in a larger discussion of theological method, it would seem logical to take up reason after considering Scripture.

Nevertheless, Wesley's understanding of experience could come immediately after Scripture because it is his most distinctive contribution to Christian thinking. Besides, the study of experience draws attention to the experimental dimension of religious truths so crucial to the life of believers and to the defense of Wesley's theology.

Then again, Wesley always assumed the orthodoxy of his theology and the continuity of the Methodist movement with the truest, most primitive form of Christianity (which he believed to develop in spiritual succession through the Church of England). He did not try to create a new theology, but only integrate reason and experience in ways that better reflected classical, orthodox beliefs. In sum, all three sources of religious authority could profitably be discussed in any order following Scripture.

3. *The Book of Discipline of the United Methodist Church* 1984 (Nashville: United Methodist Publishing House, 1984), 81.

4. *Journal* (Curnock ed.), 2:226, 22 June 1739.

5. "To James Hervey," 20 March 1739, *Letters* (Telford ed.), 1:285.

6. "To John Dickins," 26 December 1789, *Letters* (Telford ed.), 8:192.

7. Preface, §9, "Sermons on Several Occasions," *Works* (Bicentennial ed.), 1:107.

8. "The Case of Reason Impartially Considered" (1781, sermon 70), I.6, *Works* (Bicentennial ed.), 2:591.

9. Ibid., 2:591–92.

10. Preface, §5, "Sermons on Several Occasions," *Works* (Bicentennial ed.), 1:105.

11. 2 Tim. 3:16, *Notes upon the New Testament*, 794.

12. "To Thomas Whitehead (?)," 10 February 1748, *Letters* (Telford ed.), 2:117.

13. See "A Plain Account of Christian Perfection," §10, *Works* (Jackson ed.), 11:373.

14. See *Journal* (Curnock ed.), 1:91, 22 Saturday 1738.

15. *Journal*, 1:442, 4 March 1738.

16. Ibid. (Italics are Wesley's.)

17. Compare Wesley's comments on 2 Timothy 3:16 in the *Notes upon the New Testament*, 794, with Anglican formularies concerning "The Scriptures" in Articles VI–VII of the Thirty–nine Articles in Philip Schaff, *The Creeds of Christendom* (New York: Harper & Brothers, 1919), 1:592–649, 3:486–516; and Edward J. Bicknell, A *Theological Introduction to the Thirty–nine Articles of the Church of England* (London: Longman, 1919), 128–46.

18. "The Character of a Methodist," §1, *Works* (Jackson ed.), 8:340. 19. Ibid.

20. "A Clear and Concise Demonstration of the Divine Inspiration of the Holy Scriptures," *Works* (Jackson ed.), 11:484.

21. Ibid.

22. C. S. Lewis, *Mere Christianity* (New York: Macmillan, 1943), 55–56.

23. Colin Williams, *John Wesley's Theology Today* (New York: Abingdon, 1960), 27.

24. Ibid.

25. Preface, §12, *Notes upon the New Testament*, 9.

26. "The Witness of the Spirit, I" (1746, sermon 10), I.7, *Works* (Bicentennial ed.), 1:274. Cf. "The Imperfection of Human Knowledge" (1784, sermon 69), *Works* (Bicentennial ed.), 2:567–86.

27. 1 Corinthians 13:9, 12.

28. "On Faith, Heb. 11:6" (1788, sermon 106), I.8, *Works* (Bicentennial ed.), 3:496. Cf. related discussions of Wesley's theological proximity with classical Protestantism in R. Larry Shelton, 'John Wesley's Approach to Scripture in Historical Perspective," *Wesleyan Theological Journal* 16, no. 1 (1981): 37–38; and Williams, *John Wesley's Theology Today*, 26, 37.

29. "On Working Out Our Own Salvation" (1785, sermon 85), II.4, *Works* (Bicentennial ed.), 3:205.

30. Cf. Harald Lindström, *Wesley and Sanctification* (1980; reprint, Grand Rapids: Zondervan, 1983), 105–112; Williams, *John Wesley's Theology Today* 1946; Randy L. Maddox, "Responsible Grace: The Systematic Nature of Wesley's Theology Reconsidered," *Wesleyan Theological Journal* 19, no. 2 [1984]: 26; Mitsuru Samuel Fujimoto, "John Wesley's Doctrine of Good Works" (Diss., Drew University, 1986), 1, 3; and Kenneth Collins, *Wesley on Salvation: A Study in the Standard Sermons* (Grand Rapids: Zondervan/Francis Asbury Press, 1989).

31. Lindström, *Wesley and Sanctification*, 113; cf. 105–119.

32. See Shelton, "John Wesley's Approach to Scripture," 23–50.

33. Ibid., 39.

34. "The Means of Grace" (1746, sermon 16), II.1, *Works* (Bicentennial ed.), 1:381.

35. "The Means of Grace" (1746, sermon 16), III.7, *Works* (Bicentennial ed.), 1:386.

36.. Shelton states that "the *sola Scriptura* watchword in Luther is virtually the equivalent of Wesley's *homo unius libri* emphasis" ("The Trajectory of Wesleyan Theology," *Wesleyan Theological Journal* 21, nos. 1–2 [1986]: 160). Cf. Shelton, "John Wesley's Approach to Scripture," 33, 37.

37. In objection to Soame Jenyns's book entitled *Internal Evidence of the Christian Religion,* in which Jenyns denied that all Scripture is given by the inspiration of God, Wesley said: "Nay, if there be any mistakes in the Bible there may as well be a thousand. If there be one falsehood in that book it did not come for the God of truth" *Journal* [Curnock ed.], 6:117, 24 August 1776). Cf. *Standard* Sermons (Sugden ed.), 1:249–50: "All Scripture is infallibly true."

38. John Alfred Faulkner argues that the Methodist movement "was soteriological, [and] not in the first place theological in the strict sense. It came round to God and Christ and Spirit by way of salvation" *(Modernism and the Christian Faith* [New York: Methodist Book Concern, 1921], 220).

39. See John S. Simon, *John Wesley and the Religious Societies* (London: Epworth, 1921), 283–84.

40. *Journal,* 1:455, 22 April 1738.

41. "A Clear and Concise Demonstration of the Divine Inspiration of the Holy Scriptures," *Works* (Jackson ed.), 11:484.

42. Albert C. Outler, ed., *John Wesley* (New York: Oxford University Press, 1980), 28n101.

43. "Minutes of Several Conversations," Q.32, *Works* (Jackson ed.), 8:315.

44. James R. Joy shows the breadth of Wesley's vast literary interests in "Wesley: Man of a Thousand Books and a Book," *Religion in Life* 8 (Winter 1939): 71–84. Onva K. Boshears, Jr., expands on this theme in "John Wesley, The Bookman: A Study of His Reading Interests in the Eighteenth Century" (Diss., University of Michigan, 1972).

45. Thomas Langford, *Practical Divinity: Theology in the Wesleyan Tradition* (Nashville: Abingdon, 1983), 25.

46. Albert C. Outler, introduction, *Works* (Bicentennial ed.), 1:69.

47. Commentary on Deuteronomy 17:19, *Notes upon the Old Testament,* 1:638n.

48. See Wesley's quotations from 2 Timothy 3:15b in "The Means of Grace" (1746, sermon 16), III.8, *Works* (Bicentennial ed.), 1:388. Cf. "On Family Religion" (1783, sermon 94), III.16, *Works* (Bicentennial ed.), 3:344.

49. Some interpreters would disagree with this assessment of Wesley's view of Scripture. For example, Wilber T. Dayton squarely places Wesley in the tradition of biblical inerrancy ("Theology and Biblical Inerrancy," *Wesleyan Theological Journal* 3, no. 1 (1968): 35. The question, however, remains moot since Wesley did not address historical–critical issues, which arose largely in the following century.

50. Although Wesley sought to uncover "the plain, literal meaning of any text," he recognized that sometimes Scripture is obscure or "implies an absurdity." See "Of the Church" (1785, sermon 74), §12 *Works* (Bicentennial ed.), 3:50; cf. "To Samuel Furly," 10 May 1755, *Letters* (Telford ed.), 3:129, and "Upon our Lord's Sermon on the Mount, I" (1748, sermon 21), §6, *Works* (Bicentennial ed.), 1:473.

51. "The Imperfection of Human Knowledge" (1784, sermon 69), III.2, *Works* (Bicentennial ed.), 2:583.

52. "Walking by Sight and Walking by Faith" (1788, sermon 119), §9, *Works* (Jackson ed.), 7:258.

53. "The Imperfection of Human Knowledge" (1784, sermon 69), III.2, *Works*

(Bicentennial ed.), 2:583.

54. Wesley admired and credited his reliance on the exegesis of Bengel's commentary, entitled *Gnomon Novi Testamenti* (1742), in the preface to the *Notes upon the New Testament, 7.*

55. Langford, *Practical Divinity,* 25.

56. Mildred Bangs Wynkoop, "A Hermeneutical Approach to John Wesley," *Wesleyan Theological Journal* 6, no. 1 (1971): 21. Cf. Wynkoop's chapter on "A Hermeneutical Approach to Wesley" in her book *Theology of Love* (Kansas City: Beacon Hill, 1972), 76–101.

57. Shelton offers a helpful summary of Wesley's biblical hermeneutics in the article "John Wesley's Approach to Scripture in Historical Perspective," esp. 41. Cf. preface, *Notes upon the Old Testament,* 1:i–ix, and preface, §5, *Works* (Bicentennial ed.), 1:105–6.

58. Shelton, "John Wesley's Approach to Scripture," 41.

59. Preface, *Notes upon the Old Testament,* 1

60. Shelton, "John Wesley's Approach to Scripture," 42. Cf. discussion of "literal interpretation" in Elliott E. Johnson, *Expository Hermeneutics: An Introduction* (Grand Rapids: Zondervan, 1990), esp. 9–11, 31–38, 87–96.

61. Ibid. As an example, Wesley might appeal to the historic doctrines of original sin, justification by faith, the new birth, and inward and outward holiness in order to interpret difficult passages of Scripture.

62. Outler describes Wesley as having "twin principles of hermeneutics. The first is that Scripture is Scripture's own best interpreter; thus, 'the analogy of faith' (i.e., one's sense of the whole), should govern one's exegesis of each part. . . . The second is that one begins, always, with a literal translation and holds to it unless it should lead into a palpable absurdity; in which case, analogy and even allegory become allowable options" (*Works* [Bicentennial ed.], 1:473n22).

63. Shelton, "John Wesley's Approach to Scripture," 42.

64. "The Scripture Way of Salvation" (1765, sermon 43), §2, *Works* (Bicentennial ed.), 2:156.

65. *Standard Sermons* (Sugden ed.), 1:196n2.

66. "On Corrupting the Word of God" (1727, sermon 137), *Works* (Jackson ed.), 7:470.

67. "Popery Calmly Considered," 1.6, *Works* (Jackson ed.), 10:142.

68. "An Address to the Clergy," 1.2, *Works* (Jackson ed.), 10:482.

69. *Journal* (Curnock ed.), 1:471–72, §12, 24 May 1738.

70. "The Witness of the Spirit, II" (1767, sermon 11), III.6, *Works* (Bicentennial ed.), 1:290.

71. Cf. Sugden's interpretation of Wesley as one who "first worked out his theology by strict logical deduction from the Scriptures; and then he corrected his conclusions by the test of actual experience. His class–meetings were a laboratory in which he verified or modified his hypotheses." See *Standard Sermons* (Sugden ed.), 1:196n2.

72. Cf. Lindström's interpretation of Wesley's doctrine of entire sanctification, of which Lindström says: "It was from this appeal to experience, moreover, that Wesley's doctrine of perfection sprang; the latter is regarded as a corollary of the former" (*Wesley and Sanctification,* 4).

73. "A Plain Account of Christian Perfection," §19, *Works* (Jackson ed.), 11:406.

74. "The Case of Reason Impartially Considered" (1781, sermon 70),II.10, *Works* (Bicentennial ed.), 2:599. Outler notes that Wesley's use of the quote from Proverbs 20:27 reflects a slogan of the Cambridge Platonists (Bicentennial ed., 2:599n58).

75. "The New Birth" (1760, sermon 45), I.1, *Works* (Bicentennial ed.), 2:188; cf. "The End of Christ's Coming" (1781, sermon 62), I.1–7, *Works* (Bicentennial ed.), 2:473–76.

76. "The Case of Reason Impartially Considered" (1781, sermon 70), 1.6, *Works* (Bicentennial ed.), 2:592.

77. Ibid.

78. "A Plain Account of Christian Perfection," §25, *Works* (Jackson ed.), 11:429.

79. See "To Thomas Whitehead (?)," 10 February 1748, *Letters* (Telford ed.), 2:117.

80. These six rules are a summary of Arnett's study of Wesley's approach to scriptural interpretation. See William M. Arnett, "John Wesley — Man of One Book" (Diss., Drew University, 1954), 89–96. The quotation in rule five comes from William R. Cannon, *Theology of John Wesley* (New York: Abingdon, 1946), 159.

81. Outler, introduction, *Works* (Bicentennial ed.), 1:58–59.

82. Quotations taken from the letter "To Samuel Furly," 10 May 1755, *Letters* (Telford ed.), 3:129, and "Of the Church" (1785, sermon 74), I.12, *Works* (Bicentennial ed.), 3:51.

83. Gerald R. Cragg, *Reason and Authority in the Eighteenth Century* (Cambridge: Cambridge University Press, 1964), 160.

84. Edward H. Sugden, introduction, *John Wesley's Fifty-three Sermons*, ed. Edward H. Sugden (Nashville: Abingdon, 1983), 7.

85. *Notes upon the New Testament*, §7, quoted by Sugden, *John Wesley's Fifty three Sermons*, 7–8.

86. Preface to the Book of Joshua, *Notes upon the Old Testament*, 1:701.

87. George C. Cell, *The Rediscovery of John Wesley* (New York: Henry Holt, 1935), 13.

88. Williams, *John Wesley's Theology Today*, 26.

89. Albert C. Outler, *Theology in the Wesleyan Spirit* (Nashville: Tidings, 1975), 9; cf. introduction, *Works* (Bicentennial ed.), 1:57.

90. For example, see S. Parkes Cadman, *The Three Religious Leaders of Oxford and their Movements* (New York: Macmillan, 1916), 338, and Wilbur H. Mullen, "John Wesley's Method of Biblical Interpretation," *Religion in Life* 47 (Spring 1978): 99–108.

91 Mullen, "John Wesley's Method of Biblical Interpretation," 107.

# Chapter 5
## The Authority of Tradition

1. Gerald R. Cragg describes the eighteenth–century distrust in Christian tradition as follows: "Thus all forms of traditional authority were suspect. . . .Men were to be taught to rely on the evidence provided by nature or reason, not on the arguments supplied by tradition. Indeed, the history of eighteenth–century thought is largely concerned with the problem of authority" (*Reason and Authority in the Eighteenth Century* [Cambridge: Cambridge University Press, 1964], 2).

2. Preface to the third edition, §4, *Works* (Jackson ed.), 1:iv.

3. "On Laying the Foundation of the New Chapel" (1777, sermon 112), II.3, *Works* (Bicentennial ed.), 3:586.

4. Ibid.

5 "An Earnest Appeal," §2, *Works* (Oxford ed.), 11:45, quoted by Wesley in "On Laying the Foundation of the New Chapel" (1777, sermon 112), II.1, *Works* (Bicentennial ed.), 3:585. Cf. "On Divine Providence" (1786, sermon 67), §18, *Works* (Bicentennial ed.), 2:543.

6. Here Wesley quoted from the collect to "The Order for the Administration of the Lord's Supper, or Holy Communion" in the *Book of Common Prayer* in "On

Laying the Foundation of the New Chapel" (1777, sermon 112), II.4, *Works* (Bicentennial ed.), 3:586. Cf. *The Book of Common Prayer* 1559, ed. John E. Booty (Charlottesville: University Press of Virginia, 1976), 248.

7. See "On Laying the Foundation of the New Chapel" (1777, sermon 112), II.1–4, *Works* (Bicentennial 00.), 3:585–86.

8. Preface, §5, "Sermons on Several Occasions," *Works* (Bicentennial ed.), 1:106.

9. Outler, *Works* (Bicentennial ed.), 1:324n47.

10. "Of Former, Times" (1787, sermon 102), §12, *Works* (Bicentennial ed.), 3:448.

11. Ted A. Campbell, "John Wesley's Conceptions and Uses of Christian Antiquity" (Diss., Southern Methodist University, 1984), 14.

12. "A Farther Appeal, III," III.28, *Works* (Oxford ed.), 11:310.

13. "On Laying the Foundation of the New Chapel" (1777, sermon 112), I.3, *Works* (Bicentennial ed.), 3:582.

14. "On God's Vineyard" (1787, sermon 107), I.4, *Works* (Bicentennial ed.), 3:505: "The book which, next to the Holy Scripture, was of the greatest use to them in settling their judgment as to the grand point of justification by faith was the *Book of Homilies.* They were never clearly convinced that we are justified by faith alone till they carefully consulted these, and compared them with the Sacred Writings, particularly St. Paul's Epistle to the Romans."

15. "To Dr. Conyers Middleton," 4 January 1749, III.11, *Letters* (Telford ed.), 2:387.

16. "The Advantage of the Members of the Church of England, Over Those of the Church of Rome," §3, *Works* (Jackson ed.), 10:134.

17. "To Dr. Conyers Middleton," 4 January 1749, III.12, *Letters* (Telford ed.), 2:387.

18. Ibid.

19. "Address to the Clergy," I.2, *Works* (Jackson ed.), 10:484.

20. Outler, *Works* (Bicentennial ed.), 3:586n31.

21. "To Dr. Conyers Middleton," 4 January 1749, §1 *Letters* (Telford ed.), 2:312.

22. See ibid., 2:312–13. Wesley considered Dr. Conyers Middleton to have presented such a book against the fathers.

23. Luke Keefer, Jr., "John Wesley: Disciple of Early Christianity" (Diss., Temple University, 1981), 4. Keefer further argues that Wesley's primitivism "was a primary motif throughout his life, subject to development, alteration, and assessment, but never renounced."

24. For a more complete discussion of the study and uses of Christian antiquity in seventeenth– and early eighteenth–century British Christianity, see Campbell, "John Wesley's Conceptions and Uses of Christian Antiquity" 21–57; and Keefer, "John Wesley: Disciple of Early Christianity" 551–643. Cf. Umphrey Lee, *John Wesley and Modern Religion* (Nashville: Cokesbury, 1936), 132, and Outler, introduction, *Works* (Bicentennial ed.), 1:74–76.

25. John Bramhall, *The Works of John Bramhall* (Dublin: His Majesties Printing House, 1676), 407.

26. Francis Paget, *An Introduction to the Fifth Book of Hooker's Treatise of the Laws of Ecclesiastical Polity* (Oxford: Oarendon, 1907), 284.

27. Henry R. McAdoo, *The Structure of Caroline Moral Theology* (London: Longman's, Green, 1949), 4.

28. See "An Address to the Clergy," I.2, II.1, *Works* (Jackson ed.), 10:484, 492–93. Keefer and Campbell make impressive cases for the lifelong importance of tradition in Wesley's theology in their respective dissertations, "John Wesley: "Disciple of Early Christianity" and "John Wesley's Conceptions and Uses of Christian Antiquity."

29. "An Address to the Clergy," I.2, *Works* (Jackson ed.), 10:484.

30. See "To Dr. Conyers Middleton," 4 January 1749, V.I–11, *Letters* (Telford ed.), 2:368–74. Cf. "The Means of Grace" (1746, sermon 16), III.9, *Works* (Bicentennial ed.), 1:388n58.

31. Throughout the British revival and Methodist movement, Wesley staunchly affirmed his alignment with the Church of England. He was not uncritical of its theology and ecclesiology, but he declared his theological loyalty until his death. See the following:

"An Earnest Appeal," §78, 85–86, *Works* (Oxford ed.), 11:77–78, 82–83;

"A Farther Appeal, III," III.31–32, *Works* (Oxford ed.), 11:313–14;

"Minutes of Some Late Conversations," 27 June 1744, *Works* (Jackson ed.), 8:279–81;

"The Principles of a Methodist Farther Explained," III.1–9, *Works* (Jackson ed.), 8:436–44;

"To 'John Smith,'" 28 September 1745, §20, and 30 December 1745, §3, *Works* (Oxford ed.), 26:160–61, 176;

"To John Baily," 8 June 1750, II.20, *Letters* (Telford ed.), 3:289;

"To the Editor of 'Lloyd's Evening Post,'" 1 December 1760, *Letters* (Telford ed.), 4:115–16; and

"To Sir Harry Trelawney," August 1780, *Letters* (Telford ed.), 7:27–28.

In addition, see Wesley's firm commitment against schism: "I live and die a member of the Church of England, and none who regard my judgment or advice will ever separate from it." See "Farther Thoughts on Separation from the .Church," *Arminian Magazine* (1790): 216; cf. *Journal* (Curnock ed.), 4:186, 28 September 1756; and "Reasons Against a Separation from the Church of England," *Works* (Jackson ed.), 13:225–32.

32. "On God's Vineyard" (1787, sermon 107), I.4, *Works* (Bicentennial ed.), 3:505.

33. "To Sir Harry Trelawny," August 1780, *Letters* (Telford ed.), 7:28.

34. "To John Smith,'" 30 December 1745, §3, *Works* (Oxford ed.), 26:176.

35. "The Advantage of the Members of the Church of England, Over Those of the Church of Rome," §1–3, 6, *Works* (Jackson ed.), 10:133–35.

36. Cf. "Reasons Against a Separation from the Church of England," *Works* (Jackson ed.), 13:225–31.

37. Cf. Outler's discussion on how Wesley developed his own disciplined communities within the Church of England in order to renew the church without separating from it ("The Wesleyan Quadrilateral in John Wesley," *Wesleyan Theological Journal* 20, no. 1 [1985]: 11).

38. See Wesley's discussion on the orthodoxy of his views concerning the operations of the Holy Spirit, in "A Farther Appeal," V.27, *Works* (Oxford: ed.), 11:170. .

39. Vincent of Lérins, *A Commonitory*, II.[6], *A Select Library of Nicene and Post–Nicene Fathers of the Christian Church*, ed. Philip Schaff and Henry Wace, 2d series (Grand Rapids: Eerdmans, 1982), 11:132.

40. Mildred Bangs Wynkoop, *Theology of Love* (Kansas City: Beacon Hill, 1972), 66.

41. "A Letter to a Roman Catholic," §16, *Works* (Jackson ed.), 10:85. The internal quote came from the preceding paragraph in Wesley's letter.

42. Ibid.

43. Wesley keeps doctrinal statements to a minimum, generally professing the inspiration of Scripture and creedal affirmations concerning God, Jesus Christ, the Holy Spirit, and salvation. He does mention differences between Methodism and, for example, Socinians, Arians, and the Roman Catholic Church. However, most differences had to

do with "opinions which do not strike at the root of Christianity." See "The Character of a Methodist," §1, *Works* (Jackson ed.), 8:340. Cf. 8:340–47 and "A Letter to a Roman Catholic," *Works* (Jackson ed.), 10:80–86.

44. "Prophets and Priests" (1789, sermon 121), §21, *Works* (Bicentennial ed.), 4:83–84.

45. See *Journal* (Curnock ed.),3:178, 29 May 1745. Cf. the following:

"The Lord Our Righteousness" (1765, sermon 20), II.20, *Works* (Bicentennial ed.), 1:464;

"The Nature of Enthusiasm" (1750, sermon 37), §36, *Works* (Bicentennial ed.), 2:59;

"On the Death of George Whitefield" (1770, sermon 53), III.1, *Works* (Bicentennial ed.), 2:341;

"On the Trinity" (1775, sermon 55), §2, *Works* (Bicentennial ed.), 2:376;

"On the Wedding Garment" (1790, sermon 127), §14, *Works* (Bicentennial ed.), 4:145; and

"The Character of a Methodist," §1, *Works* (Jackson ed.), 8:340.

46. See "Scriptural Christianity" (1744, sermon 4), IV.4, *Works* (Bicentennial ed.), 1:175;

"Upon our Lord's Sermon on the Mount, II" (1748, sermon 22), III.18, *Works* (Bicentennial ed.), 1:508;

"On the Trinity" (1775, sermon 55), §§1–2, *Works* (Bicentennial ed.), 2:374–76;

"On Laying the Foundation of the New Chapel" (1777, sermon 112), II.10, *Works* (Bicentennial ed.), 3:588; and

"On the Wedding Garment" (1790, sermon 127), §15, *Works* (Bicentennial ed.), 4:146.

Cf. Richard A. Muller's discussion of *adiaphora* in his *Dictionary of Latin and Greek Theological Terms* (Grand Rapids: Baker, 1985), 25–26.

47. See "The Lord Our Righteousness" (1765, sermon 20),II.3,20, *Works* (Bicentennial ed.), 1:454, 464;

"Upon our Lord's Sermon on the Mount, II" (1748, sermon 22), III.18, *Works* (Bicentennial ed.), 1:508;

"The Nature of Enthusiasm" (1750, sermon 37), §36, *Works* (Bicentennial ed.), 2:59;

"Catholic Spirit" (1750, sermon 39), I.1–6, *Works* (Bicentennial ed.), 2:82–85;

"On Patience" (1784, sermon 83), §11, *Works* (Bicentennial ed.), 3:177; and

"On God's Vineyard" (1787, sermon 107), IV.4. V.7, *Works* (Bicentennial ed.), 3:514, 517.

48. "Catholic Spirit" (1750, sermon 39), III.4, *Works* (Bicentennial ed.), 2:94.

49. "Catholic Spirit" (1750, sermon 39),II.1, *Works* (Bicentennial ed.), 2:89.

50. See Outler, *Works* (Bicentennial ed.), 1:220n7.

51. "The Advantage of the Members of the Church of England, Over Those of the Church of Rome," §1, *Works* (Jackson ed.), 10:133.

52. "A Roman Catechism, Faithfully Drawn Out of the Allowed Writings of the Church of Rome. With a Reply Thereto," Q.5, *Works* (Jackson ed.), 10:90.

53. Preface, "A Roman Catechism, Faithfully Drawn Out of the Allowed Writings of the Church of Rome. With a Reply Thereto," *Works* (Jackson ed.), 10:87.

54. Wesley's focus on soteriology in his primitivism is a major thesis in Keefer's dissertation; see "John Wesley: Disciple of Early Christianity," i. Cf. Keefer's chapter "Characteristics of Wesley's Primitivism," 644–717.

55. This oft-quoted statement of Wesley's came in response to the question, "What may we reasonably believe to be God's design in rising up the preachers called

Methodists?" See "Minutes of Several Conversations," Q.3, *Works* (Jackson ed.), 8:299.

56. Donald Joy suggests that Wesley avoided the writings of a systematic theology because its central tendency is "scholastic" and "anti–experiential." Joy offers the alternative conception of a *systemic* theology when he argues, "What we need is a different way of doing theology. I am appealing here for a wholistic theology, a theology that fully synchronizes all reality and shows up everywhere from the root system to the finally ripened fruit — just as a systemic gardener avoids systematic spraying of vegetables and fruit in favor of a way of gardening that engenders health and resistance to disease, even predators, by getting the proper nutrients and inhibitors into the *system* of every living plant." See Donald M. Joy, "'The Contemporary Church as 'Holy Community,'" in" *The Church*, ed. Melvin E. Dieter and Daniel N. Berg (Anderson, Ind.: Warner Press, 1972), 400; cf. 397–99.

57. Cf. Outler's discussion of how it was a matter of principle to Wesley not to define "doctrinal standards" too narrowly, rather than the sign of an indecisive mind ("The Wesleyan Quadrilateral," 8).

58. Cf. Jerry L. Walls, *The Problem of Pluralism: Recovering United Methodist Identity* (Wilmore, Ky.: Good News Books, 1986).

59. "A Letter to a Roman Catholic," §16, *Works* (Jackson ed.), 10:85.

60. "Catholic Spirit" (1750, sermon 39), III.1–3, *Works* (Bicentennial ed.), 2:92–94.

61. Cf. the basic tenets of Christian belief to which Wesley alludes in "A Letter to a Roman Catholic," *Works* (Jackson ed.), 10:80–86, and "Catholic Spirit" (1750, sermon 39), m, *Works* (Bicentennial ed.), 2:92–95.

62. See Outler, introductory comment, "On the Death of George Whitefield" (1770, sermon 53), *Works* (Bicentennial ed.), 2:325–29. Cf. Wesley's attack on the doctrine of predestination and all its partisans, including Whitefield, in the sermon "Free Grace" (1739, sermon 110), *Works* (Bicentennial ed.), 3:542~63.

63. See "On the Death of George Whitefield" (1770, sermon 53), *Works* (Bicentennial ed.), 2:330–47.

65. See "A Letter to a Roman Catholic," *Works* (Jackson ed.), 10:80–86.

66. "A Letter to a Roman Catholic," *Works* (Jackson ed.),.10:86.

# Chapter 6
## The Authority of Reason

1. "To Dr. Rutherford," 28 March 1768, *Letters* (Telford ed.), 5:364.

2. "An Earnest Appeal," §28, *Works* (Oxford ed.), 11:55.

3. "To Joseph Benson," 5 October 1770, *Letters* (Telford ed.), 5:203.

4. See similar quotes by Wesley concerning the value of reason for religion in "The Case of Reason Impartially Considered" (1781, sermon 70), §§1–2, II.10, *Works* (Bicentennial ed.), 2:587–88, 599–600. For more complete discussions on the role of reason in Wesley's theology, see Wallace G. Gray, Jr., "The Place of Reason in the Theology of John Wesley" (Diss., Vanderbilt University, 1953), and Rex D. Matthews, "'Religion and Reason Joined': A Study in the Theology of John Wesley" (Diss., Harvard University, 1986). Cf. articles by Stuart Andrews, "John Wesley and the Age of Reason," *History Today* 19 (1960): 25–32, and Bernard E. Jones, "Reason and Religion Joined, the Place of Reason in Wesley's Thought," *London Quarterly and Holborn Review* 189 (1964): 110–113.

5. For example, see "The Nature of Enthusiasm" (1750, sermon 37), §26, *Works*

(Bicentennial ed.), 2:55–56; "Causes of the Inefficacy of Christianity" (1789, sermon 122), §12, *Works* (Bicentennial ed.), 4:93; and "Seek First the Kingdom" (1725, sermon 134), §6, *Works* (Bicentennial ed.), 4:219.

Interestingly, William M. Arnett finds the following order of importance in Wesley's appeals to religious authority: "Scripture, primary; reason, secondary; and experience, finally." Tradition plays a comparatively less important role, according to Arnett ("John Wesley — Man of One Book" [Diss., Drew University, 1954], 67–70).

6. "The Nature of Enthusiasm" (1750, sermon 37), §26, *Works* (Bicentennial ed.), 2:55.

7. "The New Birth" (1760, sermon 45), I.1, *Works* (Bicentennial ed.), 2:188; d. "The End of Christ's Coming" (1781, sermon 62), I.3–7, *Works* (Bicentennial ed.), 2:474–76.

8. "Doctrine of Original Sin," pt. 2, objection 2, *Works* (Jackson ed.), 9:291.

9. Robert G. Tuttle, *John Wesley: His life and Theology* (Grand Rapids: Zondervan, 1978), 71.

10. *Journal* (Curnock ed.), 7:340,5 November 1787. Wesley refers to "Lord Bacon," the scientific empiricist, as possessing "universal genius" along with Aristotle.

11. Rex D. Matthews demonstrates how Aristotle provides the basic framework of Wesley's understanding of reason. Matthews says, "And this essentially Aristotelian understanding of reason as a faculty with a three–fold operation is found consistently in works written throughout Wesley's life" ("'Religion and Reason Joined,'" 17; cf. his section on "The Oxford Aristotelian Logical Tradition," 143–57).

12. See Wesley's criticism of Luther's disparagement of reason in the *Journal* (Curnock ed.), 2:467, 15 June 1741.

13. Scholars such as Robert W. Burtner and Robert E. Chiles do not hesitate to say of Wesley's thought that "essentially this may be called an empirical theology; there is nothing abstract or theoretical about it" (Burtner and Chiles, eds., *John Wesley's Theology* [1954; reprint, Nashville: Abingdon, 1982], 17).

14. Cf. Albert C. Outler, *Works* (Bicentennial ed.), 2:589n7.

15. Clifford Hindley, "The Philosophy of Enthusiasm: A Study in the Origins of 'Experimental Theology,'" *London Quarterly and Holborn Review* 182 (1957): 108; cf. 99–109.

16. Richard E. Brantley, *Locke, Wesley, and the Method of English Romanticism* (Gainesville, Fla.: University of Florida Press, 1984), 30; cf. 27–102.

17. Tuttle, *John Wesley: His Life and Theology,* 69–77, 143–55. Cf. similar ideas held by Edward H. Sugden in the *Standard Sermons* (Sugden ed.), 2:46n5; Vivian H. H. Green, *The Young Mr. Wesley* (London: Epworth, 1961), 310; Albert C. Outler's various works in "John Wesley as Theologian — Then and Now," *Methodist History* 12 (1974): 68; "John Wesley in the Christian Tradition," 30–31; and *Works* (Bicentennial ed.), 1:146n52, 276n46, 433n7, 711n122 and 2:192n29, 571n14, 589n7; John C. English, "The Cambridge Platonists in John Wesley's *Christian Library*," *Proceedings* 37 (1970): 101–4; Mitsuo Shimizu, "Epistemology in the Thought of John Wesley" (Diss., Drew University, 1980), 29n1, 111–54, 219–24; and Roderick T. Leupp, "'The Art of God': Light and Darkness in the Thought of John Wesley" (Diss., Drew University, 1985), 197–98, 224–29.

18. "To Mrs. Susanna Wesley," 29 July 1725, *Works* (Oxford ed.), 25:175. The quotation comes from Richard Fiddes, who wrote *A Body of Divinity* and defined faith as "an assent to a proposition on reasonable (or rational), grounds" (Fiddes: quoted by John Telford, *Letters* 1:24n1). Wesley soon saw the spiritual limitations of such a rationalistic definition of faith; cf. "To Mrs. Susanna Wesley," 22 November 1725, *Works* (Oxford ed.),

25:188.

19. See Umphrey Lee's comments on Wesley's experimentation with bibliomancy in *John Wesley and Modern Religion* (Nashville: Cokesbury, 1936),

140. Bibliomancy is belief in the guidance of the Holy Spirit in the act of arbitrarily opening to a passage of Scripture.

20. "The Circumcision of the Heart" (1733, sermon 17), I.7, *Works* (Bicentennial ed.), 1:405. This definition still reflects the rationalistically influenced understanding of faith Wesley had held earlier in a series of letters with his mother. See Wesley's letters "To Mrs. Susanna Wesley," 29 July 1725 and 22 November 1725, *Works* (Oxford ed.), 25:173–76, 186–89.

21. See Rex D. Matthews's extended discussion in the chapter on "Wesley's Changing Understanding of Faith," in which Wesley's mature view of faith includes (1) assent, (2) trust, and (3) "spiritual experience" ("'Religion and Reason Joined,'" 184–246).

22. "On Laying the Foundation of the New Chapel" (1777, sermon 112), II.11, *Works* (Bicentennial ed.), 3:588.

23. Outler, an introductory comment to "The Imperfection of Human Knowledge" (1784, sermon 69), *Works* (Bicentennial ed.), 2:568.

24. In response to the question "Whether anything can be religious that has not right reason to countenance it?" Wesley responded, "No. True religion is the highest reason." See "To the Editor of 'Lloyd's Evening Post,'" 1 December 1760, *Letters* (Telford ed.), 4:118.

25. "An Earnest Appeal," §36, *Works* (Oxford ed.), 11:58.

26. See "On a Single Eye" (1785, sermon 125), §3, *Works* (Jackson ed.), 7:298.

27. "To Mrs. Susanna Wesley," 29 July 1725, *Works* (Oxford ed.), 25:174. Of course, this letter reflects an early stage in Wesley's faith–thought development when he promoted a rationalistically oriented view of religious faith learned from Richard Fiddes (and Locke) but later repudiated. Nevertheless, the quote reveals Wesley's early belief in the sufficiency of Scripture as a resource for establishing reason as a legitimate and necessary source of religious authority.

28. Shimizu: quoting Wesley from the same letter, "To Mrs. Susanna Wesley," 29 July 1725. See Shimizu, "Epistemology in the Thought of John Wesley," 16.

29. "An Earnest Appeal," §31, *Works* (Oxford ed.), 11:56.

30. "To 'John Smith:'" 28 September 1745, III.11, *Works* (Oxford ed.), 26:157.

31. "Compendium of Logic:' *Works* (Jackson ed.), 14:178.

32. Shimizu, "Epistemology in the Thought of John Wesley," 51–52, drawing on information from the sermon "On Faith, Heb. 11:6" (1788, sermon 106), I.1–9, *Works* (Bicentennial ed.), 3:493–97.

33. "The Case of Reason Impartially Considered" (1781, sermon 70), II.10, *Works* (Bicentennial ed.), 2:599.

34. Ibid.

35. These two categories may seem overly broad in discussion of Wesley's philosophical and theological thought, but they represent the most prominent philosophies between which Wesley is generally discussed by scholars, and they also provide the context for discussions of the Enlightenment as a whole. Cf. the discussion of Wesley between these two philosophical traditions in Tuttle, *John Wesley: His Life and Theology*, 69–77, 143–55.

36. "The End of Christ's Coming" (1781, sermon 62), III.1, *Works* (Bicentennial ed.), 2:481.

37. "Scriptural Christianity" (1744, sermon 4), III.5, *Works* (Bicentennial ed.), 1:171.

38. Albert C. Outler, "The Place of Wesley in the Christian Tradition:' in The *Place of Wesley in the Christian Tradition,* ed. Kenneth E. Rowe (Metuchen, N.J.: Scarecrow, 1976), 30.

39. For example, see English, "The Cambridge Platonists," 101–4; and Outler, "The Place of Wesley in the Christian Tradition:' 30–31, and *Works* (Bicentennial ed.), 1:171n122, 433n7.

40. "The New Birth" (1760, sermon 45), II.4, *Works* (Bicentennial ed.), 1:433.

41. Outler, *Works* (Bicentennial ed.), 1:146n52.

42. See Outler, *Works* (Bicentennial ed.), 1:433n7. However, Rex D. Matthews notes that the English Puritans, who also influenced Wesley's theology, had made use of the language of spiritual sense ("'Religion and Reason Joined:'" 308–313).

43. Outler, *Works* (Bicentennial ed.), 3:361n1. Here Outler notes Wesley's familiarity with the ongoing debate between philosophical idealists and empiricists concerning innate ideas. Wesley agreed with empiricism in rejecting innate ideas, but allowed for intuitive ideas or insights about our self–existence and the existence of God. These allowances were also made by Locke, who was the primary influence of the British empirical tradition in the early eighteenth century. So Wesley need not be associated with idealist traditions even though he was undoubtedly influenced by them and often used terminology resembling their philosophy.

44. Although Locke was critical of Continental rationalists such as Descartes, he accepted several ideas characteristic of Christian rationalism. For example, Locke allowed for a degree of intuitive knowledge, particularly intuitive knowledge of one's own existence. With this starting point, he then argued for the existence of a being (God) adequate to produce all the effects manifest in experience. Although Locke felt the inconsistency of going beyond his own empirical definition of knowledge, he accepted what he believed common sense required. Cf. James Gordon Clapp, "John Locke," in *Encyclopedia of Philosophy,* ed. Paul Edwards, 4 vols. (New York: Free Press, 1973), 4:497–98.

45. Alexander Fraser, in annotating Locke's *Essay Concerning Human Understanding,* clarifies that the skepticism in his philosophy is not directed against religion. With regard to religion, Fraser notes that Locke's skepticism resembles that of Francis Bacon rather than Hume.. See John Locke, *Essay Concerning Human Understanding,* 2 vols., ed. Alexander Fraser (New York: Dover, 1894), 2:380n2.

46. Locke distinguishes between faith and reason in the following way: *"Reason,* therefore, here, as contradistinguished to *faith,* I take to be the discovery of the certainty or probability of such propositions or truths, which the mind arrives at by deduction made from such *ideas,* which it has got by the use of its natural faculties; viz. by sensation or reflection.

*"Faith,* on the other side, is the assent to any proposition not thus made out by the deductions of reason, but upon the credit of the proposer, as coming from God, in some extraordinary way of communication. This way of discovering truths to men, we call *revelation"* (Locke, *Essay Concerning Human Understanding,* 2:416).

47. See "Remarks upon Mr. Locke's 'Essay on Human Understanding'." *Works* (Jackson ed.), 13:455, and "On the Discoveries of Faith" (1788, sermon 117), §1; *Works* (Jackson ed.), 7:231.

48. Locke, *Essay Concerning Human Understanding,* 2:431.

49. Locke continued to argue that intuitive knowledge is the basis of all our knowledge and our highest certainty (*Essay Concerning Human Understanding,* 1:lxxvii–ix; 2:176–78,407). Cf. further discussion by Locke concerning the role of intuition in reli-

gion in the *Reasonableness of Christianity*, 10, 13–17, 79, 90.

50. Locke objected to being called a deist, and his affirmation of Scripture as "the constant guide of my assent. . . containing infallible truth relating to things of the highest concernment" reflects one of the significant distinctions between deism and him. See Locke's postscript to his first *Letter* (1697), to Edward Stillingfleet: quoted by Alexander Fraser in his introduction to *Essay Concerning Human Understanding*, 1:1.

51. Samuel Coleridge: quoted by Tuttle, *John Wesley: His Life and Theology* 69; cf. 76–77.

52. Cf. Tuttle, *John Wesley: His Life and Theology*, 46–47.

53. In conclusion of his "Remarks," Wesley stated, "From a careful consideration of this whole work, I conclude that, together with several mistakes, (but none of them of any great importance,) it contains many excellent truths, proposed in a clear and strong manner, by a great master both of reasoning and language. It might, therefore, be of admirable use to young students, if read with a judicious Tutor, who could confirm and enlarge upon what is right, and guard them against what is wrong, in it" ("Remarks upon Mr. Locke's 'Essay on Human Understanding,'" *Works* [Jackson ed.], 13:464).

54. "The Case of Reason Impartially Considered" (1781, sermon 70), §5, *Works* (Bicentennial ed.), 2:588–89.

55. For example, Wesley often thought that Locke, "chiefly through affectation of novelty," tried to complicate terms or logic that Aristotle had already stated more simply and precisely. See Wesley's critical comments of Locke's philosophy in his "Remarks upon Mr. Locke's 'Essay on Human Understanding,'" *Works* (Jackson ed.), 13:455–64, esp. 456, 460. Rex D. Matthews delineates differences between Wesley and Locke more explicitly when he says, "Locke, Browne, Butler, and Hume collectively had emphasized *probability* as 'the guide of life.' Faith, understood as intellectual assent to propositional truth, was to be proportioned to the *degree* of evidence which can be produced in support of any given proposition" ("'Religion and Reason Joined,'" 310).

56. See Outler's comments in *Works* (Bicentennial ed.), 2:589n7.

57. Roderick Leupp attempts to substantiate that connection by investigating how Wesley's frequent use of the metaphor of *light* "operates in his thought with sufficient flexibility to combine both the empirical and the intuitive tradition" ("'Art of God,'" 224–29, esp. 228). Cf. Albert C. Outler, ed., *John Wesley* (New York: Oxford University Press, 1980), introduction, 9–10, 14.

58. Matthews dedicates an entire section of his dissertation to the subject "Intuitionism versus Empiricism." He convincingly argues for the predominance of the empirical tradition in Wesley and against Albert C. Outler's interpretation of Wesley as having tried to synthesize — with more or less success — a "two–track" epistemology of intuitive and empirical philosophies. For example, Matthews contends that "in only one place in all of his writings does Wesley himself actually use the language of 'intuition' in addition to that of 'perception,' and even that use is qualified" ("'Religion and Reason,'" 300–308, esp. 305; cf. 14–20).

59. In support of this position, Matthews says that Outler "seems to miss the point cogently made by Laurence Wood: that whereas the metaphysical systems of such important 17th–century thinkers as Descartes, Malebranche, Spinoza, Leibniz, as well as the Cambridge Platonists and John Norris, 'saw reason to be in the realm of eternal truths held in common by the human and the divine mind,' 18th–century thinkers, beginning with Locke, 'looked upon reason as an intellectual activity'" ("'Religion and Reason,'" 303: quoting Laurence W. Wood, "Wesley's Epistemology," *Wesleyan Theological Journal* 10, no. 1 [1975]: 52).

60. Matthews, "'Religion and Reason,'" 18. Howard Slaatte also sees the philosophical connection between Locke and Wesley, but he argues that Wesley moved beyond Locke, especially. concerning his "faith in God and his revelation, particularly in the, New Testament gospel" *(Fire in the Brand* [New York: Exposition, 1963], 84).

61. See Locke's "Discourse of Miracles" and "Further Note on Miracles" in the *Reasonableness of Christianity*, 78–100. Cf. Richard E. Brantley, who described the influence of Browne on Wesley's concept of faith as follows: *"Evidence* [for faith] refers not so much to sense data, and hence not so much to empiricism per se, as to the paraempirical theology of Browne, wherein data of spiritual influx impress the mind and constitute faith's unsensuous, ineffable essence" *(Locke, Wesley, and the Method of English Romanticism* [Gainesville, Fla.: University of Florida Press, 1984], 39).

62. "On the Discoveries of Faith" (1788, sermon 117), §1, *Works* (Jackson ed.), 7:231.

63. For example, see "On Faith, Heb. 11:1" (1791, sermon 132), §18, *Works* (Jackson ed.), 7:335. Cf. Gerald R. Cragg, who notes that "Wesley's interpretation of the senses is a part of the epistemology he derived from John Locke," in *Works* (Oxford ed.), 11:57n1. It is interesting that less than a half–century later, Immanuel Kant endeavored to delineate the limits of reason in order to make room for faith. In a similar way as Kant, Wesley embraced empirical philosophy, noting the limitations of sense experience, to stress the need for a higher sense — analogically speaking — of faith.

64. "An Earnest Appeal," §32, *Works* (Oxford ed.), 11:56–57. Wesley knew that the limitations of language prevent us from comprehensively articulating the nature of spiritual senses or faith. We should not try to interpret Wesley's analogy of the spiritual senses too literally; he did not intend for it to be taken as part of a critical philosophical epistemology. .

Wesley contrasted human knowledge (and language) with angelic knowledge, which is directly intuitive and does not require the "slow method which we call reasoning." As a result, "we are constrained to speak through the poverty of human language" when we speak of truths that transcend our empirical world. See "Of Good Angels" (1783, sermon 71), 1.2, *Works* (Bicentennial ed.), 3:6.

65. Cell argues that "Wesley always developed his doctrine of Christian experience, not on the low level of sense empiricism but in the higher form of transcendental empiricism" (George C. Cell, *Rediscovery 'of Wesley* [New York: Henry Holt, 1935], 93; cf. 84–86, 168–94). Interestingly, Outler uses the term "transempirical intuition" to communicate a similar idea, though he puts the stress more on the influence of intuition than of empiricism *(Works* [Bicentennial ed.], 3:361n1).

66. Matthews, "'Religion and Reason,'" 309. Roderick Leupp also finds Cell's description constructive and interprets Wesley's distinctive form of transcendental empiricism in terms of the visual words of *light* and *darkness* so commonly found in Wesley's writings ("'Art of God,'" 71–80).

67. See "On the Trinity" (1775, sermon 55),§§3,14–18, *Works* (Bicentennial ed.), 2:376–77, 383–86. Here Wesley says, "The Bible barely requires you to believe such *facts*, not the manner of them. Now the mystery does not lie in the *fact*, but altogether in the *manner."* ("On the Trinity," §14, 2:383).

68. See "The Means of Grace" (1746, sermon 16), V.4, *Works* (Bicentennial ed.), 1:395.

69. See Wesley's criticism of those who exhibit an improper zeal for *opinions* in his *Journal* (Curnock ed.), 3:178, 29 May 1745.

70. See "Remarks upon Mr. Locke's 'Essay on Human Understanding,'" *Works* (Jackson ed.), 13:456, 460.

71. See Hindley, "The Philosophy of Enthusiasm," 205–9.

72. See Outler, "John Wesley as Theologian — Then and Now," 68, and *Works* (Bicentennial ed.), 1:276n46, 146n52, 433n7 and 2:192n29, 571n14, 589n7; Shimizu, "Epistemology in the Thought of John Wesley," 111–54, 219–24; Leupp, "'Art of God,'" 197–98, 224–29; and English, "The Cambridge Platonists in John Wesley's *Christian Library*," 101–4.

73. See Brantley, *Locke, Wesley,* 48–102; and Matthews, "'Religion and Reason,'" 13–20, 121–83.

74. "An Earnest Appeal to Men of Reason and Religion," §32, *Works* (Oxford ed.), 11:56.

75. "A Farther Appeal," 1.6, *Works* (Oxford ed.), 11:107.

76. "On Living Without God" (1790, sermon 130), 008–9, *Works* (Jackson ed.), 7:351.

77. Wesley's paraphrase of Romans 8:16 in "Walking by Sight and Walking by Faith" (1788, sermon 119), §1 *Works* (Jackson ed.), 7:256.

78. See Matthews, "'Religion and Reason,'" 308.

79. "The Witness of Our Own Spirit" (1746, sermon 12), §8, *Works* (Bicentennial ed.), 1:304.

80. "The Witness of the Spirit, II" (1767, sermon 11), II.8–V.4, *Works* (Bicentennial ed.), 1:288–98.

81. "Walking by Sight and Walking by Faith" (1788, sermon 119), §4, *Works* (Jackson ed.), 7:257.

82. "An Earnest Appeal," §34, *Works* (Oxford ed.), 11:57. Note the language of scientific classification Wesley uses in description of these spiritual matters.

83. See "To 'John Smith,'" 30 December 1745, §13, *Works* (Oxford ed.), 26:180–82.

84. "John Smith": quoted by Henry Moore, *The Life of the Rev. John Wesley, A. M.,* 2 vols. (London: Kershaw, 1824–25), 2:476–77, 500, 502.

85. "To 'John Smith,'" 30 December 1745, §16, *Works* (Oxford ed.), 26:182–83.

86. Wesley discusses this issue in greater detail in a letter "To 'John Smith,'" 30 December 1745, §§12–17, *Works* (Oxford ed.), 26:180–83. Clifford Hindley observes that "Wesley most carefully collated the experiences of others, and regarded it as experimental evidence in confirmation of his own faith" ("Philosophy of Enthusiasm," 205).

87. Clifford Hindley makes this observation in arguing for how readily Wesley's experience was fitted into the scheme of empirically oriented epistemology. Of course, Hindley interprets Wesley as being confused in his use of empiricist ideas, but that may result from Hindley's analyzing Wesley's ideas only from a strict Lockean–Brownean perspective. "Nevertheless," Hindley says, "we should, I believe, value Wesley's appeal to experience as (among other things), an essentially right way of re–orientating theology in the face of philosophical empiricism; and we should view his discussion of perceptible inspiration and kindred topics as a brave first attempt to plot a course through the problems raised (and the solutions offered), by a consideration of religious experience in the no–man's–land of philosophical theology" ("Philosophy of Enthusiasm," 202, 209).

88. See Locke's discussion of the sense in which the idea of God is innate and necessary in the *Essay Concerning Human Understanding,* 1:95, 100–101, and how the existence of God is demonstrable in 2:306, 312, 324, 327.

89. Hindley argues that Browne's form of argument represents Locke's position as well and was practically universal in eighteenth–century orthodoxy ("Philosophy of Enthusiasm," 105).

90. Locke, *Essay Concerning Human Understanding,* 2:416.

91. Ibid., 2:412–13.

92. "The Imperfection of Human Knowledge" (1784, sermon 69), §4, *Works* (Bicentennial ed.), 2:571.

93. "A Farther Appeal," III.21, *Works* (Oxford ed.), 11:268.

94. "Upon our Lord's Sermon on the Mount, VI" (1748, sermon 26), III.7, Works (Bicentennial ed.), 1:580–81.

95. "On the Omnipresence of God" (1788, sermon 118), II.8, *Works* (Jackson ed.), 7:242.

96. Preface, §3, "Sermons on Several Occasions," *Works* (Bicentennial ed.), 1:104).

97. "Remarks upon Mr. Locke's 'Essay on Human Understanding,'" *Works* (Jackson ed.), 13:462. Cf. further discussion on Wesley's use of "common sense" in chap. 3.

98. See "Compendium of Logic," II.i. 1, *Works* (Jackson ed.), 14:177.

99. *Formal logic* constructs valid patterns (forms) of inference as opposed to dealing directly with content (meanings). By contrast, *informal logic* studies those inferences that (a) do not follow a precise logical form (and if they do, their truth does not depend on such a form), (b) are based on the meanings rather than the validity of the forms involved in the argument, and (c) may be true or false depending on considerations (such as empirical evidence) other than the form of their argument. See Peter A. Angeles, *A Dictionary of Philosophy* (New York: Harper & Row, 1981), 156.

100. See "Walking by Sight and Walking by Faith" (1788, sermon 119), §8, *Works* (Jackson ed.), 7:258.

101. Cf. William J. Abraham, *An Introduction to the Philosophy of Religion* (Englewood Cliffs, N.J.: Prentice-Hall, 1985), 86.

102. See Locke's discussion of how the existence of a God is evident and obvious to reason in *Essay Concerning Human Understanding*, 1:99; cf. 100–106, 114. Cf. the discussion of Locke's appeal to common sense in James Gordon Clapp's article "John Locke" in Edwards, *Encyclopedia of Philosophy*, 4:497.

103. In an editorial comment, Alexander Fraser notes that the Scottish philosopher Thomas Reid criticized Locke for inconsistency with regard to his arguments for the existence of God. See *Essay Concerning Human Understanding*, ed. Fraser, 2:310, 311n4.

104. Locke, *Essay Concerning Human Understanding*, 2:431. Cf. Locke, *Reasonableness of Christianity*, 82.

105. Robert Tuttle discusses Wesley's progressive reliance on Scripture to balance what he considered extreme positions among philosophical traditions (*John Wesley: His Life and Theology*, 46–47). Regarding Wesley's eclecticism, Mitsuo Shimizu comments, "In view of this eclectic background, Wesley is confident that his theory of knowledge can be supported from several different strands of intellectual tradition" ("Epistemology in the Thought of John Wesley," 223).

106. Richard Brantley cites inconsistencies in Locke over his confusion of Cartesian and empirical philosophy. For example, Brantley points out that for Locke, ideas are somehow both independent mental entities and the products of shaping forces. He says, "For Wesley, I suggest, as for Norris and Berkeley, and even as for Locke (insofar as Locke scattered through the *Essay* tinctures of Cartesian thought), ideas are somehow both independent mental entities and the products of shaping forces. Lockean ideas, after all, not only clarify the world, but also themselves become quasi-objective, for 'Ideas,' in Locke's twofold understanding, are not only 'Perceptions in our Minds' but also 'modifications in the Bodies that cause such Perceptions in us' (*Essay* 2.8.7; Nidditch, p. 134)." See Brantley, *Locke, Wesley*, 19.

107. See Wesley's general comments concerning Hume *in* the *Journal* 5:303–4, 5

March 1769; "The Unity of the Divine Being" (1789, sermon 120), §19, *Works* (Jackson ed.), 7:271; and "The Deceitfulness of the Human Heart" (1790, sermon 128), II.7, *Works* (Jackson ed.), 7:342. For a discussion of the general disregard by England for the revolutionary philosophy of David Hume, see Donald G. C. MacNabb, "David Hume," in Edwards, *Encyclopedia of Philosophy,* 4:74.

108. See Wesley's refutation of Dr. Hartley's "Essay on Liberty and Necessity," of which Wesley says, 'I cannot believe the noblest creature in the visible world to be only a fine piece of clock–work" ("To the Reader," "Thoughts Upon Necessity," *Works* [Jackson ed.], 10:457).

109. "A Farther Appeal," V.2 *Works* (Bicentennial ed.), 11:140. Cf. Shimizu, "Epistemology in the Thought of John Wesley," 72.

110. "The Spirit of Bondage and of Adoption" (1746, sermon 9), I.1, *Works* (Bicentennial ed.), 1:251.

111. "On Working Out Our Own Salvation" (1785, sermon 85), III.4, *Works* (Bicentennial ed.), 3:207. Cf. "Heavenly Treasure in Earthen Vessels" (1790, sermon 129), I.1, *Works* (Jackson ed.), 7:344.

112. "On Working Out Our Own Salvation" (1785, sermon 85), I.1, *Works* (Bicentennial ed.), 3:199. Cf. "Walking by Sight and Walking by Faith" (1788, sermon 119), §§7–8, *Works* (Jackson ed.), 7:258.

113. "An Earnest Appeal," §33, *Works* (Oxford ed.), 11:57; cf. §§31–35, *Works* (Oxford ed.), 11:56–57.

114. "To Richard Thompson," 16 March 1756, *Letters* (Telford ed.), 3:174–75.

115. "To Joseph Benson," 21 May 1781, *Letters* (Telford ed.), 7:61. 116. Ibid.

117. "On the Trinity" (1775, sermon 55), §3, *Works* (Bicentennial ed.), 2:377.

118. Brantley, *Locke, Wesley,* 56.

119. "Address to the Clergy," I.2, *Works* (Jackson ed.), 10:483.

120. "The Case of Reason Impartially Considered" (1781, sermon 70), I.6, *Works* (Bicentennial ed.), 2:592.

121. Wood, "Wesley's Epistemology," 52.

122. See Brantley, *Locke, Wesley,* 93.

123. See Wesley's comments in the "Compendium of Logic," *Work* (Jackson ed.), 14:161–89, and his criticisms of Locke's logic in "Remarks upon Mr. Locke's 'Essay on Human Understanding,'" *Works* (Jackson ed.), 13:456.

124. "The Means of Grace" (1746, sermon 16), II.1, *Works* (Bicentennial ed.), 1:381.

125. "Compendium of Logic," II, *Works* (Jackson ed.), 14:187–89. 126. Appendix, "Compendium of Logic," *Works* (Jackson ed.), 14:184–87. 127. "The Nature of Enthusiasm" (1750, sermon 37), *Works* (Bicentennial ed.), 2:44–60.

128. "To Mrs. Susanna Wesley," 29 July 1725, *Works* (Oxford ed.), 25:175. Mitsuo Shimizu notes that Wesley avoided the extreme position of making Christianity a science: "Wesley finds: 'I had been under a mistake in adhering to that definition of Faith which Dr. Fiddes sets down as the only true one' [*Letters,* 1:24]. Dr. Fiddes' theory of assent which 'takes in science as well as faith' is 'but a part of the definition' of faith, since faith, says Wesley, 'is on all hands allowed to be distinct from science' [ibid., 1:25]. Faith as a rational form of knowledge cannot be proved as clearly and distinctly as can science. This leads Wesley to take the evidence of the Scriptures in addition to that of reason as a source of religious truths" (Shimizu, "Epistemology in the Thought of John Wesley," 17–18).

129. Cf. Matthews, "'Religion and Reason Joined,'" 20.

130. "To John Downes," 17 November 1759, *Letters* (Telford ed.), 4:331 32.

131. See "To the Editor of the 'London Magazine,'" 1 January 1765, *Letters* (Telford ed.), 4:281–87.

132. Ibid., 4:286.

133. "The Case of Reason Impartially Considered" (1781, sermon 70), II.10, *Works* (Bicentennial ed.), 2:600.

134. Ibid., 2:593–600.

135. See "Walking by Sight and Walking by Faith" (1788, sermon 119), §9, *Works* (Jackson ed.), 7:258.

136. See "The Unity of the Divine Being" (1789, sermon 120), §2, *Works* (Jackson ed.), 7:265.

137. Although Wesley grants that cosmological and teleological arguments *demonstratively* show the existence of God, they do not reveal the *kind* of God in which we are to believe. Thus he said, "O my friend, how will you get one step farther unless God reveal himself to your soul?" ("A Farther Appeal," III.21, *Works* [Oxford ed.], 11:269).

138. See "Walking By Sight and Walking by Faith" (1788, sermon 119), §§11–12, *Works* (Jackson ed.), 7:259–60.

# Chapter 7
# The Authority of Experience

1. Wesley recognized that Christianity needs to reflect both the *vitality* and the *form* of true religion as manifested in the lives of individual believers. In the twentieth century, Reinhold Niebuhr argued for much the same approach (Niebuhr, *The Nature and Destiny of Man,* 2 vols. (1941; reprint, New York: Scribner's, 1964), 1:26–53.

2. Preface, §6, "Sermons on Several Occasions," *Works* (Bicentennial ed.), 1:106.

3. "Thoughts upon Methodism," *Works* (Jackson ed.), 13:258.

4. This frequent theme is found most prominently in the series of sermons "The Witness of the Spirit, I" (1746, sermon 10), "The Witness of the Spirit, II" (1767, sermon 11), and "The Witness of Our Own Spirit" (1746, sermon 12) in *Works* (Bicentennial ed.), 1:267–313.

5. Wesley's belief in the confirmatory role of experience is found throughout his writings. Explicit references to this belief may be found in the following passages: "The Promise of Understanding" (1730, sermon 140), I.3, *Works* (Bicentennial ed.), 4:284; "Journal," *Works* (Bicentennial ed.), 18:233–34, 248–49, 22 April and 24 May 1738; "A Farther Appeal, I," V.22–27, *Works* (Oxford ed.), 11:162–70; "To Dr. Conyers Middleton," 24 January 1749, III.1–12, *Letters* (Telford ed.), 2:383–88; "A Letter to the Right Reverend and the Lord Bishop of Gloucester," III.1–10, *Works* (Oxford ed.), 11:534–38; "Original Sin," preface and pt. 1, *Works* (Jackson ed.), 9:192–238; "A Plain Account of Christian Perfection," §19, *Works* (Jackson ed.), 11:406; and "The Case of Reason Impartially Considered" (1781, sermon 70), II.3, *Works* (Bicentennial ed.), 2:594–95.

6. Preface, §6 "Sermons on Several Occasions," *Works* (Bicentennial ed.), 1:106. The two threats were "outside religion, which has almost driven heart–religion out of the world; and secondly, to warn those who know the religion of the heart, the faith which worketh by love, lest at any time they make void the law through faith, and so fall back into the snare of the devil."

7. Using these categories should not be seen as projecting an unnecessary dualism on Wesley. He did not clearly distinguish between various kinds of experience, which leads to confusion in understanding his theology. However, there seems to be an implicit distinction between *empirical* and *experiential* dimensions of experience in his writings.

For the sake of analysis, the distinction will help to clarify aspects of his theology.

8. Some refer to *a priori* knowledge as *notional* knowledge, that is, abstract and non-experiential knowledge. Notional knowledge contrasts completely with *empirical* and *experiential* knowledge, which entail varying degrees of personal participation in the knowing process. Empirical knowledge involves personal experiences that are relatively easy to communicate, whereas experiential knowledge involves those that are relatively difficult to communicate, if in fact it is really possible to communicate personal experiences at all.

9. Richard E. Brantley, *Locke, Wesley, and the Method of English Romanticism* (Gainesville, Fla.: University of Florida Press, 1984), 46. 10. Cf. chap. 6.

11. See "An Earnest Appeal," §31, *Works* (Bicentennial ed.), 11:56: "We therefore not only allow, but earnestly exhort all who seek after true religion to use all the reason which God hath given them in searching out the things of God. But your *reasoning justly*, not only on this but on any subject whatsoever, presuppposes *true judgments* already formed whereon to ground your argumentation. Else, you know, you will stumble at every step, because *ex falso non sequitur verum* — it is impossible, if your premises are false, to infer from them true conclusions."

12. Wesley often quoted this verse from Hebrews 11:1. Twice it served as the primary passage of Scripture in his sermons "On the Discoveries of Faith" (1788, sermon 117), title, *Works* (Bicentennial ed.), 4:29, and "On Faith, Heb. 11:1" (1788, sermon 132), title, *Works* (Bicentennial ed.), 4:188.

13. "An Earnest Appeal," §32, *Works* (Oxford ed.), 11:56–57.

14. "On Faith, Heb. 11:6" (1788, sermon 106), 1.9, *Works* (Bicentennial ed.), 3:484.

15. "To 'John Smith,'" 28 September 1745, III.11, *Works* (Oxford ed.), 26:157.

16. Rex D. Matthews provides a good look at Wesley's changing understanding of faith, variously consisting of assent, trust, and "spiritual experience" ("'Religion and Reason Joined': A Study in the Theology of John Wesley" [Diss., Harvard University, 1986], 184–246.

17. Mitsuo Shimizu, "Epistemology in the Thought of John Wesley" (Diss., Drew University, 1980), 47n2.

18. Cf. ibid.

19. "A Farther Appeal, I," V.24, *Works* (Oxford ed.), 11:167.

20. Although Clifford Hindley argues that "the witness of our own spirit" as an immediate consciousness of God's working in the heart "is *empirically* indistinguishable from what Wesley describes as the Witness of God's Spirit," Wesley believed that a person could distinguish the two (Hindley, "The Philosophy of Enthusiasm: A Study in the Origins of 'Experimental Theology,'" *London Quarterly and Holborn Review* 182 [1957], 204).

21. Cf. Robert Tuttle, *John Wesley: His Life and Theology* (Grand Rapids: Zondervan, 1978), 218n9; and Albert C. Outler, ed., *John Wesley* (New York: Oxford University Press, 1980), 14, and "The Place of Wesley in the Christian Tradition," in *The Place of Wesley in the Christian Tradition*, ed. Kenneth E. Rowe (Metuchen, N.J.: Scarecrow, 1976), 30–31.

22. "On God's Vineyard" (1787, sermon 107), 1.5, *Works* (Bicentennial ed.), 3:506.

23. For example, see "To the Revd. Thomas Stedman," 1 September 1774, *Works* (Oxford ed.), 25:4.

24. Traditional Christianity generally refers to "the witness of the Spirit" as the *testimonium internum Spiritus Sancti*, the "internal testimony of the Holy Spirit." Cf. Richard A. Muller, *Dictionary of Latin and Greek Theological Terms* (Grand Rapids: Baker, 1985), 297–98.

25. "A Farther Appeal, II," III.21, *Works* (Oxford ed.), 11:268.

26. See Thomas Aquinas, *Summa Theologiae*, I, Q.2. Cf. Diogenes Allen's discussion of Aquinas's use of the analogy of proportion in *Philosophy for Understanding Theology* (Atlanta: John Knox, 1985), 143.

27. "Upon our Lord's Sermon on the Mount, VI" (1748, sermon 26), III.7, *Works* (Bicentennial ed.), 1:580–81.

28. Cf. William F. Abraham's discussion of natural theology in his *Introduction to the Philosophy of Religion* (Englewood Cliffs, N.J.: Prentice–Hall, 1985), 86.

29. See "The Spirit of Bondage and of Adoption" (1746, sermon 9),11.1–2, *Works* (Bicentennial ed.), 1:255–56; "The Means of Grace" (1746, sermon 16), V.I, *Works* (Bicentennial ed.), 1:393–94; and "The Original, Nature, Properties, and Use of the Law" (1750, sermon 34), IV.I, *Works* (Bicentennial ed.), 2:15.

30. See "The Signs of the Times" (1787, sermon 66), I.4, *Works* (Bicentennial ed.), 2:524.

31. "A Clear and Concise Demonstration of the Divine Inspiration of the Holy Scriptures," *Works* (Jackson ed.), 11:484.

32. "A Farther Appeal, III," III.28, *Works* (Oxford ed.), 11:310.

33. Ibid.

34. See "A Farther Appeal, III," III.29, *Works* (Oxford ed.), 11:311: "Accordingly our Saviour and all his apostles, in the midst of their greatest miracles, never failed to prove every doctrine they taught by clear Scripture and cogent reason."

35. "To Miss March," 14 April 1771, *Letters* (Telford ed.), 5:237.

36. "The More Excellent Way" (1787, sermon 89), §6, *Works* (Bicentennial ed.), 3:266.

37. For example, see *Journal* (Curnock ed.), 4:532, 28 October 1762, and "A Short History of the People Called Methodists," §§80–96, 101–102, 107, *Works* (Jackson ed.), 13:349–58, 360–62, 364.

38. Harald Lindström, *Wesley and Sanctification* (1980; reprint, Grand Rapids: Zondervan; 1983), 139: "In later years, clearly actuated by his experiences in the Methodist revival, Wesley altered some of the extreme statements he had made on the state of the entirely sanctified in 1740 in the preface to *Hymns and Sacred Poems*. He finds, for instance, that he had gone too far in saying that the totally sanctified did not at all need to feel any doubt or uncertainty even in particular actions, and he modifies the statement thus: 'Frequently this is the case but only for a time.' Similarly he also corrects the statement that the Holy Spirit every instant instructs them what they should do and say. 'For a time,' he says, 'it may be so; but not always.' He also altered the statement that they had no need of 'reasoning concerning it,' saying that sometimes reasoning was necessary. Later, too, he came to believe that the fully sanctified could be tempted, even grievously. As early as 1743 in *An Earnest Appeal to Men of Reason and Religion* he declares that perfect sanctification does not exclude temptations, while in 1750 in a sermon entitled *Christian Perfection* he says that such perfection 'belongeth not to this life.' For a long time he was inclined to believe that perfect sanctification could not be lost. Early in the seventeen–sixties, however, he became convinced by facts that even the entirely sanctified man could fall."

39. See George Eayrs, *John Wesley: Christian Philosopher and Church Founder* (London: Epworth, 1926), 131, 138.

40. Ibid., 131.

41. See "A Plain Account of Christian Perfection," §19, *Works* (Jackson ed.), 11:406; "To his brother Charles," 27 January 1767, *Letters* (Telford ed.), 5:38–39, and "To his

brother Charles," 12 February 1767, *Letters* (Telford ed.), 5:41; and *Standard Sermons* (Sugden ed.), 1:19602.

42. The definition of "enthusiast" comes from Samuel Johnson's *Dictionary of the English Language*, and he attributes the source of the definition to the chapter "Of Enthusiasm" in Locke's *Essay Concerning Human Understanding*, 2 vols., ed. Alexander Fraser (New York: Dover, 1894), 2:428–41, esp. 432.

43. "To John Downes," 17 November 1759, *Letters* (Telford ed.), 4:333.

44. "To the Revd. Samuel Wesley, Sen.," 10 December 1734, §15, *Works* (Oxford ed.), 25:403.

45. *Journal* (Curnock ed.), 1:471–72, 24 May 1738.

46. "The Witness of the Spirit, II" (1767, sermon 11), III.6, *Works* (Bicentennial ed.), 1:290.

47. For example, see Wesley's discussion of the order of salvation as contained in the *Notes upon the New Testament*, Rom. 6:18; "On Predestination" (1773, sermon 58), §16, *Works* (Bicentennial ed.), 2:421; and especially "The Scripture Way of Salvation" (1765, sermon 43), *Works* (Bicentennial ed.), 2:155–69.

48. Wesley: quoted by Umphrey Lee, *John Wesley and Modern Religion* (Nashville: Cokesbury, 1936), 277.

49. "The Witness of the Spirit, I' (1746, sermon 10), 1.7, *Works* (Bicentennial ed.), 1:274.

50. See "The Witness of Our Own Spirit," *Works* (Bicentennial ed.), 1:299–313.

51. "The Witness of the Spirit, I" (1746, sermon 10), 1.6, *Works* (Bicentennial ed.), 1:273–74.

52. *Journal* (Curnock ed.), 1:475, §14, 24 May 1738.

53. "The Witness of the Spirit, II" (1767, sermon 11), III.7, *Work* (Bicentennial ed.), 1:291.

54. See "The Marks of the New Birth" (1748, sermon 18), II.3, *Works* (Bicentennial ed.), 1:423.

55. See "The Witness of the Spirit, I" (1746, sermon 10), 1.6–7, *Works* (Bicentennial ed.), 1:273, and "The Witness of the Spirit, II" (1767, sermon 11), III.5, V.3, *Works* (Bicentennial ed.), 3:289–90, 297–98.

56. Unfortunately, Wesley nowhere defined the difference between the witness of the Holy Spirit and the witness of our own spirit. He seems to indicate that the two are different, but — as Clifford Hindley points out — indistinguishable in experience. Hindley argues that "Wesley failed to see that he was presenting as two experiences what were really two ways of looking at the same experience" ("The Philosophy of Enthusiasm," 209).

57. "To Dr. Conyers Middleton," 4 January 1749, II.12, *Letters* (Telford ed.), 2:383.

58. For example, see "The Witness of the Spirit, I" (1746, sermon 10), §1, *Works* (Bicentennial ed.), 1:269.

59. See *Journal* (Curnock ed.), 4:359–60, 25 November 1759, and "Minutes of Some Late Conversations," Q.16, *Works* (Jackson ed.), 8:284.

60. Lee, *John Wesley and Modern Religion*, 277: "On one side of his mind, Wesley distrusted dreams and visions and the more exotic type of experience, and he warned his followers against them. But he showed an unusual interest in such matters, even when he expressed cautious judgments about them. Indeed, his doctrine that God expresses himself in the minute details of life, supporting not only the Universe but also looking after the least things concerning his children, made for a willingness to listen at least to any story, however improbable. Wesley certainly kept alive a sense of wonder, and this

was no doubt responsible for many of the excesses among the early Methodists. "

61. For example, see "To Mary Bishop," 19 September 1773, *Letters* (Telford ed.), 6:43–44.

62. See preface, §§1–9, "An Extract of the Life of Madam Guion," *Works* (Jackson ed.), 14:275–78.

63. "Thoughts on the Writings of Baron Swedenborg," §32, *Work* (Jackson ed~), 13:448; cf. entire "Thoughts" 425–48.

64. "To 'John Smith,'" 28 September 1745, I.5, *Works* (Oxford ed.), 26:155: "I conceive, therefore, this whole demand, common as it is, of proving our doctrine by miracles, proceeds from a double mistake: (1), a supposition that what we preach is not provable from Scripture (for if it be, what need we further witnesses? To the law and the testimony!); (2), and imagination that a doctrine not provable by Scripture might nevertheless be proved by miracles. I believe not. I receive the written Word as the whole and sole rule of my faith."

65. See "The Means of Grace" (1746, sermon 16), IV.5, *Works* (Bicentennial ed.), 1:392; cf. 392n75.

66. Robert Monk, *John Wesley: His Puritan Heritage* (Nashville: Abingdon, 1966), 72.

67. Colin Williams, *John Wesley's Theology Today* (New York: Abingdon, 1960), 33.

68. Arnett says, "Theoretically the written Word is primary, but in practice the two [Scripture and experience] are not mutually exclusive" ("John Wesley — Man of One Book" [Diss.,. Drew University, 1954], 85).

69. "On Sin in Believers" (1763, sermon 13), III.9, *Works* (Bicentennial ed.), 1:324.

70. Cf. Lee, *John Wesley and Modern Religion*, 137.

71. Brantley argues that "Wesley more or less intentionally formulated the experiential common denominator for mainstream British thought and mainstream British faith: his was a most thoroughly English language of experience" *(Locke, Wesley*, 102). Cf. Brantley's chapter on the extensiveness of "Wesley's Intellectual Influence" (103–128). .

72. Scholars do not find a direct tie between Wesley and liberal Protestantism, but many interpret Wesley as anticipating the experiential themes characteristic of F. D. E. Schleiermacher and Samuel Taylor Coleridge. See Henry Bett, *The Spirit of Methodism* (London: Epworth, 1943), 144–46;

Brantley, *Locke, Wesley, and the Method of English Romanticism*, 100; Bayrs, *John Wesley: Christian Philosopher and Church Founder*, 181–83; Stanley Brice Frost, *The Doctrine of Authority in the Works of John Wesley* (London: n.p., 1938), 106–7; Hindley, "Philosophy of Enthusiasm," 202, 209; Lee, *John Wesley and Modern Religion*, 302–3; Maximin Piette, *John Wesley in the Evolution of Protestantism*, trans. J. B. Howard (New York: Sheed and Ward, 1937),478; and Martin Schmidt, *John Wesley: A Theological Biography*, trans. Norman Goldhawk, 2 vols. in 3 (New York: Abingdon, 1962), 1:57, 142; 2.1:34, 172; 2.2:33, 215, 223, 288. We need to be careful to distinguish Wesley's view of experience from that of liberal Protestantism or other modernistic thinking. Wesley always affirmed the primacy of scriptural authority and the need for fidelity to orthodox Christian beliefs. Consequently his appeals to experience did *not* unwittingly prepare the way for the modernist era. Other factors were responsible for the rise of modernism. Wesley considered the authority of experience to be of a secondary and complementary nature. He never wanted to adapt Christian beliefs to modern culture and modes of thinking as modernism was apt to do.

73. Lee, *John Wesley and Modern Religion*, 301.

74. Cf. George C. Cell, *Rediscovery of John Wesley* (New York: Henry Holt, 1935), 72–73.

# Conclusion:
# Wesley and Evangelicalism

1. Albert C. Outler, "The Wesleyan Quadrilateral in John Wesley," *Wesleyan Theological Journal* 20, no. 1 (1985): 9.

2. For example, Larry Shelton notes that Wesley's epistemology differs from both Aristotelian methodology and contemporary fundamentalism ("John Wesley's Approach to Scripture," *Wesleyan Theological Journal* 16, no. 1 [1981]: 36, 38).

3. Richard A. Muller, *Dictionary of Latin and Greek Theological Terms* (Grand Rapids: Baker, 1985), 284.

4. Gabriel Fackre, "Evangelical Hermeneutics: Commonality and Diversity," *Interpretation* 43, no. 2 (1989): 128–29.

5. See Donald G. Bloesch, *The Future of Evangelical Christianity: A Call for Unity Amid Diversity* (Garden City, N.Y.: Doubleday, 1983), 5, 48–52, and *Essentials of Evangelical Theology*, 2 vols. (San Francisco: Harper & Row, 1978), 1:ix–xii, 1–5; 2:1–5.

6. See Millard J. Erickson, *Christian Theology*, 3 vols. (Grand Rapids: Baker, 1983), 1:11–150.

7. Bloesch, *Essentials of Evangelical Theology*, 1:ix; 2:1.

8. See "Catholic Spirit" (1750, sermon 39), *Works* (Bicentennial ed.), 2:79–96.

9. Outler, "Wesleyan Quadrilateral," 17.

10. Ibid., 10.

11. Albert C. Outler, ed., introduction, *John Wesley* (New York: Oxford University Press, 1980), 28.

12. Shelton, "John Wesley's Approach to Scripture," 40. Cf. George C. Cell, *Rediscovery of John Wesley* (New York: Henry Holt, 1935), 13.

13. Bloesch, *Essentials of Evangelical Theology*, 1:20.

14. Wesley clearly distinguished a "catholic spirit" from the kind of speculative and practical latitudinarianism (or theological indifferentism) that was characteristic of the Cambridge Platonists and others whose broad–mindedness took precedence over Scripture and classical orthodox beliefs. See "Catholic Spirit" (1750, sermon 39), III.1–6, *Works* (Bicentennial ed.), 2:92–95. Cf. Jerry Walls, *The Problem of Pluralism: Recovering United Methodist Identity* (Wilmore, Ky.: Good News, 1986), 51–67.

15. Thomas C. Oden, *The Living God*, vol. 1 of *Systematic Theology* (San Francisco: Harper & Row, 1987), ix.

16. John J. Davis; *Foundations of Evangelical Theology* (Grand Rapids: Baker, 1984), 43.

17. Bloesch, *Essentials of Evangelical Theology*, 1:21.

18. This theme may be found in several places, for example, in William J. Abraham, *The Coming Great Revival: Recovering the Full Evangelical Tradition* (San Francisco: Harper & Row, 1984), and in Donald W. Dayton, "Yet Another Layer of the Onion; or, Opening the Ecumenical Door to Let the Riffraff In" (Paper delivered to the American Theological Society at Lutheran School of Theology, Chicago, 30 October 1987).

19. Outler, "The Wesleyan Quadrilateral," 17.

20. Abraham, *The Coming Great Revival*, 67.

21. Outler, *Theology in the Wesleyan Spirit* (Nashville: Tidings, 1975), 20.

22. Erickson, *Christian Theology*, 1:77.

23. Gordon R. Lewis and Bruce A. Demarest, *Integrative Theology*, vol. 1 (Grand Rapids: Zondervan, 1986), 25; cf. 24.

24. Davis, *Foundations of Evangelical Theology*, 53.

25. Bloesch, *Essentials of Evangelical Theology*, 1:19.

26. Shirley C. Guthrie, Jr., *Christian Doctrine: Teachings of the Christian Church* (Atlanta: John Knox, 1968), 292.

27., See Davis, *Foundations of Evangelical Theology,* 27–28, 52, 166–68.

28 Carl F. H. Henry, *God, Revelation and Authority,* 6 vols. (Waco, Tex.: Word, 1976–83), 1:365.

29. Colin Brown, *Philosophy and the Christian Faith* (Downers Grove, Illinois.: InterVarsity Press, 1968), 273.

30. William J. Abraham, "The Wesleyan Quadrilateral in the American Methodist–Episcopal Tradition," *Wesleyan Theological Journal* 20, no. 1 (1985): 38.

# Select Bibliography

## Works by Wesley

Baker, Frank, and Richard P. Heitzenrater, eds.–in–chief. *The Works of John Wesley,* Bicentennial ed. Oxford: Clarendon Press, 1975–83; Nashville: Abingdon, 1984–.
*Current Volumes*
Vols. 1–4: *Sermons I–IV.* Ed. Albert C. Outler (Bicentennial ed.)
Vol. 7: *A Collection of Hymns for the Use of the People Called Methodists.* Ed. Franz Hildebrant and Oliver Beckerlegge (Oxford ed.)
Vol. 11: *The Appeals to Men of Reason and Religion.* Ed. Gerald R. Cragg (Oxford ed.)
Vols. 18–19: *Diaries I–II.* Ed. W. Reginald Ward and Richard P. Heitzenrater (Bicentennial ed.)
Vols. 25–26: *Letters I–II.* Ed. Frank Baker (Oxford ed.)
*Forthcoming Volumes*
Vol. 5: *Explanatory Notes I* (1995)
Vol. 6: *Explanatory Notes I* (1997)
Vol. 8: *Worship and Prayer* (1993)
Vol. 9: *Societies I (History),* (1989)
Vol. 10: *Societies I (Conferences),* (1992)
Vol. 12: *Theological Treatises* (1994)
Vol. 20: *Journal and Diaries III* (1994)
Vol. 27: *Letters III* (1998)
Vol. 32: *Oxford Diaries* (1996)
Burtner, Robert W., and Robert E. Chiles, Reds. *A Compend of Wesley's Theology.* New York: Abingdon, 1954.
Curnock, Nehemiah, ed. *The Journal of the Rev. John Wesley.* 1909–1916. 9 vols. London: Epworth, 1938.
Jackson, Thomas, ed. *The Works of John Wesley.* 1829–1831. 3d ed. 14 vols. Grand Rapids: Baker, 1980.
Osborn, George, ed. *Poetical Works of John and Charles Wesley.* 13 vols. London: Epworth, 1868–72.
Outler, Albert C., ed. *John Wesley.* Library of Protestant Thought. New York: Oxford University Press, 1964.
Sugden, Edward H., ed. *Standard Sermons of John Wesley.* 2 vols. London: Epworth, 1921.
Telford, John, ed. *The Letters of the Rev. John Wesley.* 8 vols. London: Epworth, 1931.
Wakefield, Gordon, ed. *Fire of Love: The Spirituality of John Wesley.* New Canaan, Conn.: Keats Publishing, 1976.
Watson, Phillip, ed. *The Message of the Wesleys: A Reader.* 1964. Reprint. Grand Rapids: Zondervan, 1984.

Wesley, John. *The Arminian Magazine: Consisting of Extracts and Original Treatises on Universal Redemption.* London: Frey et al., 1778–91 (–97).

_____. *Explanatory Notes upon the New Testament.* 1755. Reprint. London: Epworth, 1950..

_____. *Explanatory Notes upon the Old Testament.* 3 vols. 1765. Reprint. Salem,. Ohio: Schmul, 1975.

_____. *Primitive Physic[k, or an Easy and Natural Method of Curing Most Diseases].* 1747. Reprint. London: Epworth, 1960.

_____. *A Survey of the Wisdom of God in the Creation: or, A Compendium of Natural Philosophy.* 2 vols. 1763. Reprint. Philadelphia: Pounder, 1816.

Wesley, John, ed. *A Christian Library: Consisting of Extracts from, and Abridgements of, the Choicest Pieces of Practical Divinity which have ever been Published in the English Tongue.* 50 vols. Bristol: Farley, 1749–55 (–84). .

Whaling, Frank, ed. *John and Charles Wesley: Selected Prayers, Hymns, Journal Notes, Sermons, Letters, and Treatises.* Classics of Western Spirituality. Ramsey, N.J.: Paulist, 1981.

## Works about Wesley and the Wesleyan Tradition

Abraham, William J. *The Coming Great Revival: Recovering the Full Evangelical Tradition.* San Francisco: Harper & Row, 1984.

_____. "Inspiration, Revelation and Divine Action: A Study in Modem Methodist Theology." *Wesley Theological Journal* 19, no. 2 (1984): 38–51.

_____. "Response: The Perils of a Wesleyan Systematic Theologian." *Wesleyan Theological Journal* 17, no. 1 (1982): 23–29:

_____. "The Wesleyan Quadrilateral in the American Methodist Episcopal Tradition." *Wesleyan Theological Journal* 20, no. 1 (1985): 34–44.

Aikens, Alden. "Wesleyan Theology and the Use of Models." *Wesleyan Theological Journal* 14, no. 2 (1979): 64–76.

Andrews, Stuart. "John Wesley and the Age of Reason." *History Today* 19 (1960): 25–32.

Arnett, William M. "John Wesley and the Bible." *Wesleyan Theological Journal* 3, no. 1 (1968): 3–9.

_____. "John Wesley—Man of One Book" Diss., Drew University, 1954.

_____. "A Study in John Wesley's *Explanatory Notes upon the Old Testament.*" *Wesleyan Theological Journal* 8, no. 1 (1973): 14–32.

Ayling, Stanley. *John Wesley.* Nashville: Abingdon, 1981.

Baines–Griffiths, D. *Wesley the Anglican.* London: Macmillan, 1919.

Baker, Eric. *A Herald of the Evangelical Revival–A Critical Inquiry Into the Relation of William Law to John Wesley and the Beginning of Methodism.* London: Epworth, 1948.

Baker, Frank. *John Wesley and the Church of England* New York: Abingdon, 1970.

_____. "John Wesley and Practical Divinity." *Wesleyan Theological Journal* 22, no. 1 (1987): 7–15.

Bangs, Carl O. "Historical Theology in the Wesleyan Mode." *Wesleyan Theological Journal* 17, no. 1 (1982): 85–92.

Bence, Clarence. "John Wesley's Teleological Hermeneutic." Diss., Emory University, 1980.

Bett, Henry. *The Spirit of Methodism*. London: Epworth, 1943.

Boshears, Onva K., Jr. "The Books in John Wesley's Life." *Wesleyan Theological Journal* 3, no. 1 (1968): 48–56.

_____. "John Wesley, the Bookman: A Study of His Reading Interests in the Eighteenth Century." Diss., University of Michi gan, 1972.

Bowmer, J. C. *The Sacrament of the Lord's Supper in early Methodism* London: Dacre Press, 1951.

Brantley, Richard E. *Locke, Wesley, and the Method of English Romanticism*. Gainesville, Fla.: University of Florida Press, 1984.

Bready, John Wesley. *England Before and After Wesley*. New York: Harper, 1938.

Cadman, S. Parkes. *The Three Religious Leaders of Oxford and Their Movements–John Wycliff, John Wesley, John Henry Newman*. New York. Macmillan, 1916.

Cameron, Richard M. *Methodism and Society in Historical Perspective*. New York: Abingdon, 1961.

Campbell, Ted Allen. "John Wesley's Conceptions and Uses of Christian Antiquity." Diss., Southern Methodist University, 1984.

Cannon, William Ragsdale. *Theology of John Wesley*. New York: Abingdon, 1946.

Carter, Charles W., ed. *A Contemporary Wesleyan Theology*. 2 vols. Grand Rapids: Zondervan, Francis Asbury Press, 1983.

Cell, George Croft. *The Rediscovery of John Wesley*. New York: Henry Holt, 1935.

Chiles, Robert E. *Scriptural Christianity: A Call to John Wesley's Disciples*. Grand Rapids: Zondervan, Francis Asbury Press, 1984.

Clapper, Gregory S. "'True Religion' and the Affections: A Study of John Wesley's Abridgement of Jonathan Edwards' *Treatise on Religious Affections*." *Wesleyan Theological Journal* 19, no. 2 (1984): 77–89.

_____. *John Wesley on Religious Affections: His Views on Experience and Emotion and Their Role in the Christian Life and Theology*. Pietist and Wesleyan Studies, no. 1 (Metuchen, N.J.: Scarecrow, 1989).

Cobb, John B., Jr. "I say, 'Keep the Quadrilateral!'" *Circuit Rider* 11, no. 5 (1987): 4–6.

_____. "Response to 'Bible as .Decisive Authority.'" *Circuit Rider* 11, no. 5 (1987): 8–9.

Collier, Frank W. *John Wesley Among the Scientists*. New York: Abingdon, 1928. .

Collins, Kenneth J. "A Hermeneutical Model for the Wesleyan *Ordo salutis*." *Wesleyan Theological Journal* 19, no. 2 (1984): 23–37.

_____. *Wesley on Salvation: A Study in the Standard Sermons*. Grand Rapids: Zondervan, Francis Asbury Press, 1989.

_____. "Wesley's Platonic Conception of the Moral Law." *Wesleyan Theological Journal* 21, vols. 1–2 (1986): 116–28.

Coppedge, Allan. "John Wesley and the Issue of Authority in Theological Pluralism." *Wesleyan Theological Journal* 19, no. 2 (1984): 62–76.

Crow, Earl P. "John Wesley's Conflict with Antinomianism in Relation to the Moravians and Calvinists." Diss., University of Manchester, 1975.

Cubie, David L. "The Theology of Love in Wesley." *Wesleyan Theological Journal* 20, no. 1 (1985): 122–54.

Cushman, Robert E. *John Wesley's Experimental Divinity*. Nashville: Abingdon, Kingswood, 1989.

Dayton, Wilber T. "Theology and Biblical Inerrancy." *Wesleyan Theological Journal* 3, no. 1 (1968): 30–37.

Deschner, John. *Wesley's Christology: An Interpretation*. 1985. Reprint. Grand Rapids: Zondervan, Francis Asbury Press, 1988.

Downes, Cyril. "The Eschatological Doctrines in the Writings of John and Charles Wesley." Diss., Edinburgh University, 1960.

Dreyer, Frederick. "Faith and Experience in the Thought of John Wesley." *American Historical Review* 88 (1983): 12–30.

Dunning, H. Ray. "Biblical Interpretation and Wesleyan Theology." *Wesleyan Theological Journal* 9, no. 1 (1974): 47–51.

_____. "Systematic Theology in a Wesleyan Mode." *Wesleyan Theological Journal* 17, no. 1 (1982): 15–22.

Eayrs, George. *John Wesley: Christian Philosopher and Church Founder.* London: Epworth, 1926.

Edwards, Maldwyn L. *The Astonishing Youth: A Study of John Wesley as Men Saw Him.* London: Epworth, 1926.

_____. *John Wesley.* 2d ed. Lake Junaluska, N.C.: World Methodist Council, Association of Methodist Historical Societies, 1966.

_____. *John Wesley and the Eighteenth Century: A Study of* His *Social and Political Influence.* New York: Abingdon, 1933.

English, John C. "The Cambridge Platonists in John Wesley's *Christian Library.*" *Proceedings of the Wesley Historical Society* 37 (1970): 101–4.

Frost, Stanley Brice. *The Doctrine of Authority in the Works of John Wesley.* London: n.p., 1938. (English translation by the author of his *Die Authoritätslehre in den Werken John Wesleys.* Miinchen: E. Reihardt, 1937.)

Fujimoto, Mitsuru Samuel. "John Wesley's Doctrine of Good Works." Diss., Drew University, 1986.

Gill, Frederick C. *On the Steps of Wesley.* London: Lutterwortb, 1962.

Gray, Wallace G., Jr. "The Place of Reason in the Theology of John Wesley." Diss., Vanderbilt University, 1953.

Green, John. *John Wesley and William Law.* London: Epworth, 1948.

Green, Richard. *The Conversion of Wesley.* London: Francis Griffiths, 1909.

_____. *The Works of John and Charles Wesley: A Bibliography.* London: C. H. Kelly, 1896.

Green, Vivian H. H. *The Young Mr. Wesley.* London: Epworth, 1961.

Grider, J. Kenneth. "The Nature of Wesleyan Theology." *Wesleyan Theological Journal* 17, no. 2 (1982): 43–57.

_____. "Wesleyanism and the Inerrancy Issue." *Wesleyan Theological Journal* 19, no. 2 (1984): 52–61.

Halevy, Elie. *The Birth of Methodism in England.* Trans. Bernard Semmel. Chicago: University of Chicago Press, 1971.

Harper, Steve. *John Wesley's Message for Today.* Grand Rapids: Zondervan, 1984.

Harrison, A. W. *John Wesley, the Last Phase.* London: Epworth, 1934.

Hartley, John E. "Old Testament Studies in the Wesleyan Mode." *Wesleyan Theological Journal* 17, no. 1 (1982): 58–76.

Heitzenrater, Richard P. "At Full Liberty: Doctrinal Standards in Early American Methodism." *Quarterly Review* 5, no. 3, (1985): 6–27.

_____. *The Elusive Mr. Wesley: John Wesley His Own Biographer.* 2 vols. Nashville: Abingdon, 1984.

Hendricks, M. Elton. "John Wesley and Natural Theology." *Wesleyan Theological Journal* 18, no. 2 (1983): 7–17.

Hildebrandt, Franz. *Christianity According to the Wesleys.* London: Epworth, 1956.

_____. *From Luther to Wesley.* London: Lutterworth, 1951.

Hindley, Clifford J. "The Philosophy of Enthusiasm: A Study in the Origins of

'Experimental Theology.'" *London Quarterly and Holborn Review* 182 (1957): 99–109, 199–210.

Horst, Mark H. "Christian Understanding and the Life of Faith in John Wesley's Thought." Diss., Yale University Press, 1985.

_____. "Experimenting with Christian Wholeness: Method in Wesley's Theology." *Quarterly Review* 7 (1987): 11–23

Hynson, Leon O. "John Wesley's Concept of Liberty of Conscience." *Wesleyan Theological Journal* 7, no. 1 (1972): 36–46.

_____. *To Reform the Nation: The Theological Foundations of Wesley's Ethics.* Grand Rapids: Zondervan, Francis Asbury Press, 1985.

_____. "The Wesleyan Quadrilateral in the American Holiness Tradition." *Wesleyan Theological Journal* 20, no. 1 (1985): 19–33.

Jackson, Thomas. The *Life of the Rev. Charles Wesley.* 2 vols. London: John Manson, 1841.

Jeffery, Thomas Reed. *John Wesley's Religious Quest.* New York: Vantage, 1960. .

Johnson, Moody S. "Toward a Theology of Contemporaneity: Tillich or Wesley?" *Wesleyan Theological Journal* 5, no. 1 (1970): 68–75.

Jones, Bernard E. "Reason and Religion Joined: The Place of Reason in Wesley's Thought." *London Quarterly and Holborn Review* 189 (1964): 110–13.

Joy, Donald M. "The Contemporary Church as 'Holy Community.'" *The Church.* Ed. Melvin E. Dieter and Daniel N. Berg. Anderson, Ind.: Warner Press, 1972.

Joy, James R. "Wesley: Man of a Thousand Books and a Book." *Religion in Life* 8 (Winter 1939): 71–84.

Källstad, Thorvald. *John Wesley and the Bible.* Diss., University of Uppsala, 1974. Bjärnum: Bjärnums Tryckeri, 1974.

Keefer, Luke, Jr. "John Wesley: Disciple of Early Christianity." Diss., Temple University, 1981.

_____. "John Wesley: Disciple of Early Christianity." *Wesleyan Theological Journal* 19, no. 1 (1984): 26–32.

Kinghorn, Kenneth C. 'I say, 'The Bible is the Decisive Source of Authority!'" *Circuit Rider* 11, no. 5 (1987): 6–7.

. "Response to 'Keep the Quadrilateral.' " *Circuit Rider* 11, no. 5 (1987): 8.

Lacy, H. E. "Authority in John Wesley." *London Quarterly and Holborn Review* 189 (April 1964): 114–19.

Langford, Thomas A. *Practiad Divinity: Theology in the Wesleyan Tradition.* Nashville: Abingdon, 1983.

Langford, Thomas A., OO. *Wesleyan Theology: A Sourcebook.* Durham, N.C.: Labyrinth, 1984.

Lawson, John. *Notes on Wesley's Forty-four Sermons.* London: Epworth, 1946.

Lawton, George. *John Wesley's English: A Study of His Literary Style.* London: Allen & Unwin, 1962.

Lean, Garth. *John Wesley, Anglican.* London: Blandford, 1964.

Lee, Umphrey. *John Wesley and Modern Religion.* Nashville: Cokesbury, 1936.

_____. *The Lord's Horseman: John Wesley the Man.* New York: Abingdon, 1928.

Leupp, Roderick Thomas. " 'The Art of God': Light and Darkness in the Thought of John Wesley." Diss., Drew University, 1985.

Lindström, Harald. *Wesley and Sanctification.* Trans H. S. Harvey. London: Epworth, 1950..

Lyons, George. "Hermeneutical Bases for Theology: Higher Criticism and the Wesleyan

Interpreter." *Wesleyan Theological Journal* 18, no.. 1 (1983): 63–78.

McCarthy, Daryl. "Early Wesleyan Views of Scripture." *Wesleyan Theological Journal* 16, no. 2 (1981): 95–105.

MacDonald, James Alexander. *Wesley's Revision of Shorter Catechism*. London: George A. Morton, 1906.

McEldowney, James. "John Wesley's Theology in its Historical Setting." Diss., University of Chicago, 1943.

Maddox, Randy 1. "Responsible Grace: The Systematic Nature of Wesley's Theology Reconsidered." *Wesleyan Theological Journal* 19, no. 2 (1984): 7–22.

Marquardt, Manfred. *Praxis and Principles of John Wesley's Social Ethic*. Trans. John 1. Farthing. Durham, N.C.: Labyrinth, 1987.

Matthews, Rex D. " 'Religion and Reason Joined': A Study in the Theology of John Wesley." Diss., Harvard University, 1986.

Meeks, M. Douglas, ed. *The Future of the Methodist Theological Traditions*. Nashville: Abingdon, 1985.

Mercer, Jerry. "A Study of the Concept of Man in the Sermons of John Wesley." Diss., Claremont School of Theology, 1970.

_____. "Toward a Wesleyan Theology of Experience." *Wesleyan Theological Journal* 20/ no. 1 (1985): 78–93.

Minus, Paul M., ed. *Methodism's Destiny in the Ecumenical Age*. New York: Abingdon, 1969.

Monk, Robert. *John Wesley: His Puritan Heritage*. Nashville: Abingdon, 1966.

Moore, Henry. *The Life of the Rev. John Wesley, A. M.* 2 vols. London: Kershaw, 1824–25.

Moore, Robert. *John Wesley and Authority: A Psychological Perspective*. Missoula, Mont.: Scholars Press, 1979.

Mossner, E. C. *Bishop Butler and the Age of Reason*. New York: Macmillan, 1936.

Mullen, Wilbur, H., "John Wesley's Method of Biblical Interpretation." *Religion in Life* 47 (Spring 1978): 99–108.

Neely, Thomas B. *Doctrinal Standards of Methodism*. New York: Revell, 1918.

Newton, John A. *Susanna Wesley and the Puritan Tradition in Methodism* London: Epworth, 1975.

Nicholson, Roy S. "John Wesley and Ecumenicity." *Wesleyan Theological Journal* 2, no. 1 (1967): 66–81.

Noro, Yohio. "Wesley's Theological Epistemology." *Iliff Review* 28 (1971): 59–76.

Oden, Thomas C. *Doctrinal Standards in the Wesleyan Tradition*. Grand Rapids: Zondervan, Francis Asbury Press, 1987.

Oswalt, John N. "Wesley's Use of the Old Testament in His Doctrinal Teachings." *Wesleyan Theological Journal* 12, no. 1 (1977): 39–53.

Outler, Albert C. "Beyond Pietism: Aldersgate in Context." *Motive* 23 (May 1963): 12–16.

_____. *The Christian Tradition and the Unity We Seek*. New York: Oxford University Press, 1957.

_____. *Evangelism in the Wesleyan Spirit*. Nashville: Tidings, 1971.

_____. "John Wesley: Folk Theologian." *Theology Today* 34, no. 2 (1977): 150–60.

_____. "John Wesley as Theologian—Then and Now." *Methodist History* 12 (1974): 63–82.

_____. "Pastoral Care in the Wesleyan Spirit." *Perkins Journal* 25, no. 1 (1971): 4–11.

_____. *Theology in the Wesleyan Spirit*. Nashville: Tidings, 1975.

_____. "Towards a Re–Appraisal of John Wesley as a Theologian." *Perkins Journal* 14, no. 2 (1961): 5–14.

_____. "The Wesleyan Quadrilateral in John Wesley." *Wesleyan Theological Journal*, 20, no. 1 (1985): 7–18.

Overton, John H. *John Wesley.* London: Metheuen, 1891.

Piette, Maximin. *John Wesley in the Evolution of Protestantism.* Trans. J. B. Howard. New York: Sheed and Ward, 1937.

Pudney, John. *John Wesley and His World.* New York: Scribner's, 1978.

Rattenbury, John E. *The Conversion of the Wesleys, A Critical Study.* London: Epworth, 1938.

_____. *Wesley's Legacy to the World.* London: Epworth, 1938.

Reddish, Robert O. *John Wesley, His Way of Knowing God.* Evergreen, Colo.: Rorge Publishing, 1972.

Rowe, Gilbert T. *The Meaning of Methodism.* Nashville: Cokesbury, 1926.

Rowe, Kenneth E., ed. *The Place of John Wesley in the Christian Tradition.* Metuchen, N.J.: Scarecrow, 1976.

Runyon, Theodore, ed. *Sanctification and Liberation.* Nashville: Abingdon, 1980.

_____. ed. *Wesleyan Theology Today: A Bicentennial Consultation.* Nashville: United Methodist Publishing House, Kingswood, 1985.

Rupp, Erriest Gordon. *Methodism in Relation to Protestant Tradition* London: Epworth, 1954.

Sangster, William E. *The Path of Perfection: An Examination and Restatement of John Wesley's Doctrine of Christian Perfection.* 1943. Reprint. London: Epworth, 1984.

Schmidt, Martin. *John Wesley: A Theological Biography.* Trans. Norman Goldhawk. 2 vols. in 3. New York: Abingdon, 1962.

Shelton, R. Larry. "John Wesley's Approach to Scripture in Historical Perspective." *Wesleyan Theological Journal* 16, no. 1 (1981): 23–50.

_____. "The Trajectory of Wesleyan Theology." *Wesleyan Theological Journal* 21, no. 1–2 (1986): 160–76.

Shimizu, Mitsuo. "Epistemology in the Thought of John Wesley." Diss., Drew University, 1980.

Simon, John S. *John Wesley and the Advance of Methodism.* London: Epworth, 1925.

_____. *John Wesley the Last Phase.* London: Epworth, 1934.

_____. *John Wesley the Master Builder.* London: Epworth, 1927.

_____. *John Wesley and the Religious Societies.* London: Epworth, 1921.

Slaatte, Howard A. *The Arminan Arm of Theology.* Washington, D.C.: University Press of America, 1977.

_____. *Fire in the Brand.* New York: Exposition, 1963.

Smith, Timothy L. "Notes on the Exegesis of John Wesley's *Explanatory Notes upon the New Testament.*" *Wesleyan Theological Journal* 16, no. 1 (1981): 107–113.

Snyder, Howard. *The Radical Wesley and Patterns for Church Renewal.* 1980. Reprint. Grand Rapids: Zondervan, 1987.

Southey, Robert. *The Life of Wesley and the Rise and Progress of Methodism.* 2 vols. New York: Wm. B. Gilley, 1820.

Stacey, John, ed. *John Wesley: Contemporary Perspectives.* London: Epworth, 1988.

Staples, Rob L. "Present Frontiers of Wesleyan Theology." *Wesleyan Theological Journal* 12, no. 1 (1977): 5–15.

Starkey, Lycurgus M. *The Work of the Holy Spirit: A Study in Wesleyan Theology.* New

York: Abingdon, 1962.

Stokes, Mack B. *The Bible in the Wesleyan Heritage.* Nashville: Abingdon, 1979.

Strawson, William. "Wesley's Doctrine of Last Things." *London Quarterly and Holborn Review* (July 1959): 240–47.

Telford, John. *The Life of John Wesley.* London: Kelley, 1910.

Terry, Milton S. *Biblical Dogmatics.* New York: Eaton and Mains, 1907.

Thompson, Edgar W. *Wesley: Apostolic Man.* London: Epworth, 1957.

Thompson, W. Ralph. "Facing Objections Raised Against Biblical Inerrancy." *Wesleyan Theological Journal* 3, no. 1 (1968): 21–29.

Thorsen, Donald A. D. *Theological Method in John Wesley.* Ann Arbor, Mich.: University Microfilms, 1988. 8817640.

Todd, John. *John Wesley and the Catholic Church.* London: Stodder & Houghton, 1958.

Towlson, Clifford W. *Moravians and Methodists.* London: Epworth, 1957.

Tuttle, Robert G., Jr. "The Influence of the Roman Catholic Mystics on John Wesley." Diss., University of Bristol, 1969.

_____. *John Wesley: His Life and Theology.* Grand Rapids: Zondervan, 1978.

Tyerman, Luke. *The Life and Times of the Rev. John Wesley, M.A.* 3 vols. New York: Harper and Brothers, 1872.

Walls, Jerry L. *The Problem of Pluralism: Recovering United Methodist Identity.* Wilmore, Ky.: Good News, 1986.

_____. "What Is Theological Pluralism?" *Quarterly Review* 5, no. 3 (1985): 44–62.

Watkin-Jones, Howard. *The Holy Spirit from Arminius to Wesley.* London: Epworth, 1929.

Wearmouth, Robert. *Methodism and the Common People of the Eighteenth Century.* London: Epworth, 1945.

Weems, Lovett Hayes. *The Gospel According to Wesley: A Summary of John Wesley's Message.* Nashville: Discipleship Resources, 1982.

Williams, Colin. *John Wesley's Theology Today.* New York: Abingdon, 1960.

Wood, Arthur Skevington. *The Burning Heart.* Exeter, England: Paternoster, 1967.

Wood, Laurence W. "Wesley's Epistemology." *Wesleyan Theological Journal* 10, no. 1 (1975): 48–59.,

Wynkoop, Mildred Bangs. "A Hermeneutical Approach to John Wesley." *Wesleyan Theological Journal* 6 (1971): 13–22.

_____. "Theological Roots of the Wesleyan Understanding of the Holy Spirit." *Wesleyan Theological Journal* 14, no. 1 (1979): 77–98.

_____. *A Theology of Love.* Kansas City: Beacon Hill, 1972.

# Name Index

Abraham, William 8, 161, 163, 166n19, 200n101, 204n28, 207n18, 208n30
Adam 60
Aldrich, Henry 24, 25, 108, 170n74
Allen, Diogenes 204n26
Andrewes, Lancelot 160n39
Anselm 13, 56, 136, 167n11
Apollos 102
Aquinas, Thomas. *See* Thomas Aquinas
Aristotle 24, 59, 108, 111–2, 117, 119, 121, 126, 194n10–11, 197,n55
Arndt, John 178n69
Arnett; William 88, 90, 143, 189n80, 194n5, 206n68
Atterbury, Francis 24–25, 169n39, 181n79
Augustine 14, 96, 167n11, 170n72
Austin (Augustine) 96
Bacon, Francis 48, 59, 194n10, 196n45
Baker, Frank 168n26
Barth, Karl 10, 160
Basil 93, 96
Baxter, Richard 24, 27, 172
Bengel, Johannes 85, 188n54
Bentley, Richard 178n75
Berkeley, George 24, 138, 200n106
Beveridge, William 24, 26
Bloesch, Donald 8, 9, 151, 158, 160, 162–163, 207n7
Böhler, Peter 26, 68, 79, 83, 88
Bonnet, Charles 185n79
Boshears, Onva, Jr. 170n71, 187n44
Boston, Thomas 66, 183n56
Boyle, Robert 20, 169, 178
Bramhall, John 96
Brantley, Richard 124–125, 131, 175n25, 178n71, 179n90, 181n15, 181n18, 184n67, 198n61, 200n106, 206n71
Brown, Colin 208
Browne, Peter 22, 30, 69, 109, 112, 115, 117, 119–20, 123, 131, 170n62, 178n75, 182n18, 197n55, 198n61, 199n89
Bull, George 25–26, 169n39
Burnett, Gilbert 29
Burtner, Robert 194n13
Butler, Joseph 197n55
Calvin 8, 14, 27, 33, 158–9, 167n16, 168n17, 181n11
Campbell, Ted 95, 178n78, 190n28

# Subject Index

# About the Author

Don Thorsen, Ph.D., is Professor of Theology in the Haggard School of Theology at Azusa Pacific University. He was educated at Stanford University, Asbury Theological Seminary, Princeton Theological Seminary, and Drew University. His doctoral dissertation was on *Theological Method in John Wesley*. He teaches courses in systematic and historical theology, church history, and spirituality on the masters and doctoral levels in the Graduate School of Theology at Azusa Pacific University.

Thorsen is the author of numerous books, anthology chapters, articles, and other publications. His best known book is *The Wesleyan Quadrilateral: Scripture, Tradition, Reason and Experience as a Model of Evangelical Theology*, which has been translated into several languages. Thorsen also published *Theological Resources for Ministry: A Bibliography of Works in Theological Studies* and *Inclusive Language Handbook: A Practical Guide to Using Inclusive Language*. In addition, he has worked as an editor with *Christianity Today, Christian Scholar's Review,* and *Light and Life Magazine*.

Having been ordained for nineteen years, Thorsen advocates ecumenism through his involvements with the Commission on Faith and Order of the National Council of Churches, Wesleyan Theological Society, Wesleyan Holiness Studies Project, and the Word Made Fresh. Thorsen is an international speaker and enjoys preaching as well as teaching and lecturing throughout the world.

Printed in the United States
86391LV00006B/1/A

9 780975 543535